Sylvanus G. Morley
and the World of the Ancient Mayas

Sylvanus G. Morley and the World of the Ancient Mayas

by ROBERT L. BRUNHOUSE

NORMAN
UNIVERSITY OF OKLAHOMA PRESS

International Standard Book Number: 0–8061–0961–0
Library of Congress Catalog Card Number: 78–160489

Copyright 1971 by the University of Oklahoma Press, Publishing Division of the University. Composed and printed at Norman, Oklahoma, by the University of Oklahoma Press. First edition.

Acknowledgments

MANY individuals have helped to make this book possible. The constant appearance of the name of J. Eric S. Thompson in the notes scarcely indicates my deep indebtedness for his patient and generous aid. Reluctantly, I forgo the pleasure of enumerating the contributions of the following individuals; to each one I express my sincere thanks for information provided in interviews or by correspondence.

Mrs. Pamela Allara, Mr. and Mrs. Gustave Bauman, Dr. Whitfield Bell, Miss Margaret C. Blaker, Mrs. Frans Blom, Mr. John S. Bolles, Dr. John O. Brew, Mrs. Laughlin Campbell, Dr. Kenneth Chapman, Sr. Manuel Cirerol, Dr. Kenneth J. Conant, Miss Margaret Currier, Mrs. Thomas E. Curtin, Professor Ralph Dexter, Dr. Bertha Dutton, Dr. Gordon F. Eckholm, Mr. Bruce T. Ellis, Miss Elizabeth Epstein, Mrs. Constance Fussell, Mr. Dudley C. Gordon, Mrs. Connie Griffith, Dr. Carl Guthe, Mrs. Robert T. Hatt, Mr. Clarence C. Hay, Mrs. John Held, Jr., Mrs. Gertrude Hess, Mr. Neil M. Judd, Mr. and Mrs. Daniel T. Kelly, Dr. J. O. Kilmartin, Mr. F. A. Kock, Mrs. Marjorie Lambert, Mrs. Boaz Long, Mrs. Samuel K. Lothrop, Dr. C. L. Lundell, Mr. Eugene B. McCluny, Mrs. Charles B. Macaulay, Mrs. Emory Marshall, Dr. Paul Martin, Dr. Alfredo Martínez Moreno, Dr. J.

Alden Mason, Dr. Frank D. Mera, Mrs. Thomas B. Miller, Mrs. Benjamin Muse, Mr. and Mrs. Jesse Nusbaum, Mrs. Lily de Jongh Osborne, Judge Medill Otero, Mr. Ross Parmenter, Dr. William Barclay Parsons, Dr. H. E. D. Pollock, Dr. Wilson Popenoe, Miss Tatiana Proskouriakoff, Miss Ruth Rambo, Mrs. Toxica de Roach, Dr. Lawrence Roys, Dr. David W. Scott, Dr. George Shattuck, Dr. Clifford K. Shipton, Dr. Ledyard Smith, Mr. Murphy Smith, Dr. John L. Sorenson, Dr. Leopold Stokowski, Mr. George Stuart, Mrs. Alfred M. Tozzer, Mrs. Charlotte Tufts, Mrs. Elinor M. Vail, Dr. Robert Wauchope, Miss Elizabeth White, and Mr. James Young.

ROBERT L. BRUNHOUSE

Mobile, Alabama
April 14, 1971

Contents

Illustrations

Maps

Sylvanus G. Morley
and the World of the Ancient Mayas

I

Introduction

SYLVANUS Griswold Morley was a man of many facets—scholar, explorer, informal diplomat, planner, and educator. He was a good friend, and he excelled in the art of living. His contributions to the scientific knowledge of pre-Columbian Maya culture is a matter of record, embodied in half a dozen volumes dealing with the hieroglyphs of that people.

The record of his adventures as an explorer through the bush and forests of Middle America, down the desolate Mosquito Coast, and among the untamed natives of eastern Yucatán is quickly fading, for he told the story in public lectures and private conversations, and the generation that heard him is fast decreasing in numbers. He left sufficient materials, however, to recapture those exciting events. His role in devising projects was known only to those with whom he conferred on a particular plan; of course, his outstanding success in this direction was the inauguration of the vast program of Maya research that centered in Chichén Itzá.

In carrying out his professional relations, he performed much informal diplomacy, creating goodwill as a by-product of lengthy visits to the nations of Middle America; this record, too, is quickly slipping into oblivion as the men who knew him pass from the scene.

Although he was no educator in the usual sense of the word, for he never taught in school or university, he was an educator of the public at large by way of many illustrated lectures and publications of a popular nature. If the full extent of his public speaking will probably never be known, such works as *The Ancient Maya* and articles in widely circulated magazines testify to his zeal for publicizing the wonders of the ancient civilization he found so fascinating.

When Thomas Gann, his close associate, dedicated one of his books to Morley, "the Little Friend of All the World," there was good basis for the tribute, because Vay, as his friends called him, took a lively, genial interest in everyone he met. Cordial personal relations and the warm feelings of friendship are too rarely preserved in the written record, but enough has survived to suggest this intensely human side of Morley.

Perhaps the most interesting aspect of the man, an aspect that his associates did not always fully comprehend, was his overwhelming love of living, the sheer excitement of everyday existence. If many individuals consider themselves satisfied when each day passes without trouble, Morley moved on another plane, intent on finding unabashed happiness in everything he did.

The world is a wonderful place to live in, despite the misfortunes one must suffer, he declared in one of his unusual moments of self-revelation. Simple as it is, this was his philosophy of life. The association with people, the occurrence of events, the surprises, and even the inevitable disappointments—these are the things that living in this world are made of, and he relished every bit of it. The kaleidoscope of life was constantly shifting parts of the pattern so that new combinations, unexpected designs, appeared. It was this fascination with daily experience that drove him to keep a diary. People and events constituted the warp and woof of the endless fabric that slowly and relentlessly came from the loom of life; every detail was a part of the total design; and his driving interest in experience itself urged him to preserve the record in written form.

His enthusiasm sprang from a combination of natural curiosity and intense nervous energy. In his early years in the Southwest he flitted about the camp so tirelessly that the Indians nicknamed him "Little Hummingbird." When he was in Mexico City or Mérida or Guatemala City, he was on the go day and night with no pause or rest between the frequent business and social engagements. It is a wonder that he bore up under the stupendous schedule he followed in Mérida in February, 1923. Moreover, he poured his entire energy into everything he did. One year he was on the panel of judges to pass on exhibits at the Inter-Tribal Ceremonial at Gallup, New Mexico. He took the assignment seriously and carried it out with his customary exhausting vigor. "At the end of the day of judging," reported Margretta Dietrich, who directed the judges, "he was still full of ideas and enthusiasm although his feet were worn out, he said, and he would never do it again without roller skates."[1]

In the field, his enthusiasm reached its highest pitch. On his first examination of the Maya ruins in Yucatán in 1907, he worked from breakfast right through the day to dinner at night, until his native assistant finally protested over the omission of the noon meal. At a new archaeological site, he was agog with excitement over finding all the stones that bore hieroglyphs. Sometimes a stela had fallen face down, and as his workmen slowly raised it in order to turn it about, he crawled underneath eagerly seeking the inscriptions, frightening the laborers who feared he might be crushed. He would climb over all ruins and temporary scaffolding around ruins, insistent on seeing everything, heedless of the danger, and worrying his companions over his safety.

Enthusiasm for people was the heart of his interest in living. His friends frequently failed to perceive this fundamental fact; they believed that his major interest was archaeology, since he talked so much about it. On at least one occasion he made the point clear. After a public lecture on the Mayas, a beautiful young woman hurried to the platform to express her appreciation.

---

[1] *Morleyana: A Collection of Writings in Memoriam, Sylvanus Griswold Morley—1883–1948* (The School of American Research and the Museum of New Mexico, Santa Fe, N.M., 1950), 56. All quotations from this volume are used by permission of the publisher.

"Oh, Dr. Morley," she blurted out, "I just adored your lecture —hieroglyphs, think of it—the most fascinating subject in the world: don't you agree?"

"Oh, no, my dear lady," he answered in a flash, "men and women are far more absorbing, just human beings like you and me. You, for example, are adorable; a Maya glyph is merely interesting."[2]

Once he confided to his diary that other people's lives are the most intriguing thing in the world. Constantly he searched for the great variety in the human race. On boarding ship at Belize in 1914, he had his cabin mate relating his experiences that ranged from amorous adventures to a promising financial deal worth $90,000 in Mexico that was knocked in the head by the revolution. The following day a young mother from Arizona confided to him the story of her unhappy marriage to a faithless rounder. These were usual examples. On the other hand, he glowed with warmth and admiration on meeting striking personalities like Lee Christmas, Frans Blom, Zelia Nuttall, and Felipe Carrillo.

He appreciated the value of fun and humor in oiling the machinery of human relations. With close friends he was not above leg-pulling and argument. Once he started verbal fireworks by observing, with a perfectly straight face, that writing *Gentlemen Prefer Blondes* would have meant more to him than deciphering hieroglyphs. Usually, however, he resorted to stories, anecdotes, and jokes. On returning to Santa Fe after months in the bush, he would greet an old friend and then launch into "Have you heard the story of . . .?" For hours on end he entertained groups before the fireside in a host's living room with an endless stream of anecdotes and incidents, and he was his happiest when everyone was laughing. His repertory of yarns ranged from Rabelaisian stories of the barroom variety through the whole spectrum to utterly banal jokes. As is often the case with an expert raconteur, the manner of narration carried as much excitement as the final punch line. Since he was naturally a kind man, his humor was light and hilarious, never edging into irony or sarcasm. Often he

[2] *Morleyana*, 118.

made himself the butt of an incident, even though it might compromise his character with persons who did not know him well. One story of this kind, centering upon a Mexican's exaggerated notion of Vay's virility, he enjoyed immensely and told to many friends; today it is repeated everywhere one meets people who knew him. On the other hand, he could be gentle in handling a near-ludicrous situation. In describing a train trip from Washington to Key West, he told of the elderly white-haired lady who shared his table in the diner. The conversation was insignificant, but his description of her mountainous bulk and the prodigious quantity of food she consumed is a genially wrought portrait, drawn with amusement and sly humor.

Had anyone told him that his own actions were sometimes humorous, he would have heartily agreed. Dr. Popenoe remembered the time that he and Morley and Herbert Joseph Spinden took the New York subway to attend a meeting at the Brooklyn Museum. "We rode and rode, and finally found we had passed our station. So we got out, and went up to the street, crossed over, and down in again. We started back, and rode a while, only to discover we had again passed our station. Vay, who was immaculately dressed in everything from spats to walking stick, jumped to his feet and screamed at the top of his voice, 'Well I'll be damned; here's three explorers lost in the Brooklyn subway!' "[3]

He had unique qualifications for the work he undertook and the social life he enjoyed. Although he was short in build, unprepossessing in appearance, and nearsighted, he was richly endowed with a warm personality that made him remarkably attractive. This was a full-bodied natural gift that explains much of his success, especially his easy association with individuals. Conscious as he was, at least as early as his college days, that he could manipulate his charm for his own purposes, it never appeared contrived or artificial. Instinctively, he knew what questions to ask, when to listen, the proper comments to make, and the amount of flattery to bestow if that seemed in order. In Latin America, where personal feelings are more openly expressed and effusive compliments

[3] *Morleyana,* 209.

expected, he fitted into the scene perfectly. He knew exactly what stop to pull on this organ he played—sympathetic agreement or coaxing, the indirect hint for a favor or ominous name-dropping, or persuasive argument. He often talked his way out of tight situations, leaving friendly feelings behind him. Names and faces, even of casual acquaintances, he remembered for years. Those persons who believed that he concentrated his efforts on archaeology and hieroglyphs failed to appreciate the agility of his mind and memory when he met any of his numerous friends; at once he could summon up everything he knew about the individual, judiciously suppressing points that might cause pain or embarrassment.

If personal charm explains his happy relations with people, other characteristics played an important part in his success. One was perseverance. In his college days he plugged away relentlessly at translating the hated Virgil, and managed to pass the examination. Alfred Kidder marveled at Vay on the first field season in the Southwest. "Persistence, endless persistence, and resolute failure to be discouraged . . . resulted in keeping Fletcher and me, sometimes from sheer sense of shame, at our work," said Kidder of that summer of 1907.[4] Once an idea became firmly planted in Vay's mind, nothing could divert him from carrying it out. He worked on the *Inscriptions of the Petén* for almost three decades, and he liked to remind anyone who fumed over delay that it took him seventeen years to get the Chichén Itzá project off the ground. His dogged persistence, however, made it difficult for an associate like Earl Morris or his chief, Alfred Kidder, to induce him to abandon a favorite brainchild that they considered unwise or impractical.

Still another trait that stood him in good stead was his excellent self-judgment. In appraising his own actions past or present, he never approached the extremes of abasement or pride. When he engaged in reminiscences or introspection—and the latter was rare—he did not judge himself severely; nor did he judge other people harshly, it should be added; he usually selected the happy memories to dwell upon. Nor did he allow himself the dubious

[4] *Morleyana*, 96–97.

luxury of pride or egoism. On scoring a success, he expressed satisfaction generally and intense pleasure occasionally, but he never crowed over a triumph. Of course, he enjoyed praise and flattery as much as any man, though he had the good sense to know how to evaluate such pleasantries.

Also, there was an engaging frank and openhanded attitude that he extended toward everyone. Since he brimmed with goodwill and honest intentions, he assumed that other persons acted upon the same motives. As a result, he made friends easily, gained the co-operation of those who worked with him, and secured the confidence of high officials he had to deal with. On occasion he could be naïve in his trust, as when he asked his new worker Gustav Stromsvik to make a key for his strongbox, never realizing that the mechanic could just as easily make another key for his own use.

With his big heart, Vay was willing to help friends whenever the occasion arose. Unhesitatingly he opened his unpublished data to J. Eric S. Thompson, who was searching for proof to clinch his discovery of the Maya Lords of the Night. He not only helped Fray Angélico Chávez to publish his book on Our Lady of the Conquest, but he presented him with an antique dress from Guatemala to clothe the statue. He enjoyed the success of his friends and associates. The report of every field season carefully credited each staff member with his achievements. Willingly, he read manuscripts of fellow scientists if they asked for the benefit of his knowledge and criticism.

His good nature was so genuine that he assumed that he must be on friendly terms with everyone. Actually, he was uneasy over any case of hard feelings regardless of who was at fault, and he labored for reconciliation. Despite the untrue charges that William Gates made against him, Vay eventually went out of his way to praise one of Gates's books in order to mend the long-broken friendship. He had good reason to believe that E. L. Hewett had treated him shabbily, but after years of coolness, Vay made the gesture that rekindled goodwill between the two men. During a long season in Central America, he had two flare-ups with the temperamental John Held, Jr.; on each occasion, Vay, though he believed he had been wronged, quickly forgot the incidents.

A strong streak of sentiment ran through his nature; consequently, memories, reunions, anniversaries, and certain places meant much to him. The recollection of his own birthday or his daughter's was to be expected, but other anniversary dates that occurred to him, like Bunker Hill Day when he was in the bush in Guatemala, suggest that recollection of the past provided his soul with necessary sustenance. Except for Lafleur's death the events he recalled were of a happy nature. Also, he valued greatly the friends he had, eagerly looking forward to meeting them after a long absence, and loath to see them leave when the time of departure arrived. His sentimental attachment to the Maya natives, stemming in part from their likable traits and in part from his esteem for the achievements of their ancestors, was so strong that he overlooked their faults and exaggerated their virtues. "My Mayas," as he referred to them, was a term of affection rather than possession. Even the ruins of the ancient pyramids and temples evoked strong emotions; every time he returned to Chichén Itzá or Copán or Uxmal he felt a grand surge of joy and satisfaction; and when he left a site, he paid farewell calls on the principal structures, for these too were friends, permanent friends who did not wander away or wither and die.

Yes, these inanimate remains provided the meat and drink of his professional work. He never ceased to marvel at the intricate carvings, the majestic piles of masonry, the pleasing proportions of the Governor's Palace at Uxmal, and the hieroglyphs, all of them no more than fragmentary suggestions of a colorful civilization that flourished for six centuries in Middle America. The fantastically accurate Maya calendar filled him with admiration: he early learned to decipher the date glyphs, and for years he concentrated on collecting every inscription he could find. His ultimate aim, of course, was to plot the history of the rise and fall of Maya civilization. For this purpose he spent season after season in Middle America, searching for new inscriptions, confirming the readings of those already reported, and enduring the hardships and dangers of life in bush and forest. Essentially, he accomplished his aim of anchoring Maya civilization in time. There are still unsolved problems on the subject, but that is because his contributions raised the study to a higher plateau, and every plateau provided new lines of sight and new horizons to explore.

"Only liars and damned fools say they like the jungle," he once said to Giles Healey.[5] Despite the many years Vay spent in the bush and forest of Mexico and Guatemala, he hated the experience. Jogging along on muleback at three miles an hour over parched trails or through the smothering atmosphere of the rain forest had no romantic glamor for him; nor did spending the night in a flea-infested *champa*, eating canned goods, fighting insects, fearing snakes, taking water from a filthy *aguada*, and always running the risk of contracting a serious tropical infection or disease. He detested it, every bit of it, but he endured it all for the sake of finding those hieroglyphs. That fact is sufficient testimony of the zeal and devotion he put into his Maya research. Burning enthusiasm, he asserted, is one of the most important qualifications for such work, and the man who did not possess that terrific drive should not enter the profession.

He hated the jungle, because he dearly enjoyed the comforts of civilization. He dressed in clothes of good quality and style, relished meals of fine food and exotic dishes, lived in a comfortable home in Santa Fe furnished with antiques, and traveled by chauffeured automobile.

Even the ill health that plagued him over the years in no way diminished his enthusiasm for advancing the knowledge of the Mayas. Seasickness seized him as soon as he placed one foot in a boat. In the early days he contracted malaria, threw it off for several decades, and then acquired it again. He was in hospitals for tests and sometimes for recovery. He suffered from colitis during the visit to Europe in 1924. The following year amoebic dysentery forced him to leave Chichén Itzá after the season had begun and to spend weeks in a New Orleans hospital; on returning to Mexico, he found that his old-time energy was too great for his

[5] *Morleyana,* 85.

emaciated frame of 109 pounds, observing that he felt as if he had a Rolls Royce engine in a Ford body. In the 1930's he discovered that he had heart trouble, and he found it difficult to slow down his pace. But he continued to travel, this time by airplane instead of by mule and boat.

He realized the vast amount of fieldwork to be done before the full facts about the ancient Mayas could be assembled. One day in the spring of 1922, as he plodded through the Petén seeking new sites, he paused to contemplate how little he had actually accomplished in his years of exploration. Perhaps all of this work must be left to the next generation, but that was a discouraging thought, for it appeared more difficult to find able young recruits than to drum up money for the expeditions.

He did everything he could to encourage work in the profession. After starting the Chichén Itzá project in 1924, he did encounter promising young men. If they lacked the requisite training, he arranged to have them spend two fall semesters at Harvard for the master's degree. In his later years in Santa Fe, he provided leaves of absence to help bright young men and women to take graduate study. Also, he raised money on his own to employ Tatiana Proskouriakoff to make accurate drawings of restorations of famous sites. He lectured widely and wrote for popular magazines to stimulate interest in the subject, and he crowned his career with the attractive book *The Ancient Maya*. As director of research facilities in Santa Fe, he did not live long enough to carry out a full-scale program; but even during his brief tenure he inaugurated a number of projects, including the extensive English translation of Sahagún.

His greatest encouragement, of course, to Middle American archaeology was the inauguration of the Chichén Itzá project, with which his name will ever be associated. Financed by the Carnegie Institution of Washington and continued for several decades, that project that he began so modestly in 1924 soon expanded into a vast multidisciplinary study of the whole Maya area. In time the results of the specialists' investigations appeared in dozens upon dozens of scholarly volumes. At Chichén his work opened a new chapter in the history of American archaeology; it made Americans aware of their own prehistory, and it subjected one pre-Columbian area to the most intensive and prolonged study ever undertaken in the field of American prehistory.

Vay Morley achieved his unique work because of a notable combination of qualities. He was scholar, explorer, informal diplomat, planner, educator, and friend. The unusual characteristic, however, that permeated all of these roles and made him truly distinctive was his tremendous personal enthusiasm.

II

The Early Years

SYLVANUS Griswold Morley came from an academic and professional family of middle-class means and comfort. His father, Benjamin F. Morley, an engineer and graduate of Pennsylvania Military Academy at Chester, Pennsylvania, taught chemistry and mathematics and served as vice-president of that institution. Sylvanus' mother was the daughter of a Belgian language teacher also on the staff of the academy. Born on June 7, 1883, Vay was the eldest of six children—Constance, Henry, Alice, Elinor, and Elizabeth were the others. In 1894 his father gave up academic pursuits and moved the family to Buena Vista, Colorado, where he became part-owner and operator of the Mary Murphy Mine in nearby Romley.

All evidence suggests that Vay was an average youngster. He attended public schools, first in Chester and later in Buena Vista. A few stories of his boyhood activities have survived. He liked to spin out tales of railroad robbers and Indian fighters; he assembled pictures of European monarchs and once attempted to work out the genealogical tree of the Bourbons. A project more predictive of his future interests was the construction of a full-size Egyptian mummy, finished with brilliant enamel coloring. Such things were far more interesting than the violin lessons taken at the behest of his mother. Even the ten cents an hour she promised him for practicing was not conducive to success, for he had two play-mates in attendance counting off the minutes by the clock. In later years he told his mother that the experience killed any interest he might have had in music.

By the age of fifteen, when he was living in Colorado, his reading interests began to show a pattern. Lew Wallace's *The Fair God* and Rider Haggard's *Heart of the World* gave vivid pictures of pre-Columbian Mexico. He also examined random articles in the *Encyclopaedia Britannica,* and went through Prescott's *Conquest of Mexico.* At this point Regis Chauvenet, a Harvard graduate of 1867 and president of the Colorado School of Mines, put him in touch with Frederick W. Putnam, eminent curator of the Peabody Museum, who did his best to cope with the large questions on archaeological subjects posed in Vay's letters and recommended H. H. Bancroft's *The Native Races,* at that time the best summary of American archaeology.

Vay attempted to carry out the suggestion, though at first he had no idea where to locate the books. It happened that at this time he was interested in the daughter of the warden of the state reformatory at Buena Vista, and there in the prison library he found a dust-covered, leather-bound set of *The Native Races.* He was allowed to lug the volumes home for his perusal. He never explained how much he derived from those fact-studded pages of uninspired prose and endless footnotes, but in later years he always had a warm spot in his heart for Bancroft's work. Incidentally, he revealed that he inscribed the initials of the warden's daughter in carbolic acid on his leg.

By the time he completed high school, he was devoted to archaeology and wanted to make a profession of it. But his practical-minded father concluded that there were no jobs in that field, and he sent his son East to enroll at Pennsylvania Military Academy and become an engineer. As Cadet 124, Vay made the best of it, joined a fraternity, and apparently had a good time. Years later he recalled incidents about Falthausen, the German teacher. Manuel Sánchez Marmol, a polite Mexican lad not well versed in English, asked fellow students the proper salutation for a teacher, and with straight faces they told him it was "Go to hell, Professor." The innocent Marmol tried it on Falthausen, who flew into a rage. But the students intervened in time to explain, and fortunately the teacher considered it a prank. Vay also remembered how Falthausen required everyone in the German course to learn the first stanza of "Die Lorelei" by heart as a prerequisite to passing; Vay claimed that those lines were the only poetry he ever memorized.

When Colonel Morley died in 1903 in an accident in the mine, Vay's mother immediately brought her children back East and took up residence near the Academy. With one more year to go, Vay dutifully followed his father's wishes and completed the course in civil engineering, with a high academic record. He received his degree in 1904.

Now he decided to follow his bent for archaeology, and he chose Harvard for his training. Why Harvard? Because Putnam, of the Peabody Museum there, had been so patient in encouraging his interest six years earlier. How much more Vay knew about Harvard and its offerings is not known, but it happened that he made a wise choice.

Already exerting his unusual ability of persuasion, he gained permission from his mother and funds from his Aunt Virginia to carry out his ambition. In later years when he maintained that he had always been lucky, he must have thought first of Aunt Virginia. The widow of his great-uncle J. Henry Morley, she enjoyed the financial means to be independent in her way of life and in the favors she dispensed. Everyone remembered her as a dowager who stubbornly retained a Victorian flavor in her clothes, wore a lace handkerchief over her white hair, and, ensconced in a chair with dignity and self-confidence, fondled a pet lap dog. She liked Vay, and as she continued to help him in the coming years, he tried to show his gratitude by pleasing her. During his college years he spent several weeks every summer at her home in Windsor, New York; and at the beginning of each semester he stopped off to visit her on his way from Swarthmore to Cambridge. On those occasions he helped her with chores about the house and sometimes accompanied her to church. Once he attentively read a paper she had written on the Five Nations, and he never failed to discuss with her his plans for the future. One year he even sacrificed Christmas Day to be with her, though it was a cheerless affair, because she could not be troubled with providing a tree or other festive decorations. She enjoyed his presence, the warmth and charm of his personality, and doubtless she shared his infectious enthusiasm as he explained his hopes for the future. In the coming years it was Aunt Virginia who financed him through Harvard, subsidized his first trip to Mexico, and responded to other occasional calls for funds.

With Aunt Virginia in the background willing to nourish his dreams, Vay packed his bags in September and took train for Cambridge.

A significant feature of Morley's character can easily be overlooked, because his gay, carefree spirit suggested that he worked from day to day without particular plan or purpose. This was not true. From his earliest days he was a goal-setter, even though his friends did not always realize it. In his own mind he established an objective to be attained, and on accomplishing it, he promptly set up another goal, and continued the process throughout his life.

At Harvard he had two objectives: preparation for a profession and a grand good time during the process. Fortunately, and as was usually the case with any aim he set, he achieved his ends. No financial problems troubled him; he carefully kept his diversions within the bounds of middle-class respectability; and he suffered from no youthful introspection about himself or about the pressing social and political questions of the day.

On becoming a student at Cambridge in the fall of 1904, he enjoyed a new freedom to which he adjusted with moderation. No longer was the twenty-one-year-old youth subjected to the discipline of a military institution; and in addition, he entered the sophomore class by virtue of transfer credits, with only a condition in Latin to be met before he became a senior. The college was still small, with a student body of eighteen hundred, although his own class of six hundred young men was the largest of the four.

Despite the number of persons on campus, his social relations were confined to about half a dozen fellow students. Harold Hassler, Henry Williford, Benjamin Gordon, and J. Gould Fletcher were his closest friends. Since Hassler, Williford, and Morley were pretty much birds of a feather, they joined in many social get-togethers. Somehow Gordon did not quite fit into the group. The Episcopalian Morley was aware that his friend was a freethinker and a Jew, and all through his life he harbored a groundless mild suspicion of Jews. All told, however, he found Gordon a good companion. The critical test of Morley's tolerance was not Gordon but John Gould Fletcher, or J. G., as he was nicknamed. Shortly after arriving on campus, Vay struck up an acquaintance with the young fellow from Arkansas. Then something happened—Vay never explained what it was—that separated them. A year later, in the fall of 1905, J. G. appeared in Vay's room, offered his hand, and once more they were friends. At most, however, J. G. played only a minor part in Morley's social life. Not until the winter of 1907 did Vay find it necessary to give considerable attention to Fletcher.

With ample funds at his disposal, Morley never complained of being pinched for lack of money. He went to plays, entertained girls, bought clothes, and ate in fashionable dining places with no concern for the cost. He tutored fellow students several times although probably not for pay. In addition, he received a scholarship of $200 in 1905 and later on a fellowship. His only earnings on campus were $36 for a small project he performed for the Peabody Museum. Otherwise, he relied on his own resources, which were generously supplied by Aunt Virginia.

Physically he was in good shape despite irregular hours and the lack of sleep common among college youth. Though he was five feet, seven inches in height and weighed about 130 pounds, he was conscious of appearing smaller than other young men of his age. Because of nearsightedness he had to wear glasses, and at best he enjoyed no more than two-thirds normal vision. He accepted the defect, like other conditions in life that could not be changed, without complaint. The only physical disabilities during his college years were minor.

Already, however, he had acquired a habit that stayed with him for many years. He dozed off unaccountably on the most unlikely occasions. One Sunday when visiting cousins at Newton Square, he fell asleep right after dinner, much to his chagrin. By the beginning of 1906, it is evident that his embarrassing habit was of long standing. His failure to gain sufficient rest at night, a fact he readily admitted, could easily explain the weakness, but it is difficult to understand why the habit persisted for years after his college days.

He had no interest in physical exercise of any kind. He shunned organized sports. In fact, he recorded only two instances when he put forth even the slightest exertion during his college years. On fair May days he occasionally went canoeing, and he admitted that once he followed Professor Putnam's orders to walk for the sake of his health.

During summer vacations, when he was at home with time on his hands and little to amuse himself, he rode horses, swam, and played tennis, but only as forms of diversion. He did not relish such activity for its own sake. Like card-playing and reading, it helped to while away the carefree days of vacation.

Since he enjoyed stylish clothes in later years, it would be interesting to know more about his tastes at Cambridge. He recorded only one incident on the subject. In April, 1905, after he had eyed a pearl-gray vest in a shop window for weeks, his resistance crumbled and he bought it. At the same time he also acquired a pair of yellow shoes, insisting that they were yellow, not tan. Sheepish over the cost of these fineries, he refused to say how much he spent for them.

In music he would accept almost anything from popular tunes to classical fare. At first he attended symphony concerts, and bought a pair of tickets for himself and a girl. At one performance he enjoyed the works of Beethoven, Dvořák, and Berlioz; on another occasion Mendelssohn appealed to him, but a Brahms symphony almost put him to sleep. When he and two classmates served as supernumeraries in the last act of *Parsifal,* he liked the dramatic music, although he confessed he did not always understand it. On the other hand, he was completely at ease with musical comedies, and of the many he saw, he took occasion to mention *Wang, Lady Teazle, Fantana, Humpty Dumpty, Clarice, Babes in Woodland,* and *Wizard of Oz.*

He also enjoyed the drama as a favorite form of entertainment. Ethel Barrymore in *The Burgomaster* and Richard Mansfield in *Dr. Jekyll and Mr. Hyde* appear in his record, though he made no comment about the performers. In only a few cases did he pass judgment, and that was of a moral nature. The first time he saw *Sappho,* he dismissed it as a second-rate affair; a year later, when he saw it again, he condemned it as immoral. Not so with Shaw's *Man and Superman,* which elicited his praise for its wit and plain talk; and, he added, it was far superior to the immoral *Zaza.* All told, his comments on theatricals indicate that he considered drama entirely for its value as entertainment, provided it did not violate his sense of respectability.

He enjoyed football games for the same reason. They provided a diversion on Saturday afternoons. In the fall of 1905 he saw seven Harvard games, and he bought a pair of tickets for the following season. Of course, he assumed that his alma mater would always win, and it usually did at the games he attended. But when Harvard lost to Pennsylvania, he could not suppress a note of angry disappointment. Later, as an alumnus, he made a special effort to see some of the major games of the season, especially the classic annual battle with Yale.

His views on religion in these years provided an interesting commentary on his general outlook. In the early part of his college life he associated with Hassler, Williford, and Gordon. The four played cards together, sometimes took their meals together, and engaged in numerous bull sessions. One of these discussions temporarily upset Vay in January, 1905, when the divinity of Christ was debated. He and Williford upheld orthodoxy, while Gordon represented the freethinkers. Vay was aghast to discover so many atheists on campus, and he was considerably shaken by the freedom of the discussion; in fact, he believed that the subject was not debatable. But upset as he was, he retained his respect for the right of others to their views, and his relations with Gordon continued friendly.

He retained his devotion to the Episcopalian faith in which he had been reared. Although the ritualistic service appealed strongly to him, his record of churchgoing at Cambridge was poor. He attended half a dozen times in 1905, only once in the following year, and thereafter he rarely mentioned the subject. On one occasion, when he took Hassler with him, the presence of a Negro sitting nearby spoiled the beauty of the service for him. At the Church of the Advent he found the ritual almost too high for his taste, but he defended elaborate ceremonial as conducive to inculcating religious principles. Apparently the years at Harvard did not alter his views.

Just as he did not consider it necessary to explain his religious ideas, so he never bothered to outline his attitude toward social drinking. It is clear that he was familiar with the use of liquor in his college days. He was happiest when, after seeing a play, he and his friends went to the New Lexington or to the Adams House for supper and something to drink. Curiously, during his first year he often refrained from imbibing at those gatherings, though that did not affect the gaiety of the occasion.

Once, and only once as far as his record shows, did he drink to excess himself. And, surprisingly, he related the entire incident, as far as his memory permitted, with clinical impersonality. One night in January, 1906, he desperately needed companionship and none was to be found. He knew he could not see the girl he was interested in for three days, and when he called another young woman, she was busy. His friend Williford had gone to the theater, and apparently he did not care to confide in any of the other students. Knowing precisely what he intended to do, he rounded up Hassler and Rogers to accompany him, and proceeded to the Lenox, where he downed a martini, a manhattan, and two Green River highballs in short order. Then he became troublesome, and when the bartender refused him more liquor, he left. With his guardians nearby, he moved on to Westminster Chambers and was soon tossed out; then on to the Lexington, where he was also refused service. By this time he was desperately sick, and the faithful Hassler—Rogers apparently had disappeared somewhere along the way—led him back to Brentwood 22 and put him to bed. The next morning he suffered from a nasty hangover. In relating the incident, he did not glorify nor condemn his escapade; it was simply something that had happened, and he described it with detachment.

At times he had to readjust his normal routine in order to entertain close relatives. When his mother came to Cambridge for eight days, he outdid himself to make her visit pleasant and diverting. He took her to the Peabody Museum and introduced her to his friend Professor Putnam. On another day he escorted her and his friend Alice to church and then to the Dunster for dinner; later that day he took his mother and the Wilson girl from the Sargent School to the theater. He had seen the *Wizard of Oz* several times and thought it would be splendid entertainment for his mother; but as she had never seen a musical comedy, he had to resort to persuasion, and then she went only reluctantly. When she was about to leave Cambridge, he was able to break the good news that he had achieved the second grade of distinction in his academic work.

When his Aunt Virginia visited him, he dropped everything to give her his complete attention. He had reserved a room for her at the Touraine in Boston, but she disliked the place, and he moved her to Cambridge. She examined his quarters in Foxcroft Hall and concluded that they were pleasant enough but shabbily furnished. He guided her about the campus, with a visit to the famous glass flowers, where she spent some time sketching them, and to the display of primitive baskets in the Peabody Museum. After church on Good Friday, he accompanied her to the New England Historical and Genealogical Society in Boston for ancestor-hunting. He entertained her for ten days, registering the deepest gratitude for her kindness and generosity. On at least two other occasions Aunt Virginia came to see him in Cambridge.

Finding him in new quarters in Brentwood 22, she provided more comfortable furniture for the suite. He listened sympathetically to her complaints of people taking advantage of her, and performed little favors like having her watercolors bound in a neat volume and running in to Boston to add more names to the family tree.

His failure to inform her of one bit of unpleasant news did not shake her confidence in him. It was the entrance condition that he put off until the last moment. When Professor Cram wrote her about it, she was aghast that her Vay had an academic deficiency to make up. But he used sweet reasonableness and soon brought her back to normal.

During the college years he gradually shifted the emphasis of social life from fellow students to young women. He continued to hobnob with Williford, Hassler, and Fletcher, but he spent more time in feminine company. For over a year he flitted about from one to another with varying degrees of interest, but by the middle of the second year he found Alice Williams, who soon absorbed his exclusive attention.

There was variety in his search for romance. Some girls, like Miss O'Reilly and Miss Griffin, whom he met at a dance, are mentioned only once in the diary. For a time he corresponded with a girl named Ruth, and this interest died. By March, 1905, he enjoyed being with Helen Aylotte, though by the next month he was escorting Miss Wilson to concerts; it appears he never got beyond the "Miss" stage with her. Briefly he took a fancy to a chorus girl and stood at the stage door in Colonial Alley to get a glimpse of his inamorata; before he had the opportunity to entertain her, she had taken off for parts unknown.

For a time he failed to find a young woman who commanded his entire devotion. During the summer vacation in Swarthmore he saw Anne Jackson, June Prevost, and Edith Walbridge. Back on campus in the fall he developed a momentary passion for Jeannie, a Smith College girl. Yes, he believed it was love at last; but by the end of the year he lost interest because she did not respond to his ardor.

By this time, Vay made a discovery. The Sargent School of physical education, conveniently located in Cambridge, was a promising place to find attractive young women. As early as May, 1905, he stopped there one evening just to see the girls dancing, and he marveled at their gracefulness. In the following fall he attended a dance at the school on November 18, a date he had good reason to remember in later years. In recording the event, he noted only that he took Miss Bellman to the dance and met Miss Barnes there; there is not a word that he also met Alice Williams that night. In fact, not until December 7 did he begin to give serious notice to Alice. That night he decided to take Chorené Barnes and Alice Williams to a play. When he called on the girls and extended the invitation, Alice accepted at once in a straightforward way without the preliminary coyness that girls usually displayed on such occasions.

For several weeks Vay could not decide between Alice and Chorené. To complicate matters, Miss Wilson and Jeannie were still in the picture. Balancing the attractions of Chorené and Alice, he gave Alice a slight edge in the matter. The next time he saw her, he was completely captivated by her divine dancing, and he mildly reproached himself for falling in love with her.

On returning from the mid-winter holidays, the first thing he did was to see her. Now, he knew he was in love. But she did not respond, and when asked why, she explained that she was committed to another man, a statement that cut him deeply. He brought his persistence into full play, continued to see her, and we hear no more about the other man.

Little did he realize that he had begun a three-year courtship. At first he was uncertain whether she really liked him, and so for some time it was a one-sided affair. But there was no doubt about his feelings. At a Sargent School dance, when she insisted on having a turn with Robert Sibley, a freshman, Vay boiled with jealousy. The next night he continued to declare his love, hoping upon hope that she would respond.

Soon he was convinced that she did love him, and then he had to be with her every free moment. He took her to the theater, to dances, and even to a lecture in one of his anthropology courses. He met her mother, and he visited at her home in Salisbury, New Hampshire. When spring came to Cambridge, he took her to Revere Beach for an outing or whiled away the hours canoeing; and sometimes he spent most of Sunday with her. When he could not arrange to see her at night, he phoned her or stopped in for a brief call during the day. He cut classes to be with her. In the middle of June, six months after meeting her, he left for home in Swarthmore and obtained his mother's consent to the engagement.

By July 5 he was back in Cambridge for the summer session. When his train pulled into the station, she was there waiting for him. Then began an idyllic six weeks. He was with her all of his free time; and when they were not together, she was constantly on his mind; he was delirious with happiness. Somehow he managed to attend classes and to pass the course that was his legitimate excuse for being in Cambridge.

The courtship continued from the fall of 1906 to the end of 1908. Although he was separated from her for nine months, when he was in Mexico and the Southwest on archaeological work, the letters sped back and forth between them. Early in 1907 he bought her a diamond and began to call her "Little Woman"; and a year later he began to make plans for marriage.

If social life, fun, and love appear to be the exclusive concern of many college students, such was not the case with Morley. He entered Harvard for the specific purpose of training for a profession, and despite his extracurricular activities he took his academic work seriously. There were lectures, assignments, examinations, and other prosaic details that could not vie in interest with the round of shows, dances, and football games; but he had a firm set of values that told him when the call of duty must be obeyed.

Several factors favored his academic work. He had a good mind; he was able to gauge his ability with remarkable accuracy; he could exert self-control when necessary; and, perhaps most important, his increasing interest in archaeology stimulated a driving zeal to master that field of knowledge.

He responded variously to the six courses he took each semester. Some of them—English courses, comparative literature, French, and philosophy—were rarely mentioned in the diary. Zoology gained notice only because the teacher did not like Vay's sketches. Though he said nothing about history of religion, he liked the teacher, Professor George Moore, for his dry humor.

In other courses he had his ups and downs. Professor Haskins tried to dissuade him from taking medieval history, the introductory course in the subject, but Vay ignored his advice. At first, all went well, but by mid-winter he had his fill of it and detested the stuff. In freshman rhetoric he and Gordon crammed the textbook by Hill the night before the final examination.

For a brief period he displayed a fleeting interest in writing. During a summer vacation he wrote two stories. "The Tales of a Western Town" and "The Fall of Jericho." His mother and his aunt applauded the efforts, but it is doubtful that he submitted the second story to *Harper's* as he had contemplated in a hopeful moment. On returning to the campus in the fall of 1905, he signed up for a course in English composition, only to discover that he and Dr. Maynadier did not agree on his achievement. Vay was confident that he was making an A or B in the course; the instructor declared it was no more than a C. Thereupon the disappointed student sought the class of another teacher, Dr. Murray, who was more to his liking. That is the last we hear of his attempts at writing in the early years.

If he showed no particular ability in composition, his performance in one foreign language was even less promising. The language happened to be Spanish, and his struggle with it is amusing in view of his future need of that tongue. He delayed studying as long as possible. When he did buckle down to Alarcón's *Capitán Veneno*, he found it dry as dust. He admitted he was unprepared for the mid-winter examination, and hardly studied for the final, realizing that he could gain no more than a C in the course. In his academic record Spanish was his poorest subject.

The entrance requirement in Latin also gave him trouble. For a year and a half he did nothing about it except to try to talk his way out of it, but the Latin Department would not budge. Time crept up on him; his senior year was approaching, and he could not register until he had cleared the deficiency. So in April, 1906, five months before the deadline, he began the task of translating three thousand lines of Virgil. At first he plodded along at twenty lines an hour, and stared at the pages that lay ahead. Sometimes he worked diligently, including entire Sundays when he could have been with Alice. Once he secured the aid of a tutor, and during the summer at home he gladly accepted the help of a friend. In September he returned to the campus, took the examination, and nine days later learned that he had passed.

It is not surprising that the teachers who influenced him were all active in the field of his future profession. Beyond that simple fact, no consistent pattern of influence from teacher to teacher emerges.

Frederick W. Putnam, long-time curator of the Peabody Museum, who never had Vay in a course, was a friend or, more accurately, his first professional mentor, for it was Putnam with whom Vay had corresponded when he was only fifteen years old. Putnam was probably the only man on the campus whom Vay knew when he arrived there in September, 1904. From then until January, 1907, the curator had the student at his home for dinner several times, forced him once to walk for his health, and helped to arrange his first trip to Yucatán. Understandably, Vay held him in high esteem.

If Egyptology had originally attracted Morley to Harvard, as is sometimes claimed, he soon changed his mind, because the several courses he took in that subject failed to strike fire in him. Perhaps Professor Lythegoe was too easy and unchallenging—Vay received an A-plus on one examination—and the several conversations he had with the man left no striking impressions. In the summer of 1906 he took classical archaeology with Oliver Tonks. It started with Egypt, which pleased Vay, and he found the professor satisfactory; but the lectures were an hour and a half long, and Vay was too deeply involved in his courtship of Alice to give the course proper attention.

Several other instructors received surprisingly scant notice in the diary, which is a fairly reliable barometer of Vay's interest. Charles Peabody taught European ethnology, and for that course Vay prepared a paper on the Basques; but he never mentioned the man or the paper in his diary. Professor Farrabee offered the introductory course in anthropology that kindled his excitement only with the lecture on Central America. The subject of Vay's term paper, "Pigmentation as an Index of Vital Superiority," was an unfortunate choice, as is evident in the pedestrian performance. Even the lecture notes in this course degenerated to a scrawl.

For a time Ronald B. Dixon held his interest, despite several unattractive traits in teaching. Dixon cultivated a cool detachment from his subject and showered an array of facts on the students. But Vay liked and respected him, and took four semester courses with him. In fact, he also signed up for American Indian languages, which was canceled because he was the only one to register for it. The first indication of Vay's fascination with the Mayas appears in a paper on deluge myths of Central America prepared for Dixon in December, 1904. Early in the essay he glowed with enthusiasm as he declared that the Mayas had the most brilliant of all aboriginal American cultures and equaled, or almost equaled, those of ancient Egypt and Assyria. In regard to the deluge myths, he concluded that they had no relation to the biblical deluge. Under Dixon, Morley enjoyed his first real excitement in the serious study of the Mayas.

If Dixon stimulated Vay at the right time, Alfred M. Tozzer cultivated the interest until it flowered into professional dedication. Though Vay had only one course with him, which he took in his second year, it marked the turning point in his academic preparation for the career he adopted. At this moment he was ready for the archaeology and ethnology of Central America and ripe for the stimulation that Tozzer offered.

Just thirty at this time, Tozzer had examined the Maya field with a fresh, scholarly approach. Shortly after he graduated from Harvard in 1900, the Archaeological Institute of America sent him to Yucatán to study linguistics. There he visited Chichén Itzá, saw Edward H. Thompson dredging curious artifacts from the Sacred Cenote, and thereupon deserted linguistics for archaeology. For three years he worked among the Lacandones of the Usumacinta River valley and became the earliest serious student to investigate that reticent, dwindling people of Maya stock. In September, 1905, he first offered at Harvard Anthropology 9 on the Mayas, which soon became famous for introducing students to that subject. Morley was one of the three students in the class.

From the start the two men were kindred spirits, Tozzer happy to talk with an interested, dynamic student, and Vay drinking in every word and marveling at the man's deep, driving devotion to his work. Morley wrote a paper on Maya jade for the course and began to read books like Fancourt's *History of Yucatán*, Brinton's *Primer of Maya Hieroglyphics*, and the formidable *Mexican and Central American Antiquities* that contained the latest German scholarship. Then, on December 6, Tozzer took up the subject of glyphs and started Vay on his future specialty. The final examination called for a solution of the Initial Series of Lintel 21 at Yaxchilán; each student came up with a different answer, all of them wrong. Vay's grade of A-minus for the semester must have reflected enthusiasm and effort rather than mastery of the subject. By the second term he was deep in the problem of deciphering glyphs, sometimes working late into the night. When he encountered obstacles, he appealed to Tozzer and was helped over the rough spots.

Morley talked with several men about Maya archaeology with varying success. Perhaps it was only coincidence, but only three days after he learned that he had received the Nichols scholarship of $200, Charles P. Bowditch invited him to his office. Bowditch, then sixty-four years old, was a respected Maya scholar of hieroglyphs, who for years had used his ample private resources to send expeditions to Maya sites, build up the library and collections of the Peabody Museum, and support fellowships for promising young scholars. Doubtless he wanted to size up and encourage this youthful enthusiast. During the conversation he gave Vay copies of his publications, spoke of Maya study, and warned that it was not all easy going. Vay indicated that he would not be discouraged. In recording this interview, Vay gave no suggestion that he fully appreciated the importance and influence of Bowditch; and three years later he committed the blunder of underestimating the power that Bowditch could wield.

Less satisfactory were his calls upon Gordon and Hilprecht at the University of Pennsylvania. George B. Gordon, curator of the museum, was a Harvard graduate who had headed the Peabody Museum expedition to Copán in the 1890's. Vay showed commendable interest in wanting to speak with Gordon, but everything went wrong. The receptionist suspected that the caller was a newspaper reporter and refused to show him in; after the error was cleared up and Vay was introduced, his friendly, enthusiastic spirit withered before the cool, impersonal Gordon, who suffered from a serious inability to get along with people. It is no wonder that Vay was unimpressed. At the same time he called on Herman V. Hilprecht, professor of Assyriology, but found nothing to report about the meeting.

In the summer of 1906 he continued to cultivate his interest in archaeology beyond the classroom, despite the many hours with Alice. He read something by Bandelier, perhaps the 1881 tour to Mexico or more likely the famous essays on the Aztecs; he delved into John L. Stephens' classic on the Mayas; and he ordered editions of Landa and Ximénez from Leipzig.

With his return to the campus in the fall of 1906, the Maya fever continued to rise. Aware that he was spending more and more time on the subject, he apologetically explained that it was not work but pleasure. Once he attempted to translate Landa's account of the Maya alphabet, the earliest and most frustrating source of information for so many Maya enthusiasts. Then he went to the Peabody Museum to examine Adelia Breton's watercolor reproduction of the murals in the Temple of the Tigers at Chichén Itzá. Next he looked into the Dresden Codex, and then asked J. W. Fewkes at the Bureau of Ethnology for copies of his publications. During this activity he also worked on the supplementary sign of God D, and became so entranced that he adopted the figure of that deity for his bookplate.

During the years on campus, curiosity or professional interest attracted him to a number of meetings and lectures. When he heard Henry James speak, he found him verbose and vague. Professor Schofield's reading of Chaucer in the original was pure music to his ears. However, he had no comment after attending a session of Professor Hart's seminar in American history. At a Boston session of the Folk Lore Society, he criticized the audience as overdressed and overfed, but enjoyed the address of Vilhjalmur Stefansson. Naturally, the campus Anthropology Club, composed of students and faculty of that department, commanded his most sustained interest. The programs consisted of reports of explorations, two of which excited his favorable comment—G. F. Will and Herbert Spinden on the Mandans, and Edward H. Thompson on the Maya ruins of Yucatán.

Within several months after hearing Thompson speak, Vay had reasons, which he did not divulge, for believing that he might soon have a trip of his own to Yucatán under the auspices of the Peabody Museum. The interview with Bowditch on December 8 certainly had some bearing on the project. The first mention of the subject in the diary appears on January 24, 1906, when Vay asked and received his Aunt Virginia's approval of the trip, apparently for the coming summer. But the next month Putnam absolutely vetoed the idea of a summer expedition, saying Vay would die of the heat. That shelved the plan for at least six months.

By the time Vay returned to the campus in September, he knew he was slated to go at the end of that semester. It is likely that Putnam gave him the good news in August, when he had the student at his home for dinner. At any rate, the trip was now a certainty.

In preparation for his adventure Vay called on Edward H. Thompson, who had spoken to the club in October. Thompson was an untrained archaeologist out of the nineteenth century, sustained entirely by his enthusiasm for the ancient Mayas. With the support of American patrons, he went to Yucatán in 1885, learned the native language, carried on explorations and wrote reports, and in the 1890's bought the vast hacienda that included the ruins of Chichén Itzá. He maintained a home in Cambridge for his wife and made occasional visits there. By the time Vay called on him, he was already dredging the Sacred Cenote at Chichén under the sponsorship of Bowditch and smuggling the artifacts out of Mexico to the Peabody Museum.

Thompson received Vay with open arms, drew up an itinerary for the trip, and gave helpful advice on the peculiar conditions of life and travel in Yucatán. Vay also met Thompson's twenty-two-year-old daughter and happily learned that she would be in Chichén when he would visit that site. Incidentally, Alice Williams received the last bit of information with a flare-up of jealousy.

In addition to seeing Thompson, Vay also made other preparations. For six weeks he went into Boston for lessons in conversational Spanish. He got along well with the pleasant, humorous teacher, and believed that he was making some small progress. To supplement the fellowship granted by the Peabody Museum and to extend the length of his visit, Aunt Virginia forwarded him $650. The first thing he did was to buy a diamond ring for Alice. In the meantime, he assembled equipment for the trip, and one afternoon Tozzer dropped into his room to inspect the gear and give him letters of introduction to several persons in Yucatán.

The final academic hurdle came late in January, when Vay took an oral examination for graduation with honors. Half of the board, Tozzer, Peabody, and Dixon in anthropology, were all for granting him *magna*; but three other professors had to be reckoned with, Schofield in comparative literature, Moore in history of religion, and Chase in Egyptology. Schofield dissented from the second grade of honor, and so Vay emerged *cum laude*. He received the A.B. in absentia on February 27.

Just past noon on Thursday, January 31, the *Edwin Brandon* moved out of New York harbor, carrying him to Yucatán.

III

Apprenticeship

MORLEY relished every moment of his four months in Mexico in 1907. After some disappointment over the low, sandy, brush-covered countryside of Yucatán, he entered Mérida, the largest city of the peninsula, where the new and old joined in mutual toleration and respect. The main streets displayed modern asphalt paving, and automobiles honked their way among carriages and people. Ancient churches held services at intervals day and night, and their bells rang relentlessly; he entered the cathedral on the main plaza several times to hear the music. Dark-complected natives sauntered about the streets in their picturesque dress, while a small set of wealthy Creoles flaunted diamonds and the latest Parisian fashions as they drove with liveried servants up and down the fashionable Paseo de Montejo to take the late afternoon air.

He had arrived in time to witness the colorful four-day carnival season, with festivities round the clock. A parade occurred every day, each time with a different theme; the one he enjoyed most was the Battle of the Flowers with floats representing ferris wheels, shell chariots drawn by butterflies, and other fantasies. Masqueraders on floats merrily tossed to the bystanders confetti, colored ribbon, candy, fans, and toys. All night dances and balls occupied everyone except the Indians, who leaned through open windows, watching their masters and mistresses and listening to the music of the orchestras. On the first night of the carnival, Vay attended the Ball of Fantastic Costumes, which he found to be a misnomer, for the young women appeared in evening dresses; and those sirens fascinated him with their white skin, lustrous dark hair and long eyelashes, graceful movement and entrancing beauty. Then on the last night he went to the *Baile de Etiqueta*, which he found magnificent, though he was unable to speak Spanish or partici-pate in the dance steps that were strange to him.

In Mérida he also met interesting people. The Jameses, whom he probably learned of through Tozzer, became his closest friends and offered him their hospitality on many occasions. Williams James managed a furniture store, and his wife knew local archaeol-ogy and had a modest collection of interesting artifacts. By coinci-dence, Morley discovered that the Selers were occupying the room next to his in the Gran Hotel. One of the respected authorities on Central American archaeology, Eduard Seler was director of the American Division of the Berlin Museum of Folk Art and at the moment was collecting objects for his museum. His wife Caecillie was a woman of considerable ability, though Vay was struck more by her defiance of convention by smoking in public.

Vay also looked up Teobert Maler, the Austrian explorer of Maya ruins, who supplied valuable reports on sites for the Pea-body Museum. Now in his early sixties, he lived in eccentric retirement in Mérida, spending his time in beer saloons and tink-ering with photography. Though he was usually suspicious of visitors, he responded quickly to Morley, who visited him several times. Once Vay bought a Lacandón incense burner from him for a song, and sometimes he bought photographs as an indirect way of helping the former explorer.

Also in Mérida Vay encountered E. H. Thompson, American consul and owner of Chichén Itzá, who had mapped out his itin-erary. Some years earlier Thompson had been made chief of a secret society of Indians who perpetuated ancient rituals, and he exercised his power to order a performance of old native dances for the last day of the carnival. It is possible that he did this as a favor to Morley. At any rate, Vay enjoyed the ceremony of the ten natives, who wore brown cloth masks, long robes, and headdresses topped with turkey feathers, and wielded tin rattles and feather fans.

Finally, Vay left the city to visit the ruins. As a beginning, he made a one-day trip to Acanceh to examine recently discovered low-relief stucco figures of deities, squirrels, birds, and bats. The frieze was in a dark room, and, unable to make photographs, he spent hours copying the figures, which he exuberantly compared to the reliefs of ancient Assyria. Already he had learned that on visiting a town where he was not known, it was good policy to see the *jefe político* first. In Acanceh this approach produced excellent results, including a fine native meal with the official.

After this slight experience at firsthand investigation, he set out on a two-week jaunt to Uxmal, Labná, Kabah, and Sayil, along the way taking in other places like Xcorché, Kivic, and the Cave of Loltún. It was hard work; the days were hot and the trails dusty; at the ruins he spent many hours measuring, photographing, and drawing plans, fascinated by everything he saw and sometimes growing eloquent over a building like the Governor's Palace at Uxmal.

Every day brought new experiences and more of that "conditioning" he sought in Yucatán. In preparation for the trip he hired an assistant, Adelberto Alvírez, who could speak Spanish and English, and commissioned a driver and a two-wheeled *volante* to provide the transportation. Alvírez was an alert young fellow, who quickly learned how to clear the bush for photographing, set up the camera, and help in measuring. But even Adelberto could do little to ease the trials of traveling and exploring. In the bush, *garrapatas*, or ticks, abounded in unexpected places, and they delighted to cling to human flesh. One might tolerate a few of them, but large numbers could drive a person half mad from irritation. They clung unseen in large clusters to the underside of branches, and the traveler unwittingly brushed them off as he cleared a path. The two men tried to whip myriads of them from their clothing with switches. Sometimes Vay anointed himself with the only preventive, a concoction of tobacco soaked in alcohol. In addition to *garrapatas* there were thorns and brambles to be avoided; and occasionally vines, saplings, and brush intertwined so closely as to reduce visibility to ten feet.

In the bush, trails went off in every direction, and even the experienced native sometimes was lost. Twice Morley fell into that predicament. On the way to find Kivic, some nine miles distant, the Indian guide took him and Adelberto through cornfields and up low hills; the trail grew increasingly rough and then petered out. After four hours of wandering about, Vay realized that the guide was lost and that the party had no food or water, so he wisely ordered a return to home base. A few days later, after emerging from an inspection of the Cave of Loltún, Vay relied on Adelberto's confidence that he knew the trail to the nearest hacienda and dismissed the local guide. They wandered about on horseback, going this way and that, returning to a fork in the trail, and ended in a thicket. Again they had no food or water with them, the sun was broiling, and Adelberto frantically insisted on following each new trail. Finally, Vay began to mark the way with sticks and stones, and managed to return to the main trail and the cave, where they secured drinking water. At that moment the local guide, who was returning to the hacienda on foot, found them and led them crestfallen to their goal.

Gradually, Vay adopted some of the local customs. By the time he reached Uxmal, he had acquired native sandals, which relieved his swollen feet after the day's plodding over ruins. He learned also to sleep in a Maya hammock, a convenient device that could be hung between poles, trees, or doorframes. Experience taught him that the mud walls of a hut assigned to him in a native village might be thoroughly infested with fleas; if the insects won the battle, he retired to the open air for sleep. There were times when the pests kept him awake well after midnight. Consequently, he never passed up the opportunity to stay overnight at a hacienda, where he might enjoy some comforts of civilization like a shower bath. Indian food he took to quickly, first tasting it at the meal he had with the *jefe* of Acanceh; thereafter, he relished hot tortillas, beans, venison, and chocolate.

Some days his work at the ruins absorbed him so completely that he forgot lunch and worked from six in the morning until six in the evening without food. When this happened the second time, Adelberto lectured him severely, with liberal quotations from biblical texts, on the injustice of working a whole day without nourishment. The reprimand was effective, and Vay took better care of himself and his attendant in the future.

The village of Santa Rita provided an unforgettable experience that increased his love of the Mayas. Arriving there just before dusk, he secured a good dinner and lodging for the night. Then the peaceful beauty of the place gradually stole upon him as he looked at the changing scene—the noiseless bush surrounding the settlement, Indian huts outlined against the radiant moon, the flickering light from open hearths, a barking dog creating a ripple of canine replies, children playing in and out of the shadows, and men and women speaking quietly in doorways. As time passed, the fires died down, the children disappeared, the voices ceased, and the village rested quietly in the moonlight.

In following his plan of visiting the least important sites first, he made a brief and disappointing inspection of Mayapán. Now he was ready for the more promising places, and he moved on to Chichén Itzá for a lengthy stay, already arranged with E. H. Thompson. Vay could not have found a more desirable situation for archaeological research, because his living quarters were right in the midst of the ruins. Day after day he investigated, measured, and photographed the major monuments: the Temple of the Tigers, the Ball Court, the Caracol, the Monjas, and all the others. Thompson's daughter entertained him at the main house, and one evening for diversion the two climbed the Monjas to munch onions and crackers as the sun set. When Thompson arrived several days later, he explained everything he could about the place. He recounted his discovery of the High Priest's grave, showed Vay structures he had uncovered, explained the colors used by the ancient artists, demonstrated the making of molds, and escorted him to the Sacred Cenote.

The dredging of artifacts from the depths of the Sacred Cenote, already in progress for several years, was Thompson's greatest coup and eventually the cause of his downfall. One afternoon Vay sat on the bank of the *cenote* writing letters as the dredge lifted loads of mud to the surface and workers pawed through the debris to recover objects that Indians had cast into the pool as sacrifices centuries ago. That afternoon he saw a wavy ceremonial dagger that had been brought up. Periodically, Thompson shipped the best specimens to the Peabody Museum at Harvard by friends on their way back to the States, and when Vay left Mexico he too carried out one of these missions.

At Chichén, Morley met two interesting Englishmen. Channing Arnold and J. T. Frost were completing their examination of the site about the time Vay arrived. They had just come from the wild lands of Quintana Roo, inhabited by the unconquered Indians who continued to resist Mexican domination; his hair stood on end as he listened to stories of blood and murder in the dangerous region. Several months later, when he again encountered Arnold and Frost at Progreso, they invited him to contribute a chapter on Palenque to their forthcoming book, but he had to refuse because he had been unable to visit that site.

He completed almost all of his archaeological investigations by the end of March, so that the travels of the remaining two months took on the flavor of a tourist excursion. In Mérida he attended his first bullfight and vowed it would be his last, as he recalled the sickening spectacle of callous brutality. He did not dream that in years to come he would become "conditioned" to the national sport. Then he headed for Mexico City by way of Progreso and Vera Cruz, stopping off at Mitla, Monte Albán, and Puebla; in his estimation those ruins lacked the grandeur of the monuments of Yucatán.

In Mexico City he enjoyed himself immensely. He fell in with George Guyer, Boaz Long, and Arthur Bowles, three young Americans in the city, and they spent evenings together at dinner or at the theater. In Guyer's apartment they gathered for a balcony view of the parade and Battle of the Flowers; at the height of the festivities Long threw a handful of *centavos* to the milling crowd below and brought everything to a stop, as peons searched for the money and looked for more. Finally, the police appeared and asked the Americans to desist from their little game because of the traffic jam it created.

Morley visited the places that everyone must see on the first trip to the city. One morning the bells of the cathedral moved him to step from the sunlit *zócalo* into the dim, cavernous interior of the venerable edifice, where lighted candles, clouds of incense, the swelling music of choir and organ, and the multitude of kneeling Indians and their masters held him spellbound. Nearby he found the National Museum and gazed for the first time at the classic exhibits of Mexican prehistory—the Calendar Stone, the Indio Triste, the large fragment of the Palenque tablet, and Le Plongeon's Chacmool. Other days passed in photographing churches and visiting the Guadalupe Shrine, Chapultepec Park, and old bookstores for copies of Las Casas and Sahagún. Just before he left, he called on Mrs. Zelia Nuttall, eminent archaeologist, in her magnificent residence in Coyoacán. She gave him a graceful and charming reception, which formed the basis of many other visits to her home in later years.

When the final day of departure from the city arrived, he made another visit to the cathedral and the museum—his ritual of paying farewell calls on monuments that impressed him—said goodbye to his friends who gathered to bid him bon voyage, and was off for the States.

On returning from Mexico, Vay spent some time at home, then hustled about to prepare for a two-month field season in the Southwest. That experience in July and August, 1907, initiated him in dirt archaeology and introduced him to Edgar L. Hewett, a pioneer in the field, who was to influence his professional life for the next few years.

Hewett, at the age of forty-two, was just entering his career in archaeology. After teaching and administrative work in public schools and teachers' colleges, he had gone abroad for graduate training. In 1906 he was associated with the Archaeological Institute of America, and the following year he became director of its affiliate, the new School of American Archaeology at Santa Fe. Dynamic and bristling with ideas, he always had a number of irons in the fire. He was half a century ahead of general practice in his belief that undergraduates could be used to advantage in actual digging. He wrote to Professor Tozzer at Harvard about the "opportunities for field work and training"[1] during a summer in the Southwest, and asked for three young men who would be interested in that experience.

Tozzer chose the candidates with little ceremony. He inserted a note in the Harvard *Crimson*, calling for volunteers who had specialized in anthropology to come to his office in Thayer Hall at a stated time. Only three students showed up for the interview —Morley, Kidder, and Fletcher—and after a casual conversation they were accepted. Obviously, Vay met the requirement, but how Kidder and Fletcher qualified remains a mystery. Kidder was preparing for medicine, and Fletcher had been a college drop-out since January. But Tozzer was an obliging man; he had been asked for three undergraduates and he sent three.

In the case of Alfred V. Kidder, the choice was a happy accident. Twenty-two years old at the time, the Michigan-born student had been educated at private schools in Switzerland and Boston, and was completing his junior year at Harvard. His preparation for medicine was not going well. He detested chemistry, which was required for admission to the medical school. He had taken one course in anthropology, Professor Dixon's introduction to the American Indian, in his second year because the class hours suited his convenience. Kidder was able, adaptable, and self-sufficient. The arduous fieldwork and the outdoor life in the summer of 1907 appealed to him so much that he deserted medicine for anthropology.

John Gould Fletcher was of a different stripe. He joined the

---

[1] Edgar L. Hewett, *Campfire and Trail* (University of New Mexico Press, Albuquerque, copyright 1943 by Edgar L. Hewett), 150.

expedition only because he had nothing else to do. A moody, introspective youth from a well-to-do family in Arkansas, he had entered Harvard in 1903, and in the normal course of events would have graduated four years later. But he was an unhappy young man, uninspired by his courses and so much at odds with fellow students that he had very few friends. In January of his senior year he refused to take the term examinations and so ended his hope for a degree. Since his mother was upset by this turn of events, he could not go home; therefore he stayed on in Cambridge, hoping to find something to do. By this time Morley was his closest friend and the only person in whom he would confide. Vay tried to help him, suggested that John's interest in archaeology was almost as great as his own, and encouraged him to apply for the summer work.

The three students agreed to go on the expedition with little more than a vague idea of what they were in for. They had no knowledge of the vigorous, driving methods of Hewett, who could inspire and frustrate those who worked under him. A rugged individualist, he believed that hard challenges made or broke a man, and he proceeded to supply the challenges.

The plans called for the students to meet Hewett at Jim Holley's ranch in the McElmo Canyon of southwestern Colorado on July 3. Kidder started west several days before the other two and met Hewett on the night of the first in Bluff City, where the director supervised a group of students from the University of Utah in the San José watershed. Hewett and Kidder began a horseback trip for the McElmo, camping out at night and resuming the journey the next morning.

In the meantime Morley and Fletcher reached Cortez by train and were surprised to find no word from Hewett. On July 3, while Kidder was suffering from the horseback ride, Vay and J. G. were on a stage that brought them to Hill's ranch. After supper that evening Hewett appeared and led the two students over the three-mile stretch to Holley's ranch, which was to be their headquarters for the next few weeks. They would take their meals, prepared by Mrs. Holley, in the house and sleep nights in the open area nearby.

41

The students soon learned that everyone slept out-of-doors. The Holleys spread mattresses and quilts about the ground, and the visitors bedded down in cots they had brought. During the first night a windstorm swept over the place, dumping Fletcher out of his bed, though he continued to sleep through it all.

The Fourth of July was no holiday, as Hewett hurriedly introduced the men to their work. They rose at four to make the most of the good morning hours, pitched their tent, and unpacked their duffle bags. Hewett pulled out a map and showed them the region with its mesas, canyons, and streams. Then he led them on a walk, too briskly paced for their comfort. "We panted after him," Kidder remembered, "up the mesa at the McElmo's junction with the Yellow Jacket. From its towering prow we could see Mesa Verde and Ute Peak in Colorado; the Abajos and the distant Henry Mountains in Utah; the tall, red buttes of Monument Valley and the blue line of the Lukachukais in Arizona. None of us had ever viewed so much of the world all at one time, nor so wild and barren and broken a country as lay about us."[2] Hewett explained that the ruins were usually found on mesas at the meeting of important streams. So they tramped through the sagebrush out to the point of a mesa, and sure enough, there was a defending wall with its tower and a pueblo a little beyond. Mr. Hewett knew what he was talking about. They continued to walk and to climb over rocks, while the master pointed to cliff dwellings, pictographs, and evidences of another ruined pueblo. Then they trekked three miles back to camp in terrific heat.

In the afternoon when it was too hot for physical exertion, they lolled about in the shade. Hewett talked about archaeology and made a strong impression on them.

On the fifth Hewett left them. Before riding away, he gave brief instructions. Morley was put in charge of the group, though he was modest enough to believe that this involved no more than copying the field notes at night. Hewett waved his arm in a grand sweep over the landscape, and casually said, "I want you boys to make an archaeological survey of this country. I'll be back in three

2 *Morleyana*, 95–96.

weeks."[3] Then he rode off to Bluff City, two hundred miles down the San Juan River.

The trio went to work. All ruins had to be described, photographed, and mapped. Vay took notes, the most boring and tedious of all the tasks, and aided Kidder in drawing plans of buildings, while all three worked together on measuring. Fletcher, clumsy with his hands, soon demonstrated that he could do little more than hold the measuring tape. Vay had learned surveying and horseback riding at military school. Kidder also had some experience with horses. It seems that Fletcher could ride, but he was really not at ease with animals.

Vay's persistence soon amazed Kidder. "He never let up. Heat, cracking sunburn, thirst, saddle soreness, rock bruises, cactus stabs, nothing discouraged him," Ted remembered. "I can see him now, a quick, small figure in high boots and khakis and an enormous straw hat that was always falling off, stumbling about among the fallen walls and along the rimrocks, perilously close to nasty drops. Why he never broke his neck . . . is a mystery—he never looked where he was going. He'd trip and go down, and pick himself up and keep on, cheerfully whistling."[4]

Sunday, July 7, was the first of several unfortunate days for Fletcher. The men rose at four as usual, the moon still shining; and they were off to their work by five-thirty. They rode a buckboard to the entrance of Ruin Canyon, tied the horses, and went their separate ways to examine the top of the mesa. After crawling over more than a mile of rocks and cliffs, Morley and Kidder found no ruins and returned to the wagon. Then they called for J. G. and finally found him at some distance. But when he descended from the mesa to join them, he took an unfortunate jump and rolled down over the stones, suffering a cut on his knee, a broken tooth, a skinned upper lip that swelled painfully, and torn trousers. The three men continued their work, returned at the usual time for lunch, and then rested in the afternoon.

[3] A. V. Kidder, "Reminiscences in South West Archaeology, I," *The Kiva*, Vol. 25 (April, 1960), 12. All quotations from this article are used by permission of the publisher.
[4] *Morleyana*, 96.

In the evening Vay and J. G. went to a neighbor's to look for horses. On their return, as Fletcher dismounted, his refractory mule, which he had chosen in spite of Vay's advice, dragged him for many yards until he finally relinquished the rope. The accident added more knee cuts, a scratched face, and a hand unmercifully burned by the rope. With trembling, angry voice he cursed Vay and the mule.

These misfortunes demoralized the sensitive Fletcher. He did not show up the next day when Vay and Ted rode out of camp at daybreak. But on returning from their work that afternoon, Vay learned that J. G. had written a complaining letter to Hewett, which embarrassed and annoyed Vay.

Hewett later explained the incident. "The first cow man who came down the river brought me a doleful letter from Fletcher. They were in dire condition—totally unprepared for the life they had fallen into; quite ignorant of the work assigned to them. Would I kindly return and give them a few weeks of instruction in camp life and in the rudiments of archaeological field work? The next cow man to drift down the river brought me a spirited letter from Kidder and Morley. They had learned of Fletcher's lamentations and wanted me to know it was a minority report. They were not infants; they begged me not to come back to their rescue and assured me that they would survive and have something to show me." And Hewett added, "I said, 'Well, this looks interesting. It may be possible to live down a Harvard education.' "[5]

It must be said for Fletcher that, banged up as he was, he pulled himself together after a day of recuperation and joined his companions once more in the routine of reconnoitering, measuring, and mapping. However, a few days later there was another incident. On returning from some ruins they had examined, J. G. began to complain about something, and Kidder, having had enough of that sort of thing, told him to go to hell. At that, J. G., shaking with passion, poured forth a volcanic eruption of anger. Even Vay, who could tolerate much, discovered the limits of his

[5] Hewett, *Campfire and Trail*, 152.

endurance with J. G.'s antics, and made some harsh comments in the diary about the incident. Less serious was an episode two days later. As they ascended Bridge Canyon, Fletcher insisted at every defile that they were on the wrong trail; but Morley and Kidder, who knew where they were going, ignored the advice and came out at their goal.

If Fletcher was a misfit in the summer expedition, Morley was the natural leader. Kidder, too modest to record his own achievements, praised Morley as "the sparkplug of our three-man team." Vay alone knew "what an archaeological survey was all about." When Ted concluded that "we did a pretty good job," he added, "But it was all due to Vay. He was an indefatigable worker, full of energy, invariably cheerful, whistling and singing as he stumbled about the ruins. Very nearsighted, it was a miracle that he didn't break a leg or pitch himself over any of the cliffs. . . . His example kept us going, in spite of the great heat, and various minor discomforts, the worse of which was the clinging of the swarms of flies at the Holleys'."[6]

Good as his word, Hewett showed up on July 25, three weeks after he had left the young men to carry out the stiff assignment. He later crowed over the success of his policy of throwing a person in the water to teach him to swim. "A bewhiskered trio laid before me well-made maps of that six-mile square, archaeological remains meticulously described in orderly notebooks, potsherds accurately classified, and a two-hundred page report that I am still proud of," he declared thirty-five years later.[7]

Then he moved the team to Mesa Verde for another three weeks to concentrate on two structures, Spruce Tree House and Cliff Palace. Kidder and Fletcher measured the remains and noted the direction of the walls, and Morley drew the plans and took notes. Hewett continued to amaze them with his physical vitality; on August 4, Vay noted that on returning to the camp that day the director walked so fast he nearly killed them.

At Mesa Verde they met Jesse Nusbaum, a tall, striking young

6 Kidder, "Reminiscences," 12, 13.
7 Hewett, *Campfire and Trail*, 153.

fellow just out of the State Normal School at Greeley, Colorado. Sociable, friendly, and with an uncanny know-how in solving practical problems, he got along well with the Harvard boys, and became a lifelong friend of Ted and Vay.

In the middle of August, Hewett moved the team down to the Santa Clara Canyon of New Mexico to work on the ruins of Puyé mesa. Here they were ordered to excavate, a new and thrilling experience for the budding archaeologists. Puyé "kept us very busy for it was the first piece of digging for either Morley or me," Kidder explained later. Hewett wanted "to try us out and to make us learn for ourselves." The result was "very good for us although it might have been hard on the ruin. But, thanks again to Morley, we did a pretty good job."[8] In fact, Vay published the results of their excavations in a paper three years later.

Fletcher was still in the group but not of it. He was unable to acquire the knack for that kind of work; as Ted said, his "fingers were all thumbs,"[9] and he was useful for nothing more than holding the measuring tape. Completely unmoved by dirt archaeology, he hated everything about the job. More accurately, he disliked himself because of his clumsiness. Every day was monotonously the same, with rocks, cliffs, heat, and the cursed tape measure. Touchy and irritable, he exploded at the least quip at his expense. A humorous reference to his plight with the refractory mule set him off in a burst of anger. One day in the field he walked off the job and returned to camp; that afternoon Ted told him off, but he refrained from recording the details.

As the weeks passed, J. G. developed a resentment against everybody. He was irritated at Vay's humor and his jokes; he envied the exactness of his archaeological work; and he concluded that the man had no creativity, doubtless an unconscious reflection of what the young poet esteemed in himself. Also, he found Kidder too reserved and distant. And Hewett was no more than a slave driver, forcing them to work over those dreary piles of rock. By the end of August, Fletcher left the team and took train to nearby

8 Kidder, "Reminiscences," 28.
9 Kidder, "Reminiscences," 13.

Santa Fe, telling Vay that he would no longer be one of Hewett's "niggers." Later on, in the more congenial atmosphere of Europe, Fletcher developed his talents in poetry.

Now that the records of the participants of the summer of 1907 are available, the story of Fletcher's part in the expedition comes into focus. He was just not made for that kind of work. More surprising is the fact that in writing his autobiography he omitted large portions of his experience that would have provided a more convincing explanation of his emotional trouble.

In the last days of the season Hewett began to talk to Kidder and Morley about possible jobs in the future, hinting at a $1,000 scholarship that might be available. After Ted left, Hewett had a conversation with Vay, dangling hopes and possibilities but carefully promising nothing. Morley was goggle-eyed at the prospect of a job under Hewett.

The summer of 1907 left its mark on each of the young men. J. G. deserted the expedition with a hatred that burned bitterly in his sensitive soul for the rest of his life. Morley and Kidder learned to know and respect each other, and formed a lasting friendship. They also met an invaluable man in Jesse Nusbaum, who adopted archaeology as a career and made contributions that were never adequately recognized. Ted Kidder shifted from medicine to the study of prehistoric America, adding a remarkable scholar to the ranks of twentieth-century archaeology. The summer showed Vay that fieldwork was to his taste and confirmed him in his professional choice; and he also gained the respect of Hewett.

Morley worked under E. L. Hewett from 1908 to 1914, years of apprenticeship during which he acquired the practical aspects of the profession of archaeologist. Although Hewett was at times an exasperating employer, Vay did his best to get along with him, and in the end received valuable training in archaeology as well as in crusading for the old Mexican colonial style of architecture in Santa Fe.

During his last year at Harvard, when Vay was taking graduate work, he had an increased sense of urgency, a striving to get things done. Immediate plans called for the completion of the master's degree, getting a job, and marrying Alice.

Graduate study was almost incidental to his other activities. A fellowship and some aid from Aunt Virginia spared him financial concern. As for research, he examined the Maya codices and produced two papers, one on the death deity and the other on the four major gods found in those records. His master's thesis on the deities was submitted on 168 four-by-six cards, complete with text, line drawings of glyphs, and conclusions.

Other projects took up most of his time. By the middle of the winter he was writing several reports on the summer excavations, which were never printed. He collaborated with Kidder on what he called a book, possibly the article by the two men that appeared belatedly in 1917. He also studied the Initial Series and the Supplementary Series, and looked into the inscriptions of the Naranjo stelae.

Social life continued with customary vigor. He saw Alice constantly, went to the theater, and entertained his Aunt Virginia and also his mother. He attended several meetings of the Anthropology Club and at one of them reported on his summer experience in the Southwest. Conscious that he should improve his Spanish, he signed up for a course at the Berlitz School in Boston, but he put off going for the lessons and probably never did appear.

Looking toward the completion of his academic work by June and his desire to marry Alice, he began to hunt for a job. Eagerly he grasped at any news of an opening. At the Peabody Museum he heard of the founding of the new school in Santa Fe, with $3,000 earmarked for work in Central America. When he learned of the creation of the Mesa Verde National Park, he at once inquired if that meant jobs. Early he enlisted the aid of Alice's grandfather, Senator Jacob Gallinger of New Hampshire, to arrange interviews for him with officials of the Smithsonian Institution and the Carnegie Institution of Washington.

The prospect that E. L. Hewett dangled before him in the

summer of 1907 was best, and in February, 1908, Hewett told him to come to Washington for conversations. The visit was successful from every point of view. Hewett introduced him to William H. Holmes and Frederick W. Hodge, key men in the Bureau of American Ethnology, and also to lesser lights in that organization; he took him to the National Museum for a view of the Tuxtla statuette; and then he got down to business. Hewett assured Vay of a full-time job at $600 the first year and $1,200 thereafter, which meant that he could seriously consider marriage. When Senator Gallinger heard of the terms, he gave his consent to the match. Vay and Alice promptly went to the New Willard and celebrated the good news with a sumptuous meal. In view of the promised job, there was no need to meet Secretary Walcott at the Smithsonian or the president of the Carnegie Institution.

Before the end of 1908, Vay had accomplished several aims. On leaving Harvard with the M.A. in June, he secured the job with the School of American Archaeology in Santa Fe that Hewett had offered him. And then, taking advantage of the holiday season, he married Alice Williams on December 30.

His title was Fellow in Central American Archaeology for the Archaeological Institute of America, and his immediate superior was Hewett, director of the new organization in Santa Fe. This man, under whom Vay spent the six years of his apprenticeship, was a curious personality. He was a good teacher by example, and he bubbled over with ideas and knew how to carry them out. He was constantly on the go, initiating and implementing projects at different places; he knew the people worth knowing in the profession, had a knack for lobbying, and was wholeheartedly devoted to the archaeology of the Southwest.

People who worked closely with Hewett discovered another side of the man. He was a rural, rugged individualist from Illinois with the traits of a captain of industry who had somehow got into education instead of business. At thirty-three he was a college president, and five years later he deserted academe to become a pioneer in the prehistory of the Southwest. He developed his own methods of investigation (in marked contrast to later "scientific" approaches), organized expeditions, and set up courses of instruction on the subject. He exuded confidence and the sense of infallibility often found in self-made men. A product of the West, he envied the East; as director of the small, struggling School of American Research, he resented the prestige of the Peabody Museum. At the camp at Frijoles in 1908 when Allie Tozzer, of the Harvard faculty, was denied a second helping of bacon, it was not because Hewett was stingy. If he never set out to make enemies, his reflexes did so instantaneously.

Respect and forbearance go far to explain how Vay could work with this man for six years. From the beginning Hewett recognized Morley's ability and was happy to have him on his staff, although he rarely complimented him in public. In turn, Vay respected the energetic drive and positive achievements of the director; and with great tolerance for the vagaries of human nature, he swallowed slights, overlooked rude actions, and patiently countered unreasonable demands. Even when the parting of the ways came in 1914, he did not completely close the door on a resumption of the friendship in the future.

Under Hewett, Vay engaged in a variety of activities. He continued on summer digs in the Southwest for several years and also participated in Hewett's summer school, held at Rito de los Frijoles and later in Santa Fe. In the camps he made friends easily with fellow workers and with students of the outdoor school. Already he was an unforgettable personality. His khaki field outfit and his sandy hair gave him a tan appearance from head to foot. Also, his short stature and his restless energy distinguished him from other members of the staff. As he flitted about from one thing to another, the Tewa Indian laborers nicknamed him *Kohe-'e*, Little Hummingbird. As soon as they realized his lack of fluency in Spanish, they continued to tease him. An Indian would offer him a worthless potsherd with the grave observation. "*Señor Morley, esta cosa es muy buena.*" And Vay always replied, "*Esta cosa es muy buena por nada!*"[10] The incident occurred many times a day.

[10] *Morleyana,* 90.

One of the students at the summer school in 1908 recalled scenes at the camp. Hewett was "bug-eyed with the excitement of exploring an untouched and important site." The staff workers "talked over their discoveries around the camp fire at night," but Morley "was always writing love letters on his knee." "He was the butt of much kidding and would look up with twinkling blue eyes, and, in a high squeaky voice, fire some witty answer at his tormentors."[11]

In one of the summer camps some of his friends perpetrated a huge joke on him. He was already intensely devoted to the study of the Mayas, and he hoped to discover some artifact in the excavations in the Southwest that would indicate a relationship between the ancient inhabitants of that region and the pre-Columbian Mayas of Middle America. As he talked about this favorite theme, Jesse Nusbaum casually questioned him about what he expected to find, and Vay eagerly described the figures most likely to appear. Then Nusbaum set to work at night and secretly contrived an artifact, antiqued it, and buried it in the ground directly in the path of Vay's excavation. Some days later Morley rushed back to camp, triumphantly waving the "proof" he had been seeking. That night he gave a learned discourse on the significance of the find. It was several months before anyone had the courage to enlighten him.

In 1909, Hewett sent him to Mexico to study the orientation of the ancient structures at Maya sites. After taking measurements of some two dozen buildings at Chichén Itzá and Uxmal, he moved on to Kabah. He set up his quarters in the central room of the Palace of the Masks, and the first night he came down with a violent attack of malaria. A nearby quack doctor proved useless, and Vay thought he was going to die. But a local native and his wife fed him sour orange juice and gave him hot baths and massages that brought him around. As soon as he was able to travel, he hastened on to Mexico City. There he suffered another attack of malaria, with his temperature rising to 105 degrees. Except for a visit to Teotihuacán, that closed his second visit to Mexico. The

[11] *Morleyana*, 103.

trip provided only limited scholarly results. Although he later said that he had determined the orientation of almost fifty structures, a report on the subject never appeared, probably because he failed to complete the investigation. But he did announce the discovery of an elaborate complex of buildings at Uxmal that disclosed careful and detailed planning by the ancients.

As far as Vay's future was concerned, his most important work in these early years occurred during the field seasons of 1910 through 1912 at Quiriguá. When Hewett took Morley and Jesse Nusbaum to Guatemala early in 1910, he had no idea where he would excavate; then he happened upon Victor M. Cutter, manager of the Guatemala Division of the United Fruit Company, who urged him to work at Quiriguá, located on a large tract the company had just acquired for banana plantations. In the end, Cutter set up a park of seventy-four acres that included the ruins, provided native labor to clear away the vegetation, and gave the archaeologists the use of the company's commissary and hospital. After the first year the company also paid half the expenses of each annual expedition.

This was Vay's first experience with excavation in Middle America, and he discovered that removal of vegetation from the site was a formidable task. Cohune palms covered the ground, and majestic mahogany and ceiba trees, towering more than one hundred feet, grew out of mounds that contained ruins, and sometimes threatened to crash on the elaborately carved stelae. Gangs of workmen, using cables and tackle blocks, strove to remove those trees; and in some cases the monuments barely escaped destruction. When Vay returned for the second season, he found the land he had cleared overgrown with brush fifteen to twenty feet high.

During the 1910 season, Hewett, Morley, and Nusbaum, the photographer, paid a two-day visit to Copán. During the brief stay for no more than a preliminary examination of the ruins, Vay proceeded to make friends among the natives, who always gave him a happy welcome on later visits.

Not until 1912 did noticeable archaeological results appear at Quiriguá. Earl Morris, a student from the University of Colorado, worked on a shapeless mound and uncovered a seven-room structure. Around the building ran a band of hieroglyphs that Vay deciphered and dated as of the sixth century A.D.

Since Hewett was absent much of the time during the third season, Morley carried the whole burden of administrative detail of the Quiriguá expedition. He was employer, timekeeper, paymaster, interpreter, and in charge of meals. This time his wife and daughter accompanied him. But his daughter fell sick for a time, and Alice was unhappy. He had trouble with the house servants, and at the same time the field workers became discontented and began to leave. At that time he was preparing for the reception of Secretary of State Knox, who paid a brief visit to the ruins. These experiences, trying and exhausting as they were, gave him valuable training for larger administrative tasks in the future.

Because the natives would not work during the week preceding Easter, Morley and Morris suspended their labors at Quiriguá and spent an unforgettable Holy Week at Copán hunting glyphs. As the two men entered the town, the natives rushed to greet Vay with open arms; Juan Ramón Cueva, *alcalde* and prominent man of the place, provided quarters in a clean room, probably the new jail that had not yet been occupied, facing the central plaza. Doña Julia Zúñiga agreed to provide the meals and became Vay's official cook on all future visits.

He sought missing fragments of inscriptions that he had noted in 1910. He knew that the natives had used broken parts of stelae in a modern stone fence bordering the road between the town and the ruins; so he and Earl searched the wall for inscribed pieces, and whenever one appeared he tore it out and copied the figures in his notebook. He continued the search in the modern village, where stones from the ruins had also been generously incorporated into house walls.

In the meantime Morris worked at his assignment of tidying up the grave of John G. Owens, a member of the Peabody Museum expedition who had died of tropical fever at Copán in 1893 and was buried at the foot of the Hieroglyphic Stairway. Earl found a large stone slab, managed to get it to the spot and place it over the grave, and planned to chisel Owens' name and date of death on it.

"Earl," said Morley, coming up to him, "I've found an inscription I never saw before on a step in a stairway down toward the south side. Only the left end glyph shows up. I hope you can uncover the rest of it for me this afternoon."[12]

During these days at Copán it was evident that Vay was sick, though he refused to admit it or to give up working. At night he moaned and tossed with malarial fever, and had to endure the band's practicing the "Dead March" from Saul for the Good Friday service. In the morning he was always up and about, sometimes dragging himself with great effort.

Meanwhile Earl secured a native and a shovel and went to work uncovering the partly exposed inscription. During the operation "we uncovered a crack between two of the blocks, from which a crowd of black bees boiled. The Indian was determined to pry out the blocks to reach the honey in the nest behind them. It took strong argument to induce him to leave them alone until the *patrón* could draw and photograph them as they lay. We plastered mud over the crack," and exposed the group of glyphs by sunset.[13]

The next morning, two days before they were scheduled to leave, Vay came up to Morris, who was completing the chiseling at Owens' grave, and remarked that he had almost finished copying the exposed inscription.

"Got most of it," he said. "Can finish easily this afternoon."

He clasped Morris' shoulder and suddenly went limp.

"My God, Earl, I don't want to go like Owens did. Let's get out of here."[14]

Earl recognized a crisis and knew how to deal with it. By two o'clock he had found enough mules somewhere to take them out, had the luggage packed, and had begun the flight from Copán. He goaded his animal with a sharp stick and lashed the others with a rope to keep the pace as fast as possible. Late in the after-

---

[12] *Morleyana*, 155.
[13] *Morleyana*, 156.
[14] *Morleyana*, 156.

Sylvanus Griswold Morley shortly before his death. Collections in the
Museum of New Mexico.

Part of Hewett's summer school class in anthropology and archaeology in Rito de los Frijoles, 1910. Seated, left to right: Morley, Kenneth M. Chapman, J. P. Adams, Jesse Nusbaum, Nate Goldsmith, and Junius Henderson. Standing, left to right: Wilfred Robbins, Donald Beauregard, J. P. Harrington, F. W. Hodge, Edgar L. Hewett, Neil Judd, Miss Woy, and Miss Freire Marrecco. From *El Palacio*, 1927, Museum of New Mexico.

Group at Hawikuh, Zuñi, New Mexico, in 1920. Seated, left to right: F. W. Hodge, A. V. Kidder, Standing, left to right: Morley, Edwin F. Coffin, Jesse Nusbaum, Aileen O'Bryan, Eleanor Hope Johnson, Neil Judd, Earl Morris, and Deric O'Bryan (young boy). Courtesy Daniel T. Kelly.

Morley on Expedition of 1915. When Morley sent this picture to Robert
S. Woodward, then president of the Carnegie Institution, he identified it
only as "Scene in Camp." Morley is at the right; the other men are natives
who accompanied him. Courtesy Carnegie Institution of Washington.

John Held, Jr., who accompanied Morley on naval intelligence expeditions during World War I. This photograph was taken about 1920. Courtesy Mrs. John Held, Jr.

Entering the Cave of Loltún, February 24, 1923. The party, preceded by natives, descends a makeshift ladder to the cave. Courtesy Mrs. Elinor Vail.

In the Cave of Loltún. Shortly after this picture was taken, panic spread among the visitors, and Governor Carrillo mounted the rock and gave a stern command to restore order. Courtesy Mrs. Elinor Vail.

With the departing guests at Progreso, February, 1923. Left to right: Dr. Merriam, Mrs. James, Morley, unidentified lady, Alma Reed, E. H. Thompson, Elinor Morley, and Jean Hiland. Mrs. James, Morley, Thompson, and Elinor Morley saw the visitors off to their boat. Courtesy Mrs. Elinor Vail.

noon they stopped at a miserable inn for food. Vay slept by fits and starts, and when he woke inside the hut, he found a chick pecking at his spectacles and then witnessed filthy actions of a child and a dog. Revolted at the sight, he rushed from the room to his mule.

By nightfall Earl got him as far as Jocotán, where the *commandante* turned over his office for their sleeping quarters. Soon they discovered that the cowhide plaiting of the bedstead where Vay was to sleep teemed with bedbugs. He looked about the room in disgust. "With one movement of his arm he swept the *commandante*'s desk free of papers, pens, inkwells, everything, and on that hard surface he writhed and twisted through a miserable night."[15]

The next morning they made the most of the cool hours for traveling, but when they entered the plain the heat mounted and so did Vay's fever. As Earl saw him riding along, at times only half-conscious, he feared he would fall from the saddle. So he tied his feet together beneath the animal, and moved the *mulada* on as fast as possible. By early afternoon they reached Zacapa and found quarters in the railroad barracks. They had covered the route in half the normal time.

"When the rope was untied," Morris explained, "Morley slid into my arms like a bag of salt. I carried him through an open doorway to a cot that showed invitingly within. In those days the bar at the far end of the barracks offered the most refreshing drink it has been my lot to quaff—fresh lime juice squeezed into simple syrup, served in a huge tall glass with ice and carbonated water. A lump of ice rubbed over Morley's cheeks and forehead brought him to full consciousness. He tugged at the straws with the avidity of a nursing lamb and when the glass was drained, closed his eyes in what I hoped would be a long and restful sleep. I went round to the bar for a drink on my own account. Upon my return I witnessed as forceful a demonstration of the relentless drive and unquenchable spirit of the man as I was ever to behold in years of subsequent association. There he sat with shirt open, one

[15] *Morleyana*, 158.

trouser leg on, one off, huddled over the ubiquitous notebook. He said, 'They'll wreck that inscription for the honey behind it. Got to draw those terminal glyphs before I forget . . . .' At that point he slumped forward in a dead faint."[16]

Morley made one more annual expedition, that of 1913, under the direction of Hewett. It was unique among his trips to Yucatán, because this time the director commissioned him and Jesse Nusbaum to prepare an extensive photographic record for use at the San Diego Exposition that was scheduled to open in 1915. Alice and daughter True accompanied Vay to Mérida and lived there while the men visited Maya sites to take pictures.

After enjoying the carnival season in the city, Vay and Jesse set out on their assignment. Morley had ambitious plans to photograph the daily life of contemporary Mayas and also to film a drama enacted before the ancient pyramids and temples. When he visited Chichén Itzá, he began to select the major actors for the play, striving to use only pure Maya types. But the fate of that project is unknown; later reports of the expedition fail to mention the film drama.

They did shoot considerable footage of contemporary life and ancient ruins. After weeks at Chichén, they moved on to Valladolid to record the *cenote* and the local market, famed for its henequen hammocks. Uxmal was too unhealthy for more than a few days' stay, and they proceeded to Campeche. On the way back to Mérida they stopped at the Santa Cruz hacienda, and while Nusbaum made a detailed record of henequen cultivation for the commercial side of the San Diego Exposition, Vay managed to discover a date inscription.

Then the two men made a daring trip into the region of the *sublevado* Mayas. Ever since the War of the Castes in the mid-nineteenth century, Mexico had failed to conquer the natives in the eastern part of Yucatán, despite alternating policies of persuasion and persecution. In 1913 the government sent General Eguía Lis, military commander of the peninsula, to make peace overtures to the *sublevados*. Lis had had one meeting with the

[16] *Morleyana,* 159.

chiefs and was about to make a second trip to complete negotiations when Morley arranged to go with him to be under the
protection of his soldiers.

Two purposes lay behind this dangerous venture. If Nusbaum
could take motion pictures of a meeting between Lis and the
Maya chiefs, it would enrich the pictorial record of contemporary
native life in Yucatán that Hewett had ordered. Also, Morley
wanted to visit Tulum in order to verify the reading of a date inscription first reported by John L. Stephens in 1840 and deciphered by George Howe in 1910. Howe read the date as A.D. 290,
which Morley considered entirely too early, and he believed that
Howe had made some error.

The military expedition sailed from Progreso along the northern
coast, rounded Cape Catoche, and landed at San Miguel on Cozumel Island. Vay and Jesse, attired in their field outfits of khaki
trousers and knee-length boots, attended a native dance there.
With Tulum as their major aim, they rented a sailboat to take
them across the short stretch of water to the mainland. But the
local official in San Miguel refused to clear them for Tulum because of danger from the *sublevados*. Then they said they would
go to Chacalah, twelve miles from Tulum, and they secured reluctant permission to depart. They headed, of course, straight for
the ancient walled city.

Quickly they realized that they could not count on the help and
protection of the three soldiers and five sailors who accompanied
them. The men got drunk, and a storm tossed the vessel about in
the night. On approaching the wall-crowned bluff of Tulum, they
encountered a reef parallel to the coast, and between the reef and
the shore an expanse of six hundred feet of high seas. The captain
refused to cross the reef. So Vay, Jesse, and three soldiers launched
a dugout canoe they had brought with them, and filled it with
supplies. As the small craft shipped water in the high seas, the
Mexicans cursed their fate, and the Americans used stronger
words in two languages to urge them on. The canoe rode one swell
and had almost reached shore when a high wave capsized the boat
and poured cameras, lunch, guns, and supplies into the water.

They fished out the articles, realizing that the guns were out of commission—not much loss as they were old-fashioned muzzle-loading shotguns—and that the cameras and photographic plates were damaged. A man was sent back to the sailboat for the rest of the soldiers and five remaining dry plates. Then the party, constantly apprehensive of an attack by the natives, gingerly explored Tulum.

They were able to do little more than wander over the site for a few hours. Everywhere they had to hack their way through scrub palms and thorny bushes, along the rocky bluff that led them to the outer walls as well as inside the enclosure. Before the main *castillo* a cleared space appeared, but it was not particularly welcome because it indicated that natives regularly visited a shrine they had set up in that structure. No photographs were taken; everyone was too busy watching the brush for Indians about to attack them.

After five hours of furtive exploration, fortunately with no evidence of hostile natives in the vicinity, they put off in the dugout. Morley tells the rest of the story: "Toward evening the party returned to the beach and made preparations for boarding the boat. The sinking sun painted the principal temple a golden yellow, and the green sea, pounding the rocky shore below its base, every now and then threw a cloud of spray swirling in the air. In silence, as we found it, we left the ancient city until some more fortunate time.

"During the stay on shore the sea had risen and it was with grave doubts that the writer entrusted himself to the dugout canoe again. Twice this unseaworthy shell was capsized before getting beyond the breakers, and it was only with the most energetic bailing that it reached the sailing boat at all. The sun was just setting as the last of the guard was climbing over the heaving gunwale and the anchor was weighed.

"A gale was blowing dead ahead. Time after time the captain tried to tack out to open sea, but as often was buffeted back by the mountainous waves. In one of those encounters the little boat, caught in a hollow between two lofty crests, was battered down it seemed to the very bottom by an avalanche of water. To the writer in the hold, too ill to raise his head, it seemed as though a young Niagara had broken over him. Under this continuous assault, the boat sprang a leak and it was all the wheezy little pump could do to hold its own. The bilge water rushing from end to end, as the boat one moment was stern up and the next stern down, sounded as though the whole Gulf of Mexico had been shipped and was riding back and forth.

"By seamanship worthy of the highest praise, by teamwork little to be expected in such a ragged, misfit crew, the boat was gradually coaxed out to open sea where, although the swell was heavier, the perilous white-caps were fewer. A night of pitching and tossing followed, and it was the middle of the morning before San Miguel was sighted."[17]

"No Broadway hotel," remarked Nusbaum, "ever looked better to us, or more inviting, than the little thatch roofed cantina where we took our belated noon-day meal."[18] That night the Mexican gunboat, now making its return trip, picked up the two men and brought them back to Progreso after thorough punishment from a *norte* along the northern coast.

All told, the trip yielded limited results. Nusbaum secured only a handful of pictures and apparently failed to record the interview between General Lis and the Maya chiefs. The stone with its questionable hieroglyphic inscription could not be found. Vay was able, however, to report certain features about the ruins of Tulum: it was a walled site, unusual among the ancient Mayas; all of its structures had flat roofs; and its decorations consisted of stucco carving and wall paintings. These things made it attractive for future investigation.

Another result of the trip was the seriocomic attention it received in Morley's hometown newspaper. Some enterprising journalist, reading the plans of the excursion, played up the potential

[17] Morley's report from Edgar L. Hewett, *Ancient Life in Mexico and Central America*, 163–64, copyright 1936, by the Bobbs-Merrill Company, Inc., reprinted by permission of the publishers.
[18] Winifred Hogaboom, "The First Story of Morley's and Nusbaum's Excursion to Central America Last Winter," *Santa Fe New Mexican*, July 25, 1913.

danger that the explorers faced. On April 15, the *Santa Fe New Mexican* carried a front-page article headed "Two Santa Feans Visit Bad Men on Cozumel Isle," which sounded the ominous question whether the natives of Cozumel and Tulum were cannibals. Two days later the question became a fact, as the paper announced, "Grave Danger in Visiting Isle of Cozumel. Peril of Morley-Nusbaum-Luis Expedition in Facing Cannibals Who Have Eaten Other Explorers. Mrs. Morley Alarmed over Husband's Fate." Accompanying the article was a picture of Nusbaum, with a caption suggesting that he might have been devoured by man-eaters.

Not until ten days after the first article appeared did the paper allay the fears it had created by explaining that the two men were safe and on their way back to the United States. Still a week later it quoted from a report attributed to the *Boston Globe* that emphasized the escape of the men from a perilous situation. In July, weeks after the men had returned home, the Santa Fe paper ran a long account of the whole expedition to Yucatán, based on information provided by Nusbaum. There is no doubt that Vay and Jesse thoroughly enjoyed the public notice as well as the alarm their adventures created.

During these early years of his career, Morley engaged in one cause that took him beyond the bounds of archaeology, a crusade to preserve the old native style of architecture in Santa Fe. Early in 1912 a city planning board was created to support the movement, and Morley was one of the eleven members.

In the course of time he became a chief spokesman, perhaps the major aggressive leader, of the crusade, supported always by other members of the committee, many of whom were his friends. Hewett offered the co-operation of the school; Bronson M. Cutting, publisher of the local newspaper, helped to publicize the cause; M. A. Otero, former governor of the state, added the weight of his name; and there were others, like Samuel Cartwright and Harry Dorman.

Vay threw himself into the cause with the same enthusiasm with which he searched out glyphs in Central America. He talked to all kinds of local organizations on the theme that Santa Fe would enjoy fame and prosperity from its old buildings rather than from more modern ones. He admitted that his mission was to teach the people to value their own heritage.

Soon he was given full responsibility for the campaign, and he enjoyed the challenge. He proposed an exhibition for the purpose of informing the public how civic improvement could be achieved; the Chamber of Commerce sponsored his idea, made him director of the project, and asked him to co-operate with the planning board. Since the exhibition was scheduled for November 18, he had only eleven weeks to prepare for the public show.

He went into high gear. To his friends he assigned particular tasks; and as those persons toiled away, he made his rounds, rushing in on each assistant to inquire about progress and fussing about like a hen over its chicks. New ideas constantly popped into his mind. One was a lamp post he designed that would be in keeping with the old style; another called for replacing the Victorian bandstand on the plaza with a structure conforming to the colonial style.

The exhibition opened on schedule in the old Palace of the Governors and continued for two weeks. There was everything he had planned—models of buildings as they should be restored, drawings of proposed improvements, and photographs of structures in the best colonial form.

He also sensed that concrete results could be effective, and so he pointed to old houses that had been historically refurbished; moreover, he started a campaign to supply architectural plans for persons wishing to build homes in the tradition. In fact, he had already bought an old adobe house in Santa Fe and renovated it so as to emphasize its original lines. He showed how modern conveniences could be incorporated into such houses without altering the style. The Chamber of Commerce offered prizes for the best architectural plans, and after the competition the winning designs were also displayed for public inspection. In the meantime, Jesse Nusbaum began the task of restoring the Palace of the Governors, the most historic of all the old buildings in the town.

Morley published an article early in 1915 that stated the fundamental aspects of the old style. He made good use of photographs and drawings, introduced sufficient history to explain the indigenous nature of the colonial form, and once more emphasized the telling point that modern living could be adapted to the old architectural style without compromise to either.

He gave dynamic leadership to the campaign at the right moment. He supplied the crusader's zeal; he stimulated the coterie of believers with faith, vitality, and enthusiasm; and he was astute enough to combine the practical with the esthetic. Unlike many professional men, he intuitively knew how to appeal to the general middle-class public.

IV

The Carnegie Institution
of Washington

FROM any point of view, Morley's appointment to the staff of the Carnegie Institution of Washington in 1914 was the significant milestone of his entire professional career. It placed him in the niche he was cut out to fill, it came when he was young enough to make the most of his talents, it allowed him greater professional freedom than any other post he could have found, and it initiated a new chapter in the history of American archaeology. Incidentally, the appointment eventually brought coveted public notice to the Institution because of his work on the Mayas.

He showed intuitive good sense in seeking the post at the time he did, though he was remarkably young for appointment by such an institution. He had the ability to measure himself accurately; he had the self-confidence, unspoiled by egoism or boastfulness, that comes with maturity. And as events proved, he evaluated himself correctly.

The Carnegie Institution of Washington naturally attracted his attention. It had ample resources for research, it required no other duties, such as teaching, and scholarly results were published without thought of income or royalty. The offices were housed in a stately stone edifice that reflected the dignified and serious work it carried on. With an endowment of $22,000,000, the organization spent over $925,000 for research in 1914, and its income continued to mount year after year. The powers of its charter were generously vague, restricted only by the requirement that it engage in investigation, research, and discovery, and apply the knowledge gained to the improvement of mankind. From the start, however, the trustees trained their sights mainly on the natural sciences, and by 1914 eight of the nine major departments belonged to that category. The president, Robert S. Woodward, astronomer and physicist, had early abandoned the policy of grants to individual scholars to be used as they saw fit in favor of a system of creating departments in various disciplines, staffed by specialists, who worked under some supervision toward the solution of specific problems. Although a board of trustees, composed of outstanding men from various fields, was responsible for the funds and their use, the executive committee and the president formulated policy and presented it to the trustees for approval. As a result, one or two trustees on the powerful executive committee could exert unusual influence on policy, as was the case in Morley's appointment. In the early years the C.I.W. would have nothing to do with the newfangled fields of anthropology or archaeology. When five learned societies drew up a joint appeal in 1907, asking for $20,000 to study anthropology on the American continents, the answer was a flat no.

The movement that led to Morley's appointment originated within the C.I.W., and was largely the work of one man, Barclay Parsons. As a successful civil engineer, who had a large part in building the New York City subway, the East River tunnel, and the Cape Cod canal, Parsons must have startled his colleagues on the executive committee when he proposed a department of Central American archaeology early in 1909. But nothing came of the idea, because he chose the wrong specialist, Hiram Bingham, to draw up the specific plans.

Parsons had become interested in Central American archaeology by accident. As a member of the Panama Canal Commission he stopped off in Yucatán on one of his trips from the Isthmus and viewed some of the Mayan ruins; it is possible that he visited

64

Chichén Itzá at the time Edward H. Thompson was dredging artifacts from the Sacred Cenote. Parsons' interest was generated independently of Morley; not until several years later did the two men meet and realize that they had a common bond.

If Parsons had lost his first round in the battle, events conspired to give him another chance. Although the minutes of the executive committee fail to indicate what was going on unofficially, it is evident that pressure came from some quarter to patronize anthropology. During 1912 a proposal to create such a department was deferred several times. News had leaked out at the beginning of the year that a sizable sum would be authorized for anthropology, and the executive committee finally took such action by the end of the year.

When Morley first heard the rumor late in January, 1912, that is, almost a year before the appropriation had been voted, he jumped at it like an answer to a prayer. He saw no future in the job he held under Hewett, and he harbored an ambitious plan to excavate Chichén Itzá that required more than the modest budget on which the School of American Archaeology operated. Unfortunately, his work kept him from Washington, for he spent half the year in the field and the other half in Santa Fe. But he had two friends in the national capital, F. W. Hodge at the Smithsonian Institution and W. H. Holmes in the United States National Museum; and both men had acquaintances in the C. I. W. In addition, he had the support of Charles D. Walcott, one of the inspirers of the C. I. W. and a member of its executive committee, who was also secretary of the Smithsonian Institution and an official of the National Museum. This trio of Hodge, Holmes, and Walcott managed to wield considerable influence directly and indirectly in C. I. W. affairs dealing with archaeology. Thus Vay's policy of urging his cause through these channels proved in the end to be the wisest approach.

In a letter to Hodge, who was always sympathetic, Vay set forth his qualifications and the arguments for the Chichén Itzá project. The statement was convincing because of his ability to speak of himself and his achievements without false modesty and also without boasting. Calmly he set forth the points. Yes, his age might count against him (he was only twenty-nine), but specialized college training and five years of experience in the Maya field could compensate for relative youth. In addition, he had some administrative experience in fieldwork, for he had largely been in charge of the last Quiriguá expedition. As for those who could speak of his ability, he counted on favorable opinions from the men at the Peabody Museum, Spinden and Wissler at the American Museum of Natural History, and, of course, his employer Hewett. The proposed project at Chichén Itzá would cost at least $10,000 a year for five to ten years, but he was willing to settle for half that amount and raise the remainder by his own efforts. Moreover, he had arranged for a lease on the hacienda buildings at Chichén Itzá, which would save money for constructing quarters for the staff. Finally, the recent revolution in Mexico, which might worry a sponsor, could be discounted, because Yucatán was quiet and undisturbed by events in other parts of Mexico.

Excited at the prospect and confident that he had a first-rate idea to offer, he found it hard to wait until he learned that the trustees had approved the grant for archaeology at their annual meeting in December, 1912. At once he arranged for an interview with President Woodward. The meeting was a complete failure, and Vay left dejected and defeated, never realizing that the president was not in a position to encourage his plans. The trustees had left all action in the matter of applying the grant in the hands of the executive committee, and that committee would not meet for three weeks. Fortunately, Morley was also ignorant of Woodward's general hostility to the Chichén Itzá project. Despite the cool interview, he did not lose faith in his plan nor did he lose hope that the C. I.W. might adopt it in the future. Soon he was in Yucatán for another busy field season, and in the process he collected additional arguments in support of the project.

While Vay bided his time in Yucatán, a curious story was unfolding behind the closed doors of the C. I.W. The executive committee had asked the trustees for $20,000 for anthropology, but the motion the trustees passed had a different twist. They appropriated that sum for an investigation of what might be done in anthropology, including archaeology and ethnology, in the American continents, with a report to be made to the board in a year. Parsons as usual took the initiative, and the executive committee followed his suggestion of appointing Woodward, Walcott, and himself a subcommittee to carry out the intent of the motion. Regardless of the wording of the trustees' action, Parsons continued to speak in terms of Central American archaeology.

The subcommittee was at sea about how to proceed. Billings, president of the board, believed that they should appoint a scholar to investigate the field and prepare a program, but the three members could not agree on the scholar. The names of Morley, Bingham, and Jenks entered the discussions; Parsons, however, ruled out Bingham, because his field was South America. To complicate matters, Woodward had no faith in Jenks and Morley, asserting that their work was no more than collecting artifacts for a museum, whereas "the Institution should try to do some better work than that already being well done by museums."[1] Nor did he believe that Jenks or Morley had sufficient qualifications to head a department of anthropology. Unable to agree on one scholar, the subcommittee decided to employ Jenks and Morley to draw up individual reports, and Woodward, apparently on his own initiative, invited W. H. R. Rivers, of England, to provide a third report. A survey of the anthropological needs of the various continents was divided between Rivers and Jenks, while Morley was assigned Central American archaeology. Whatever its merits, a plan had emerged.

Morley was in Yucatán, about to leave for the dangerous Tulum trip, when he received Woodward's invitation of February 24, asking him to come to Washington in the near future to draw up his report. Delighted as he was with the letter, he restrained the natural impulse to take off at once for the States. He was working for Hewett on a special assignment in the field, and an early de-

[1] Woodward to Parsons, Jan. 28, 1913, Morley File, C.I.W.

parture would require an explanation to his employer, which he did not care to make. So Vay put off the meeting until he returned from the field season.

One morning in early June five men sat around the big mahogany table in the board room of the C.I.W. building on P Street. They were Woodward and Parsons for the subcommittee, Jenks from Minnesota, Morley from Yucatán, and Holmes as consultant. No attempt was made to bring Rivers from England, and for some reason Walcott did not appear. The ground rules were agreed upon. Rivers would cover the anthropological needs of Europe, Asia, Africa, and Australia; Jenks was responsible for the American continents and the Pacific Islands; and Morley would handle Central America. The reports must be ready for the printer by early fall, so that copies could be submitted to the trustees a month in advance of the annual meeting in December.

Each scholar was paid on a different basis. Rivers received $1,500; Jenks, $1,000 and traveling expenses; and Morley, $200 a month and expenses as long as he was engaged on the task. In the end he received $1,053 for his work and had the temporary title of research associate.

Morley met Parsons for the first time at this conference, and at once they struck up a friendship that was to endure over the years. Soon Parsons was advising Vay on points to be made or to be avoided in his report, and one of those suggestions required a month of additional research and writing.

In August, when Morley was busy drawing up his report in Santa Fe, he informed Woodward of a development that surely startled and perhaps nettled the president. On his way back to the States, Vay had stopped off in Mexico City on May 9 and applied for a concession to excavate Chichén Itzá. Three months later he received an official letter, stating the conditions on which the grant would be made, and one of the conditions required him to give the name of the institution sponsoring the project. Morley asked Woodward how to reply to the letter. It would be interesting to know what the president thought on receiving this news. The reports of the three specialists had not been completed; the executive committee had not acted on the plans; and finally, as will be evident, Woodward was cool to the Chichén project. He had good right to feel that the young man was making a bold attempt to jump the gun. He restrained himself, however, in replying to Morley, warning him not to name the C.I.W. in any way, and suggesting that he tell the Mexicans that he was not ready to make a full report. When the time came, Woodward added, the C.I.W. itself would negotiate directly for a concession. Morley followed the advice, and was careful to send a copy of his reply to Woodward. All things considered, this negotiation for a concession is another evidence of Vay's diligence and tenaciousness, although it was a premature step at this stage of his relations with the C.I.W. It so happened that ten years were to pass before a concession was drawn up.

The three reports, surprisingly completed and printed by November 1, reveal the competition Morley faced. William H. R. Rivers, forty-nine years old and a fellow in St. John's College, Cambridge University, had made an enviable name in psychology and anthropology with his work in the Torres Straits and on an important expedition to Melanesia in 1908. He proposed an ethnological study of Oceania, with the telling argument that the native culture of that area was about to disappear forever. Albert E. Jenks, forty-four years old, was professor of anthropology at the University of Minnesota and had many investigations to his credit. He pointed to various regions of the Western Hemisphere and the Pacific Islands where fruitful anthropological studies could be carried on. Each man took a different attitude toward Morley and his proposal for the archaeological excavation of Chichén Itzá. In attempting to strengthen his own cause, Rivers belittled the study of American prehistoric culture, and as a dedicated diffusionist argued against the indigenous growth of native culture in America. Scarcely did he attempt to disguise his disparagement of the Chichén Itzá project. On the other hand, Jenks agreed that the project was one of many such investigations that could be fruitfully prosecuted in the Western Hemisphere.

Vay's report appeared last in the volume, probably because of his relatively young age of thirty and his briefer experience as a scientific investigator. Although it is perhaps of little significance, it is interesting to note that Rivers and Jenks had academic identifications attached to their names, while no such attribution appeared after Morley's name.

His report is impressive for the direct, forceful presentation of his ideas. By contrast, the papers of Rivers and Jenks exude a strong academic flavor; Rivers went out of his way to demolish prospective enemies, and Jenks balanced one proposal against another with such cool impartiality that a reader might wonder if he really championed any plan. Not so Morley. He argued the case for the excavation of Chichén Itzá with clarity and conviction. In addition to the main text of his statement, he added appendices and excellent photographs, two maps and a panoramic sketch, which enhanced the effectiveness of his case. The table of contents carefully and logically arranged, looked like a lawyer's brief, while the text was simple, clear, and devoid of scientific jargon. Near the end of the paper he astutely included such details as the daily wages of labor in Mexico in order to emphasize the economic advantages of working there.

Some later critics hold that Rivers really had the most pressing program, particularly since the native culture of Oceania was about to disappear. True as this might be, Morley gave the most effective presentation. Nonspecialists reading the three reports cannot fail to be impressed by the sharply etched picture he presented. Rivers and Jenks, on the other hand, covered broad geographical swaths, wrote with scientific coolness that smacked of a graduate-school lecture, and left a nebulous and confused impression as compared with the sharp, vivid impact achieved by Morley. If the two ethnologists had better projects, and that depends on one's point of view, Morley was their master in effective presentation of his case.

An incident clearly revealed Woodward's attitude toward the three papers. When Holmes was asked to read the reports, he bristled on encountering Rivers' declaration that science would gain by delaying archaeological exploration. At once he sent

Woodward a four-page refutation of the preposterous idea, added a similar rebuttal prepared by Aleš Hrdlička, of the Smithsonian, and insisted that the offensive statement should be deleted before printing. Woodward shot back a tart reply; he was pleased to have the comments of Holmes and Hrdlička, but after all they are no more than individual opinions; the doctors do not agree in archaeology; in fact, no one agrees in this field; and the influence of Rivers' statement has been exaggerated. The executive committee was in no haste to take action. At its meeting on October 16 the reports were officially received, and Woodward was fair enough to display plate proofs of the illustrations accompanying Morley's report. Parsons, wholeheartedly sympathetic to the Chichén Itzá project, wrote Morley an encouraging account of the meeting, and predicted approval of the plan and the beginning of the project in the near future. At the end of October he prodded Woodward to call the executive committee together to decide which plan to recommend to the trustees. Woodward, who had no enthusiasm for what he knew was in the cards, delayed the committee meeting until two days before the trustees assembled.

As Morley waited until mid-December for the verdict, he worried over two dangers that could defeat him and his plan. One was the attitude of Hewett, his employer. Over the years Morley had done his best to get along amicably with that dynamic but exasperating man, and he was confident he had succeeded; thus he assumed he could count on Hewett's support in the C.I.W. affair. Slowly, however, Vay became suspicious. He knew that at one time Hewett had been angry, perhaps jealous, over his employee's application for the $20,000 grant for Maya research; in fact, there was a rumor that Hewett himself had earlier attempted to get financial aid from the C.I.W. and had failed. Although Morley did not consider these things serious, he was alarmed when Hewett failed to give him a promised letter of recommendation before leaving Santa Fe for Washington early in October. From long association over the years, Hewett was personally acquainted with all of the archaeologists and anthropologists in the national capital; and if he was intent on mischief, Vay realized that he could damage his cause. By mid-November, Morley learned that his suspicions were entirely true.

The other possible danger came from events in Mexico. Late in 1910 Madero proclaimed a revolution, and eight months later Porfirio Díaz, long-time president and overly favorable to foreign concessionaires, resigned and fled, and Madero came to the helm. Anti-Americanism flared up, and the United States insisted on protecting its nationals there and accumulated numerous claims against Mexico. The injection of economic reform into the revolution added still another complication to the internal Mexican situation. The revolution did not end, as many foreigners had expected, but dragged on in a state of indefinite political instability.

Morley realized that fearful Americans would hesitate to deal with Mexico under these conditions, although he boldly attempted to argue that the alarm was unfounded, at least as far as the proposed Chichén Itzá project was concerned. Early in 1913, when he was in Mérida, he consulted with his friend William James and concluded that the time was ripe to seek a concession from the Mexican government. James was on good terms with Vice-President Piño Suárez as well as with the governor of the state of Yucatán. Moreover, the new Mexican official in charge of national antiquities was an upright man in contrast to his predecessor, the scoundrel Batres, and he could be approached with confidence. Unfortunately for Morley, Piño Suárez was murdered three weeks later. However, Vay's negotiations in the summer for a concession to excavate Chichén Itzá indicate some sound basis for his contention.

Then in November, 1913, he gave another optimistic appraisal of the situation. Even United States intervention, he asserted, would not affect the work at Chichén Itzá for several reasons. Yucatán was separated by geography and race from the rest of Mexico. Moreover, Yucatán depended so strongly on the United States for the market of its all-important henequen crop that it would secede from the mother country rather than break economic ties with the United States. As events proved, Morley correctly feared the adverse effects of the Mexican situation on his project, but that factor played no part in the trustees' decision on his plan.

Two days before the trustees' meeting, the executive committee found it high time to formulate a recommendation on the three reports. Parsons and Walcott voted for Morley's plan. Woodward filed a minority report in favor of Rivers' plan, declaring that the exploration of antiquities should be carried on by the nation in which they are found, and that artifact-collecting is the business of museums and not the proper task of the C.I.W. In spite of Woodward's report, the committee recommended $20,000 for archaeological work in Central America, the money to be expended under the direction of the committee. Almost unanimously the trustees approved this recommendation.

Happy as Morley was with the decision, he realized that he had won only half the battle. His plan was approved and money was provided to support it, but the director of the project had yet to be selected. That matter the executive committee would take up on January 15. Could he gain the job? For a month he had to face that question, living nervously from one day to another, the tension increasing as the time of decision approached. Events disclosed that he had good reason to worry.

At once he supplied Hodge and Parsons with detailed information about his qualifications, supported by arguments to indicate that the project could be launched at once despite the internal trouble in Mexico. Hewett was still in the East, and Morley had no idea what he was up to. Hodge warned Vay to maintain absolute secrecy about the C.I.W. matter in Santa Fe, and Vay took unusual precautions on that score, but somehow news of his candidacy leaked out.

The real threat to Morley's cause came from an unexpected quarter. Sometime between the middle of December and the middle of January the executive committee sent one of its members, probably Parsons, to the Peabody Museum for the advice of Bowditch and Putnam on the Maya project. The two men praised the plan, but recommended A.M. Tozzer as the best archaeologist to carry it out. Apparently, Bowditch could not forgive Morley for his 1909 article on the Naranjo inscriptions, which Bowditch considered his own preserve.[2] When this proposal that Tozzer should replace Morley was brought back to Washington, Holmes got wind of it and informed Vay by telegram on January 9. At once Vay replied that if Tozzer's smuggling of *cenote* objects to the United States were known, the man would not be acceptable in Mexico. There was also the rumor that the committee might compromise by making Fewkes head of the project with Morley as his assistant, an arrangement that Vay was willing to settle for if he could not get the top post.

January 15 arrived. In Santa Fe, Vay had been spending tense days and sleepless nights awaiting the fateful date, willing to be relieved by any decision, even an unfavorable one, that would end the anxiety. He was sick at heart to learn that Bowditch, Putnam, Wissler, and worst of all, Hewett, whose devious connivings never were completely unraveled, had worked against him.

In Washington the executive committee, together with Holmes as consultant, went into session. The pros and cons regarding Morley were aired and alternative plans were proposed, but Holmes managed to counter the sentiment against Vay; and the committee informally agreed upon him to head the project. Of greater concern was the question whether an expedition should be attempted because of the strained relations between the United States and Mexico and the expected collapse of the Huerta government. Oddly, the minutes of the committee make no mention of Morley; the only entry posed the question whether an expedition to Mexico was advisable at that time.

Thus the executive committee took action with a question mark. There was no need for haste, for the committee was not required to report to the trustees for eleven months. On January 15, then, the committee tentatively chose Morley to head the project; but when the expedition could be launched was unsettled; conditions in Mexico were unstable, and the situation was complicated by imminent American intervention. These facts naturally caused the Carnegie officials to investigate before attempting to

2 For details of this affair, see Chapter VIII.

work in Yucatán. Woodward doubtless believed that there was no reason to inform Morley of his appointment, much less to employ him, until an expedition was possible. Certainly this was a commonsense approach from the point of view of the Carnegie officials, although it left Morley dangling as far as a job was concerned.

Out in Santa Fe, Vay gradually wakened to the dubious nature of his success. When his faithful Eastern friends telegraphed that he had won the post, life became worth living once more, tensions relaxed, and again the world appeared pleasant and expansive. He awaited an official notice, perhaps a request to come to Washington for instructions. Days passed and no letter came from Woodward. In the meantime Hewett returned to Santa Fe and demanded whether Morley was working for him or not. Vay was in a quandary. Should he give up his job with the American School before he was assured of the Carnegie post? Hewett was so eager to settle the matter that he wanted to pressure the Carnegie Institution into employing Morley at once. Fortunately, Vay dissuaded him from the rash idea.

At last, Holmes wired Morley that he could count on the Carnegie job, but that everything was held up by the internal situation in Mexico. Then Morley salvaged what he could from his old job, a mere $200, because Hewett had promised most of his salary to Earl Morris; and Vay arranged a trip to the Petén region at his own expense. Still no word from Woodward or Parsons.

At way stations in the Petén bush and forest Morley wrote to Holmes and Hodge about his adventures in traveling and discovering glyphs. One of those letters Holmes sent to Woodward with the note, "With a mere pittance from his own meager income he is pushing his investigations into the very heart of the Maya country."[3]

The political situation in Mexico grew worse by the spring of 1914 and Woodward and his associates gave up all thought of a Chichén Itzá expedition. They were advised to wait until Huerta fell, but before that occurred American sailors were arrested at

[3] Holmes to Woodward, June 5, 1914, Morley File, C.I.W.

Tampico and President Wilson ordered the shelling and occupation of Vera Cruz. Vay, isolated from almost all contact with the outside world, learned little or nothing about these events.

Slowly the Carnegie officials moved toward clarifying Vay's position. After all, there was no need for haste in the matter; in May the committee reluctantly discussed the question of employing the man. Parsons initiated the proposal to take Morley on the staff and put him to work collecting information on existing materials of Central American archaeology, obviously a makeshift arrangement because immediate work in Mexico was impossible. The subcommittee was given power to determine when to do this.

Woodward had not changed his views about archaeology. He told Holmes that Morley's work would be no more than artifact collecting for museums, and that it would be better to turn the money over to the museums themselves for that purpose. The Carnegie Institution, he repeated, had no museum, it could not store collections, and it was not justified in stocking museums.

Down in Guatemala, Vay kept his friends informed of his whereabouts and of the time of his return to the States. Once again Parsons jogged Woodward, with the reminder that Morley would be in Washington in July. And the three men on the subcommittee agreed on the salary to be offered and the work to be assigned. But still no letter from Woodward to Morley.

Vay arrived in Washington, according to his schedule, on July 8, and stayed over into the next day. He visited Holmes and Hodge and Fewkes, and they discussed the Chichén Itzá project. He even went out to the C. I. W. headquarters on P Street and talked with Gilbert, the secretary, and Barnum, the editor. If he had planned to call on Woodward it was out of the question, because the president was at Woods Hole. As he left Washington that day for his mother's home in Swarthmore, he had no more assurance of the job than he had had six months earlier.

Then Woodward's letter reached him on July 14, offering him the job and asking him to come to Washington for a conference. Although the message was half a year overdue, it filled him with the feeling of satisfaction and victory. It offered him $200 a month to compile a bibliography of Central American antiquities until the trouble subsided in Mexico. Ten days later he was in Washington and had three interviews with Woodward, who gave no hint of his real feelings about archaeology. Although the president was required to carry out a task he did not believe in, he was a gentleman and treated Vay handsomely.

For hours the two men talked together, and it is likely that Woodward did more listening than speaking. Morley bubbled over about the stelae he had found in the Petén, showing photographs and carefully drawn diagrams of them to Woodward, and expatiated on plans for an exhaustive book on Maya chronology. At this point he gained an important concession that influenced his scholarly career. The Chichén Itzá project, for which he had been hired, had been indefinitely postponed and he was slated to carry on a dreary desk job of compiling a bibliography as a time-filler until conditions cleared up in Mexico. At the moment he was deep in the collection of date glyphs in a comprehensive way, and it would be ideal if he could convince Woodward to let him proceed with that project. Before the interview Vay had consulted Holmes, who advised him to present the project on chronology; Holmes realized what Vay could not have known, that Woodward really did not care what he worked on as an interim task. But for Morley the decision meant the forwarding or the suspension of his first scholarly contribution.

Woodward listened, now and then interjecting a flattering remark, and rolling over the idea in his mind, as Vay rattled on exuberantly. With good judgment Woodward discarded the plan of a bibliography and told the young man to go ahead with the chronology; the C.I.W. would publish the study as soon as he completed the research and prepared the manuscript. Woodward also showed concern for Vay's health, for it was obvious that malaria had worn him down, and suggested that he should carry on his work in the more salubrious climate of Santa Fe. In fact, as the third and last interview came to a close, Morley suffered a violent attack of malaria.

A few days later, when Woodward summarized the understanding in writing, he was kind and considerate. He urged Vay to find a specialist to treat the malaria; casually he suggested that conditions in Mexico might delay the Chichén Itzá project for some years; and as a parting gesture of friendship he sent him one of the recent C.I.W. publications, Huntington's *The Climate Factor as Illustrated in Arid America,* that contained interesting ideas on the Mayas that were new to Morley. Thereafter the two men got along amicably. Vay had made another conquest by the force of his personal charm and enthusiasm; and he never hinted at any unfavorable attitude toward him by Woodward.

Parsons was enthusiastic over the outcome. Woodward sent him an account of the interviews with the conclusion that Vay would produce "a very important memoir concerning the chronology of the Mayas." Of all this Parsons heartily approved, and he was happy over the projected book by Morley. "This will serve to get us started and started in the best possible way," Parsons observed to Woodward, doubtless with a glint in his eye, "by proving that we are after scientific results and not to make a collection."[4]

Whether he realized it or not, Woodward made a significant contribution to the archaeological work of the Carnegie Institution by his opposition to collecting artifacts. It so happened that his policy became a trump card when seeking concessions. Customarily, museums wanted to bring away the finest specimens and the largest possible number of objects to enhance their exhibits. But from the time of World War I, Latin-American countries surged with nationalistic fervor and resented such cultural imperialism. Thus the Carnegie Institution's policy of study, restoration, and publication of the scientific results coincided perfectly with the new sensitive feelings of Latin-Americans. As a result of Woodward's policy Morley was able to carry on work where he wished; Mexico, Guatemala, and Honduras benefited by restored, attractive ruins; the scientific world profited from the

---

[4] Woodward to Parsons, Aug. 20, 1914; Parsons to Woodward, Aug. 26, 1914; Morley File, C.I.W.

elaborate reports published by the Institution; and thus a new chapter in American archaeological research was opened.

Morley carried out the expedition of 1914 to Petén under discouraging circumstances. He had received no official confirmation of the job with the C. I. W. Hewett went ahead and employed Earl Morris in his place, and later claimed that the expedition had been made under the auspices of the school, which was technically true, though Morley supplied four-fifths of the cost from his own pocket.

Despite the bleak outlook, Vay felt that he had strong reasons to make the trip. He had never visited the Petén region, and his work on Maya chronology depended on firsthand examination of inscriptions there. Also, if the C. I. W. took him on, the Chichén Itzá project would indefinitely postpone a visit to the Petén. Underlying the rational explanation, however, was the urge to get things done; he felt that he could not lose a single season in the bush.

He left Santa Fe on February 7 for the most extensive expedition of his early years. In five months he visited more than a dozen archaeological sites, ranging from Tikal and Santa Rita in the north to Piedras Negras and Yaxchilán in the west and Quiriguá in the south.

In British Honduras he took a motorboat up the El Cayo and joined Herbert Spinden, who accompanied him to most of the important sites. Joe, as Spinden was known to his friends, had received his A.B. degree from Harvard a year before Morley, and had engaged in fieldwork in North Dakota and Idaho for the Peabody Museum for several years. Vay first met him at the Anthropological Club when Spinden and Will explained their work with the Mandans. By 1909, Joe was assistant curator at the American Museum of Natural History, and four years later he made an important contribution with his *Study of Maya Art*. Spinden was unforgettable. He had blue eyes and white hair, weighed over two hundred pounds, liked to argue, and had a way of splashing into the news at regular intervals.

With a native guide and cook as their only attendants, the two men made a ten-day excursion to Naranjo in the northeastern corner of the Petén. They suffered the usual trials of exploration. Pack mules plodded along the trail at no more than twelve miles a day, the camp had to be set up at a water hole half a mile from the ruins, and Vay suffered from insects and a heavy cold. But he had a good harvest of dates—seven new decipherable Initial Series and corrections of readings made by his predecessors.

At Naranjo he accidentally learned how to work with troublesome carvings. One afternoon as he labored over a stela trying to decipher the difficult lines, a rain shower overtook him; but he was so intent on his task that he kept on working, and at once the inscription, clear and clean-cut, seemed to spring up at him. Thereafter, he applied water to bring out the lines of recalcitrant carvings.

Although he learned that a native revolt was in progress in Tabasco, Chiapas, and Campeche, Guatemala appeared to be quiet; so he and Joe set out for sites on the Pasión and the Usumacinta rivers. At first all went well. With a letter of recommendation from the *jefe político* of Flores, the Americans could count on considerate treatment along the way. They struck south to La Libertad, where Dr. Otero offered a fine dinner and comfortable overnight quarters. Next day at Sayaxché, Don Ramauldo provided a boat, rowers, guides, and provisions for the river trip. Joe and Vay felt like royalty riding in the four-ton mahogany *Gaviota* with a shelter to protect them from the heat, while four rowers toiled in the broiling sun to pull the craft upstream to Seibal. There Vay assembled five glyph panels, found a Cycle 8 date, and a variant form of Kankin.

By the time they got to La Florida on the Usumacinta, they heard the ominous news that rebels were seizing mules and camp supplies farther down the river. Although Vay was only one day from Yaxchilán, he reluctantly turned back, and went up to Altar de Sacrificios, where he found new stelae, and to Aguas Calientes, which he considered his own discovery.

Then he returned to Flores to wait for the rebels to quiet down.

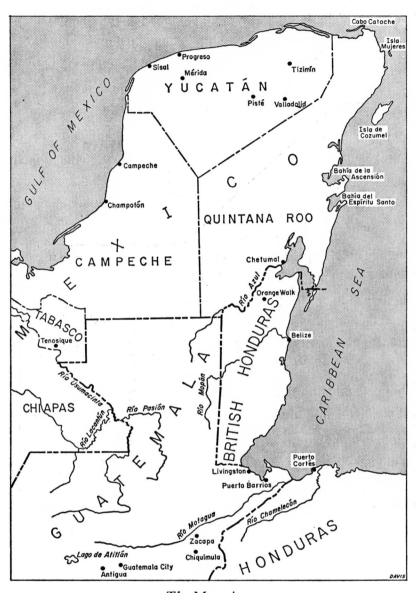

The Maya Area

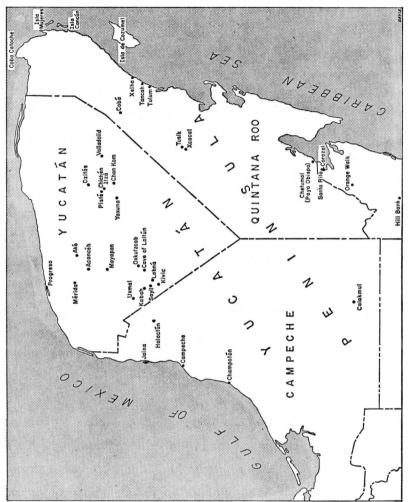

Yucatán and Adjacent Areas

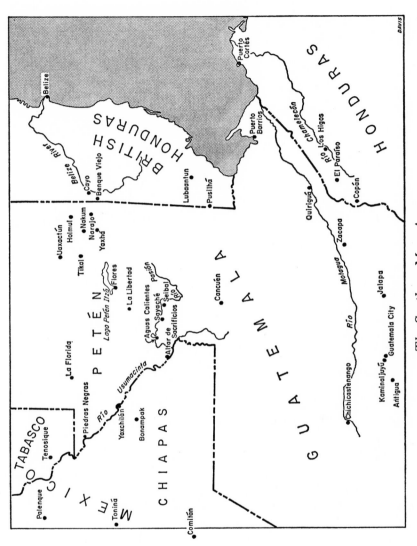

The Southern Maya Area

A ten-day trip to Tikal yielded a Cycle 10 Initial Series. Once more back at Lake Petén, he and Joe looked over the area, and Vay concluded that the peninsula, not the island of Flores, was the site of Tayasal, last stronghold of the Mayas. When news arrived that the rebellion had petered out, he did not rush off at once, but made another ten-day trip, this time to Ixkún. From the various sites he had visited, he could chalk up eleven new Initial Series and an equal number of Period Ending dates.

At this point in his travels, fifty-seven days after he had left Belize, he drew up a record of the expedition to date. With a hankering for statistics, he spilled over with figures that provide interesting information about the progress of travel. He had covered 464 miles by mule, averaging 20 miles a day, and 274 miles by water, which came to 33 miles a day. He spent seventeen and one-half days examining ruins, or less than one day of scientific work for two days of preparation and transportation.

Traveling and camping in the bush was a trial. The Petén mule was hard on human flesh and bone, it ruined water holes with alacrity, and it was a miserable companion in the heavy bush where sunlight failed to penetrate the thick foliage. Along the trail there were nuisances and sometimes dangers. Unnoticed lianas caught the rider about the neck or waist; twice they dragged Vay from his mount, breaking his saddle; in one of these accidents he was thrown to the ground and the next mule in the train stepped on his hand and sprained it. Also the undergrowth bristled with thorns and spines, ranging from the size of a needle to that of a large fishhook.

There were also insects and snakes to cope with. Vay brought with him a medicine chest filled with antidote for snakebite and ointment to soothe stings. Sometimes he found washing with carbolic soap an effective deterrent for insects. His greatest fear, however, was of snakes. Although he rarely encountered them himself, he was always expecting to meet them, and he carefully treasured every story of snakebite he had ever heard. He could report one casualty on the return from Ixkún, when a mule died within an hour after a snake had attacked it.

He and Spinden divided the scientific work along lines of mutual interest. Vay sought new inscriptions and copied them, while Joe gave his attention to art and architecture, often drawing complete figures that he found. Both men had planned to make a full photographic record of the monuments, but the moist, hot climate played havoc with the film. Hesitating to trust the camera, they drew furiously day after day to preserve a pictorial record of their discoveries.

Finally, Vay and Joe made the second trip down the Usumacinta, and spent the month of May at Piedras Negras and Yaxchilán, with no danger from the rebels.

Back in El Cayo by June 6, the two men started across British Honduras. At Banana Bank, Spinden left Vay, and Vay took a mule and headed for Santa Rita Corozal. On June 13, as he made his way north, he had a hard day. He was ten and one-half hours on the way, much of the time in incessant, heavy rain and on a road that was often submerged in water. At Hill Bank he came to the home of "Red" Frazer, manager of the Belize Estate and Produce Company.

In later years Frazer recalled the meeting for J. Eric S. Thompson: That afternoon Frazer's manservant "came to him to say that there was a gentleman to see him. As this colored servant called everybody a gentleman, Frazer supposed that it was someone looking for a job. He told his man to send him around to the back door. 'He is a white man, sah,' was the reply. Frazer went to the door and there stood a short, little man in a huge poncho, with rain cascading off him; the very heavens had opened that afternoon. The sole of one of his boots was tied up with string and there was a hole in his hat, through which his hair was showing. It was Vay. He was alone except for his mule. . . . Frazer recalled that he couldn't stop him talking, as he was shivering with cold and was wet from head to foot; he looked very ill. Frazer had almost to shove him into a hot tub, for he was so intent on telling Frazer what he had been doing that he wouldn't retire to have a bath. Frazer recalled that the only dry thing about him was his notebook, which was carefully wrapped in waterproof. Vay wanted to push on to Corozal next morning, but Frazer thought he was in very bad shape."[5] Since Morley was only five feet, seven and Frazer well over six feet tall, only imagination can picture Vay in his host's clothing. The next day Vay recuperated and luxuriated in reading—he had not read for four months—and made arrangements to go to Corozal by motorboat.

Dried out and refreshed, he proceeded according to plan. At Corozal he met Gann, and they visited Santa Rita, site of Gann's discovery some years before. Gann was an interesting person, and became a close friend of Vay. Sixteen years older than Morley, he had been born in Ireland, educated in England, and after a few years as a medical practitioner migrated to British Honduras to become district medical officer of that colony, a post he held for almost three decades. Since official duties left much time on his hands, he carried out archaeological explorations there and in neighboring areas. He published his professional report in 1895, and later won respect by finding those Maya murals at Santa Rita and later by discovering the ruins of Lubaantún. In contrast to Morley, Gann was cool and reserved, although once the ice was broken he was a good companion. If archaeology and mutual respect brought the two men together, they also had card-playing and bachelorhood in common in the years to come.

After a visit to Quiriguá to investigate any new glyphs that had turned up since his last visit, Vay embarked at Puerto Barrios on July 3 for the States. On shipboard the Fourth of July received scant notice, which disappointed a man who enjoyed merrymaking. But as the vessel approached the Mississippi, a warm feeling of satisfaction and gratification came over him as he saw the Stars and Stripes. The last night aboard everyone was on deck, and as the boat came up the moonlit river, boys on the banks and in dories sang out the inimitable, "Throw us some bananas." The chorus rose and fell, and finally mingled with the croaking of the frogs. It was good to be back again.

[5] J. Eric S. Thompson to the author. The story also appears in J. E. S. Thompson, "1914. The Carnegie Institution of Washington Enters the Maya Field," MS; it was published in Spanish in *Estudios de Cultura Maya*, IV (México, 1964), 173.

The expedition of 1914 had peculiar significance in Morley's career. It marked the end of his apprenticeship and the beginning of his professional independence. It was the first trip taken on his own initiative and without directions from Hewett. Likewise it was Vay's initial opportunity to work on the great project for a Maya chronology. In that elaborate undertaking his scientific instinct was correct in seeking to provide a historical framework for ancient Maya culture, which in turn was a necessary foundation for the future prosecution of Maya studies. Also, one of his aims in making the expedition sprang from a devotion to scientific accuracy. Earlier, working with photographs of glyphs made by predecessors, he quickly ran into uncertain readings, and he suspected that the record was incomplete. Only firsthand examination of the original inscriptions at the sites could provide accurate interpretations, and additional search in the field might turn up unknown inscriptions. Finally, the expedition demonstrated Morley's confidence in himself and his optimism for the future.

By November, 1914, Vay became very uneasy. That was the time when plans for the forthcoming field season were completed. But no proposal came from the C. I.W. In fact, when Morley had been employed, nothing had been said about annual expeditions to Central America. So he sent a report on the Hieroglyphic Stairway at Copán to Woodward and a letter to Parsons about his trip earlier in the year to the Petén. When Woodward did not take the hint, Vay made a direct approach early in December by submitting a plan for work at Copán and La Honradez, suggesting that the expedition would cost $750 to $1,000.

With a specific proposal in hand, Woodward was favorable and secured the agreement of Parsons and Walcott, and asked Morley to come to Washington in January to forward the plans. The meeting turned out better than Vay could have hoped. His plans were approved, he was told to buy his outfit and supplies at Abercrombie and Fitch, and Woodward voluntarily raised the budget of the expedition to $2,500.

The C. I.W. was generous but not extravagant, and Vay quickly learned that it drew a sharp line between business expenses and those of a personal nature. When Abercrombie and Fitch prudently inquired whether the Institution would pay for the items Vay selected, approval was forthcoming. But as early as March the C. I.W. bursar laid down the law to Vay. All bills must be itemized, and a personal bill from the Cosmos Club, with charges for drinks, cigars, barbering, laundry, and the tailor, was flatly disallowed. Vay explained that the bill had been sent to the Institution by mistake; and thereafter, he was careful to pay all personal expenses himself.

The 1915 expedition extended over four and one-half months and took him to La Honradez, Copán, and Cancuén in search of glyphs. As his assistant he chose J. P. Adams, surveyor on the Quiriguá expedition of 1911. By February 3, Vay was in New Orleans, where Adams joined him, and the next day they sailed for Belize.

In British Honduras he made a short trip up to Corozal to see Thomas Gann. Vay was happy to read his friend's manuscript that was published three years later as *The Maya of Southern Yucatán and Northern British Honduras*, noting that it combined material from Landa with archaeological finds.

On the boat trip back to Belize, a twenty-pound fish jumped through the window, soared across the room, and fell to the floor—so he described the incident in his diary. Later when he gleefully told friends of the experience, they were skeptical, and to this day his friends repeat the story with raised eyebrows.

At Belize he and Adams took the *Critic*, a motorboat, up the Belize River to El Cayo. Along the way bamboo thickets covered the banks except for an occasional handful of thatched huts. In the river itself mahogany logs and alligators were a common sight. At night the Negro crew, with good voices and strong English accent, filled the air with *Tipperary, Midnight Chou Chou*, and *Get Out and Get Under*.

El Cayo was the last link between civilization and the wilderness; there the *chicleros* from the Petén gathered to carouse and celebrate before returning to their lonely work; and from there river launches carried the chicle out to Belize for export. In El Cayo, Vay acquired the animals and supplies for his trek to La Honradez. After he and Adams joined up with some *chicleros* on the way out, the entire group consisted of eight persons and nineteen mules. Along the route Vay acquired a native guide to help find the site.

The trip to La Honradez required a week. At first the trail passed through tropical forests of large trees, dense undergrowth, trailing lianas, and corozo palms. After the Río Holmul was crossed, the aspect of the country changed. Now there were hills, some of them close to four hundred feet high, and low bush, supported by a shallow layer of soil. Because the guide misled them, they wandered about lost for three days before reaching their destination.

Morley was amazed to find the whole area between Holmul and La Honradez covered with small mounds; wherever the chicle trails went—and they had been cut with no reference to the mounds—those vestiges of ancient civilization abounded.

The five-day stay at La Honradez had mixed results. Drenching rain prevented exploration for several days. More disappointing to Vay was the fact that only a few of the inscriptions he found could be read; only five of the stelae presented decipherable glyphs. Not only did the soft stone weather easily, but the Mayas had hewn the pieces in a way that encouraged erosion on the sides of the stelae. He did learn that the city had flourished in the fifth and sixth centuries A.D.; and its art, architecture, and hieroglyphs placed it clearly with the other Maya centers of the south that flourished at the same time.

Taking the right trail back, they returned to El Cayo within a few days, and then started for the second site, Copán, by way of Belize, Puerto Barrios, and Quiriguá. At the last place the United Fruit Company had erected a $300,000 hospital, which Vay had marveled at in 1914, and now he found a golf course within walking distance. At the hospital he met Dr. Jessie McPhail for the first time, a man who became one of his best friends during the next thirty years.

Going across country by mule, Morley and Adams arrived at Copán for four weeks of serious work. The Americans received a warm welcome from the natives, and were assigned quarters in a corner of the schoolhouse. Vay arranged for meals at Doña Julia's, but after a day or two he and Adams could not stand the atmosphere—too much drinking, sour odors, and inebriates lying about the place. But how to leave her house without hard feelings? He explained convincingly that he and Adams had brought a large quantity of provisions and wanted to use them. This was acceptable to Doña Julia, and they left her table with everyone happy. Fortunately, the Americans had their own cook, Andrew, a Negro from Belize; and under careful supervision he boiled the drinking water and prepared the food so that Vay could boast that none of the party became sick.

Then there was the matter of the five-dollar fine. On the first day when he returned from the ruins to his quarters in the schoolhouse, he was summoned to appear at the town hall to show the passports. Without taking time to change his field clothes, he went at once. When he entered the room, the police official took one look at the machete he was carrying as part of his equipment, and announced a fine of five dollars for coming armed into the hall of justice. Vay pleaded ignorance of the law, but made no headway. So he returned to his quarters, left the machete, and brought the five dollars to the official. Then his passports were finally examined. When Juan Ramón Cueva, the *alcalde*, learned of the incident, he remitted the fine at once; and Morley in turn proposed presenting the money to the municipality, but the *alcalde* would not agree.

In short order the Americans were invited to have something to drink. Vay seized the first opportunity to offer the initial toast to the officials of Copán; the natives graciously responded with a health to scientific foreigners; and as the final round he offered a toast to Honduras, happiest republic of Central America.

Scarcely had that ceremony ended when the Americans were invited to a ball that night. Affairs were now moving in Morley's favor, and he proceeded to make the most of the occasion. He dressed in his best tropical clothes, appeared at the *baile* all smiles and graciousness, and made a point of dancing with each señorita. Everyone was happy, and not a word was said about the fine. Thereafter he was careful not to infringe on the laws of Copán.

The archaeological results were encouraging. He found six altars and two stelae not before reported. He drew inscriptions that had never been published, worked on the Hieroglyphic Stairway and the temple door, and found a new temple half a mile from the main group of structures. He did, however, endure a wild goose chase, when a native, claiming to know of two stelae, led him out into the country for ten miles, and pointed triumphantly to a natural crag as the goal. Utterly disgusted, Vay returned as fast as possible.

Leaving Copán, the two explorers took a roundabout way to Cancuén. They went up to Puerto Barrios, then to Livingston and down the Río Dulce into Lago Izabal, then up the Río Polochic to Panzas. After sleeping in a railroad bunkhouse at night, they pushed on to Sepacuite, where they met a curious archaeologist by the name of Burkitt.

Robert J. Burkitt had an air of mystery about him. Born in Ireland, and educated at Dalhousie College in Nova Scotia and then at Harvard, he was on the Peabody Museum expedition to Copán in 1894. Thereafter he lived at Sepacuite in Guatemala, and was known as Mr. Brown. Garbed in khaki clothes, woolen cap, and high, laced moccasins, he carried his jacket carefully folded over his arm, wearing it only on entering a church. He made photographs and drawings, spoke Kekchi, and published a few brief but excellent articles on archaeology. Vay discovered that one of his peculiar traits was a frantic addiction to phonetic spelling.

On leaving Burkitt, Morley and Adams pushed north across the Cajabón for the ruins of Cancuén. Four days before they reached the site, Adams announced that he was leaving in order to reach home in time for the birth of the first Adams baby. On May 8 the two men parted, Vay remaining to complete his work. Adams arrived home on June 1, half a day before the anticipated event. Vay regretted losing his agreeable, good-natured companion, but he sympathized completely with the young man's feelings.

On May 11, when he was within one mile of Cancuén, he suddenly discontinued his diary, and so we have no personal record of his experience there. A month later he informed Woodward that he had completed the expedition, having covered five hundred miles through forest and bush, with one-fifth of the travel afoot without the aid of trails.

At this time Morley was experiencing grave personal problems. He had been married for less than seven years, and divorce was impending. He did not venture into matrimony again for twelve years. His one consolation was his daughter, Alice Virginia, whom he always called True. She was his only child, and he loved her dearly.

He never discussed his marital troubles with his friends, and he later said very little about Alice. Undoubtedly they were deeply in love when they married, and he had expressed concern when she was ill. Twice she had accompanied him on field expeditions, in 1911 to Quiriguá and two years later to Mérida. He remarked afterward that the marriage had begun to go to pieces in 1913, though in the Petén in 1914 he was happy to receive what he called splendid letters from his wife and daughter.

Alice was granted a divorce in October, 1915. She claimed desertion on the basis of Morley's absence in Central America since the beginning of the year, and he did not contest the suit. Although he had known divorce was in the offing, the actual news of it upset him physically and emotionally for some time. For the first six months he had custody of his daughter, whom his mother cared for in Cambridge. Either he did not appeal or failed to win an appeal for complete custody of the child, and she returned permanently to Alice. He feared that his daughter would be turned against him, although he continued to do everything he could to retain her love and affection.

As the months passed, his views on his first experiment with matrimony changed as his outlook on life altered. A year after the divorce he visited Alice in Salt Lake City and believed that she shared his feeling that they should have put up with each other for the sake of the child, though he admitted that the two of them were happier since the separation. Then he reflected that the sufferings of the unhappy union were a cheap price to pay for the existence of his daughter.

Unexpectedly he saw True briefly in August, 1923, when she was fifteen years old, and he was overwhelmed with joy. As he returned from the long, arduous stay in Mexico that year, he headed for the Southwest. On the way he received a wire from his daughter to meet her in Albuquerque. Hastily he changed his plans. At noon on the thirty-first True came to his room in a hotel in Albuquerque, and Gann, who was traveling with him, tactfully withdrew. As Vay looked at her, he saw a tall, slender figure, in long dress and with bobbed hair; and he even detected in her some of his own mannerisms. She asked him to stay for an amateur performance of *The Magic Flute* that night, in which she would perform the first number.

Of course, he agreed. She appeared with a flute and was garbed in one of the old jaguar skins he had brought from Central America years ago. To the accompaniment of other dancers, she performed her number, and then the roses he had ordered were taken up on stage to her. After the performance she came to his room to talk with him once more. He gave up his quarters to her for the rest of the night, as he was taking a train just after midnight; and proud, contented, and happy, he left Albuquerque.

The few requests made on her behalf he agreed to regardless of expense. When she wanted to attend a summer camp, he replied that of course she could if she wished. He sent her to the National Cathedral School in Washington, even though he had to cut expenses elsewhere to meet the cost. Actually, he yearned to make sacrifices for her.

By the early 1920's he realized that his outlook on life had changed. He toyed seriously with the idea that perhaps he was not designed to be a husband because he had too many interests and a consuming passion for archaeology. Now he declared that before the war he had been old-fashioned, conservative, unworldly, and an innocent boy when he had married. Perhaps, he thought, he had failed in his domestic life just as he had succeeded in his profession. Despite protestations of joy in his work, however, he longed for a wife and a home, but the memory of his first domestic failure hindered him from taking the step until 1927.

V

Death in the Bush

THE expedition of 1916 was the most memorable of all of Vay's annual excursions into the field—memorable for failure, success, and tragedy. On embarking at New Orleans, he believed that everything would go well if he remained in good health. On that score he felt confident, because for the first time his staff included a physician. As it happened, the doctor was of more service to the natives than to members of the staff.

Despite some changes in plan, Vay visited Copán, Tulum, and Uaxactún. But the first objective of his itinerary, Ocosingo, proved to be a disappointment. After traveling over the highlands of western Guatemala, he found an army in his path; five to six thousand Guatemalan soldiers were guarding the boundary against incursions of Mexican bandits. Since the military authorities sternly refused to allow anyone to approach the border, he had to turn back with nothing to show for his pains.

Next he headed for Copán. This visit produced only a few fragments and a stela of A.D. 260. The personnel of the expedition included W. H. Holmes, whom Morley met by appointment in Guatemala City.

William Henry Holmes was one of the highly respected men in archaeology. Trained as an artist, he produced outstanding drawings of Maya cities, and Vay induced him to come along to

95

make a panoramic view of Copán for the frontispiece of Morley's book that was nearing completion. Apparently it did not occur to Vay that he was taking a great risk in bringing the seventy-year-old artist with him. But other members of the staff were worried about Holmes's condition. He had not been on a horse for over a decade, and the expedition moved slowly along the trail under the burning sun. When they stopped at the end of the first day, they stretched the exhausted man on a cot. Shortly he managed to extract a bottle from his luggage, took "a big swig of Scotch, sat up, and made a beautiful drawing." The recovery was more than temporary. Next morning before breakfast he was out climbing over the hills and returned with a completed watercolor. "After that we did not worry about Holmes," observed Samuel K. Lothrop, another member of the party.[1]

A gentleman of the nineteenth century, Holmes did not surrender to the informality of camp life. Garbed in a heavy woolen suit, stiff collar, and necktie, he compromised only by wearing leggings. Traveling along the trail on a mule, he continued to sketch the countryside.

Young Samuel K. Lothrop was just beginning a brilliant career in American archaeology. Educated at Harvard, he had had a field season in New Mexico the year before joining the Carnegie expedition of 1916. As an assistant at Copán, he prepared stones for photographing and drawing, and under Holmes's instruction learned the art of panoramic drawing.

Dr. Underhill, the physician, played an important role during the stay at Copán, where he extended medical aid to many of the inhabitants. News of a white physician in the village brought everyone to the Americans' quarters in the schoolhouse, which quickly became a clinic and consulting room. Sometimes this medical service played right into Vay's hands, as when a patient's grateful husband furnished information leading to the discovery of a new Initial Series stela.

Dr. Underhill's lack of Spanish involved Vay in this medical service. Consultations between doctor and patient had to pass

1 *Morleyana*, 126.

through him as interpreter. Vay could explain headaches, back-aches, and other simple troubles, but his Spanish broke down when it came to problems with internal organs like the liver and kidneys. Fortunately, most of the cases were chronic complaints that the doctor could easily diagnose, and generally he managed at least to alleviate the pain. To show their gratitude, the natives left gifts of eggs, fowl, and the produce of their gardens at the schoolhouse.

In later years Lothrop recalled the return trip from Copán to Zacapa, a distance of twenty-three leagues. Holmes and Lothrop made the journey by mule in fourteen hours, interrupted by camping out during the night. The next day Morley covered the same distance without break, cutting the time by half an hour—and killing his mule from exhaustion.

The third trip of the season stirred Vay with more than usual expectation. He planned a second assault on Tulum. In 1913 he and Nusbaum had failed to find the hieroglyphic inscription mentioned by Stephens and deciphered by Howe. After Vay returned, he learned why he had failed to find the stone. Howe had carried the fragments of it to the beach, intent on taking them away with him; but he feared an attack by *sublevados*, hastily buried the fragments, and escaped in a dory. This news sent Morley in search of Howe. He found him in Boston some months before he left for the 1916 expedition and learned the exact spot where the pieces had been concealed on the shore.

On his former visit to Tulum, Vay had also found mural paintings that he considered very promising, and so he arranged to have Thomas Gann join the party to copy the pictures. Years before Gann had made accurate transcriptions of the murals he found at Santa Rita Corozal.

By March everything looked favorable for the second attempt on Tulum. The Mexican government had made progress in calming the *sublevados*, the dry season was at its height, and the five members of the expedition, by devoting themselves to assigned tasks, could gather much information in a short time.

At Belize, Vay chartered the *Corozal*, a choice difficult to understand. After the former tugboat had served at New Orleans and had been condemned, someone brought it to Belize, cut it in half, added a middle section, and used it in the coasting trade. The captain boasted that it was a good boat—thirty years ago. His claim that she could do nine knots an hour was more than optimistic, for with boilers crowded she never made more than six. "Only Morley would have chartered her for a voyage on the open ocean," Lothrop lamented later, adding that the party "soon found out that Morley knew even less about ships than mules."[2]

When the forty-ton vessel, carrying a total of seventeen persons, put out to sea, she rolled and rolled, and Vay promptly became seasick for the duration of the trip. "He did not realize," explained Lothrop, "that the food was inadequate because he could not eat it. As a matter of fact, our cook, knowing how his ship wallowed at sea, cooked most of his food before sailing. He stupidly placed everything on the table as we got under way and the first wave outside the cays sent all of it crashing to the floor. None of us had much to eat thereafter."[3]

After two days the boat anchored inside the reef at Tulum. Underhill stayed with the crew, who absolutely refused to go ashore for fear of Indians, while the other members carried out their assignments at the ruins. Morley and Gann, dreading seasickness more than *sublevados*, had their cots and food carried through the high surf to a camp set up at the base of the cliffs. Vay found the coveted inscription and deciphered it as A.D. 290, which had been Howe's reading, but this date raised a problem, for it was about one thousand years earlier than the buildings at the site. Carpenter took almost one hundred photographs, Gann traced fifteen figures from the murals and made notes on the colors, and Lothrop gathered data for a map, ground plans, and elevations of the structures, and prepared a panoramic drawing of the whole city. All told, much information was gathered for a preliminary report.

An incident during one of the first nights illustrates how Vay

[2] *Morleyana,* 127.
[3] *Morleyana,* 127.

could engage in practical joking, even where possible danger was involved. After he and Gann had set up their camp at one end of the beach, they agreed with the men on board that they would signal with a flashlight in case they were attacked by Indians. Lothrop tells what happened:

"On board the *Corozal* a couple of hours later, the captain informed us that the light had flashed madly from the camp to the far end of the beach and then was seen no more. Gann and Morley had obviously signaled to us as they tried to escape the Indians and then had been struck down. On the chance that they were wounded but not dead, Arthur Carpenter and I persuaded some reluctant members of the crew to row us towards the beach. We anchored just outside the surf and waited in the bright moonlight, a perfect target for an unfriendly native on the cliff top.

"Minutes passed which seemed hours. The beach at the base of the overhanging cliff was in deep shadow. We saw no movement of any kind. Carpenter, a brave man as he proved again when the Carnegie expedition was shot up in the Petén, sat in the stern nearest the beach. He suddenly stripped, swam through the surf and disappeared into the shadows. Undecided, I waited. Had the Indians got Carpenter too? What should I do?

"At long last Carpenter swam out again, the angriest white man I have ever seen. His sudden appearance had given Gann and Morley the fright of their lives and they had nearly shot him. The conversation between these three *maestros* of invective must have been classic. The light? Very simple. Morley and Gann had used it as they strolled up the beach and they had returned to their camp by moonlight.

"Starting the long row back to the ship, we felt let down. Suddenly the light on shore started to flash again. Carpenter screamed with rage, grabbed a rifle and sent a bullet into the cliff above the camp which showered Gann and Morley with limestone fragments. No light showed on shore again for the rest of our stay at Tulum."[4]

The voyage back to Belize added still another chapter to the

4 *Morleyana*, 128–29.

history of the decrepit vessel. "The *Corozal* weighed anchor," explained Morley, "and put out past the reef to open sea. A norther was raging outside, and for the next twelve hours it was doubtful whether or not the ancient craft would weather the storm. Huge waves crashed over her bow, and all but beat her to the bottom. She lost her copper sheathing and when within some ten miles of Belize her coal gave out. Fortunately the sea had fallen sufficiently to enable the crew to put off in a dory to a key nearby where mangrove wood was cut, and with scarcely enough fire to keep up steam, she crept into Belize one morning, after an absence of eight days."[5]

Vay had to change plans for the projected fourth trip of the season. Originally he expected to visit Piedras Negras, then descend the Usumacinta and leave Mexico at Laguna del Carmen. But an internal disturbance flared up in the northwestern part of the Petén by the middle of March and was spreading toward Flores. If he had to abandon his plan for Piedras Negras, he told Woodward, he would make a trip to Naranjo in the northeastern part of the Petén.

In the meantime the personnel of his staff changed. Dr. Underhill and Sam Lothrop left for the States. Vay searched for a new physician, and induced Moise Lafleur, a young doctor from New Orleans then working for the United Fruit Company, to join the party.

By the middle of April, Vay was prepared to investigate not Naranjo but a new site he had learned of. When and how he first got wind of the place, later called Uaxactún, is not clear. Carpenter, sent out by the Peabody Museum, remembered that he had met Morley in a café in New York City the preceding fall, when they discussed merging their two expeditions for a trip into the Petén "after some reported ruins." But as late as April 9, 1916, Morley gave no suggestion to Woodward that he was looking for a new site; he spoke only of going to Naranjo.

[5] Morley, "The Ruins of Tuloom, Yucatan," *American Museum Journal*, Vol. 17 (1917), 203–204, published by The American Museum of Natural History, New York; quoted by permission of the publisher.

The expedition, consisting of Vay, Carpenter, Lafleur, and two Negro servants, Andrew and Marius Silas, arrived in El Cayo on April 20. They spent five days securing supplies, mules, and guides. By the time Vay set off on the trip, he had two guides, José, who eventually led him to Uaxactún, and Jacinto Rodríguez, who promised to show him four stelae at some undesignated place.

The first day out of El Cayo, as the expedition took the trail to the northwest, Jacinto, to whom Vay had paid some money in advance, twice deserted the party for the congenial grog shops of El Cayo. On the morning of the second day, Vay sent the rest of the party ahead, while he and José returned to El Cayo to round up the deserter, As he entered the village, the news he heard quickly put all thought of Jacinto out of mind. Forty revolutionaries had captured Plancha Piedra and seized the chicle and mule trains there; and there were rumors that Laguna de Yalache had also been occupied. These revolutionaries were Mexican *chicleros*, gathered from El Cayo and Benque Viejo, who were protesting against the Guatemalan government for injustices in the chicle business. Trinidad Flores, their leader, proceeded to collect the duties in the area he occupied.

The rumor of the rebel seizure of Laguna frightened Morley, for Carpenter and Lafleur were at the moment on their way to that village. He and José started for Laguna just before noon, pushing along as fast as their mules would carry them, and were almost at their goal when night fell and they lost the trail. In the dark bush they floundered about, trails seemed to lead everywhere, they tangled with low branches and lianas, and at times retraced their steps to pick up hoofprints. José lighted a candle that offered little help, as it flickered and sputtered and cast wild silhouettes. After half an hour of wandering, they arrived at the edge of the village of Plancha. Soon they fell in with Arthur and Lafleur, who had not heard the news or encountered any revolutionaries.

Before turning in for the night, the eight members of the party, including servants and guides, each armed with shotgun or revolver to repel attack, agreed that the better policy was to continue into the Petén rather than return to El Cayo. So the next morning they took the trail to the northwest, and soon forgot the threat of revolution.

During the next seven days Morley had his hands full of routine details just to keep the expedition on the move. The trail led over hills and through *bajos*, those lowlands of tangled lianas, logwood, creepers, vines, rotting vegetation, and mud dried in hard hummocks. In some places *garrapatas* attacked man and beast like a pestilence. Also Vay lived in mortal fear of snakes; he searched his cot at night, imagined he heard them slithering nearby as he went off to sleep, and insisted that he felt their presence as his mule passed through the marshy ground of a *bajo*.

His patience suffered the greatest trials from mules, muleteers, and guides. Every morning strayed animals had to be rounded up, which delayed the start of the day's journey. Once four lost animals were not recovered until ten-thirty, and the muleteer declared that it was too late to begin the day's trip. Always there seemed to be excuses for not proceeding. Even when the pack train was in movement, it might be suddenly halted. A mule would unaccountably dart off into the bush, creating confusion and delay, or a guide would announce at noontime that they must stop and camp because the next water hole was twelve miles away. Moreover, guides had a habit of getting lost in the maze of trails and blandly refusing to acknowledge their predicament.

One guide, however, was an exception. José, who came along to identify the ruins of the new site, proved faithful to the end, even though he was sick most of the time. Morley found him remarkably dependable and honest, and valued his aid. But José suffered from recurring malarial fever, his temperature rising to 103 degrees at times. Lafleur would dose him with quinine with only occasional success. The day before they reached the site of the new ruins, which José alone could identify, he was in low spirits and quite ill from the fever. In fact, he was not certain that they had reached Bejucal, the point from where he was to lead them to the monuments. If he grew worse and could not locate the site, the whole expedition into the Petén would be a complete loss.

On the morning of May 4, when they were close to their destination, José was too sick to have the least interest in thinking of ancient ruins. Lafleur went to work and applied drugs and stimulants to revive his spirits and give him strength, while Morley used all of the charm and persuasion at his command to urge him on. Finally the efforts of the two men took effect. José made an attempt to ambulate, seemed to gain strength, and went off in search of the ruins, Lafleur at his side to encourage and, if necessary, to administer more medicine.

Vay waited and waited, passing the time trying to determine his location in the Petén. Lunch time came, and no sign of José and Lafleur. The hours dragged on into the afternoon. At four o'clock the two men emerged from the bush. Yes, José had found the site, and Lafleur reported two carved stelae and a plain one. Optimism spread through the camp, and Vay waited for the morrow, eager to see what he would find.

But that night worry gnawed at Morley's soul. José developed a hot fever, he grew delirious, he groaned and cried, he moaned that he would die in the desolate bush. Morley's conscience twinged, as he felt entirely responsible for José's plight. Lafleur applied hot compresses, gave him morphine, and put him to bed. By ten he quieted down, and Lafleur decided to get some rest himself.

At eight the next morning Vay and five of the party set out to examine the find. After a two hours' hike they came to the edge of the site and spotted the first stela. Yes, Morley admitted, José was correct; there is a stela with a figure, and the figure is well preserved. Then he looked for glyphs. The three on the front were eroded, those on the sides too far gone to be legible. His spirits sank in despair—all of those miles through the bush, the trouble with the mules, the eternal pestilence of insects, and this was the result.

They wandered through the bush. There was a decapitated stela with no glyphs, and here a plain slab. Monuments but no glyphs. Then a shout from Carpenter. Running to his side, Vay found a stone with an Initial Series, the carving clear and sharp. Another stone lay flat on the ground, and as he began to read the date on it, he heard another shout and approached a second stela with an Initial Series.

After a hurried lunch he and one of his boys climbed a mound to examine a building; not bad, although the façade had fallen in. In the meantime Carpenter began to cut through the bush around the base of the mound, and shortly Morley descended, followed him, and saw a leaning stone nine and one-half feet high. Carpenter carefully restrained himself so as to let Vay get to the monument first and "discover" it. Vay could scarcely believe what he saw; it was the famous Stela 9 with a Cycle 8 Initial Series. Not until five days later, after a scaffold had been erected against the stone to facilitate careful examination of the carved figures, did Morley confidently determine its date as A.D. 50, the oldest inscription known at that time.

Then came the more prosaic work of gathering measurements for a map of the site, sketching plans of the structures, clearing away the undergrowth for photographing and drawing the inscriptions. On two occasions Morley summoned all hands to turn or raise fallen stones so that he could read the glyphs on them. Proud of the new site he had brought to light and happy with the archaeological material it contained, he knew that he had achieved a great success. In later years he sent annual expeditions to excavate Uaxactún, which yielded valuable archaeological information.

The expedition left the site on May 11, heading southeast on the return trip to El Cayo. Once more Vay had to turn his thoughts to the unrest farther down the trail. At some time in the past he had become acquainted with Trinidad Flores, the chicle contractor who was now leading the revolutionaries. In fact, Morley carried a letter from Flores into the Petén and delivered it to one of his agents at San Clemente on May 2. At that time Vay learned that the rebels had given up Plancha, but had moved north and occupied Laguna.

On the second and third days of the return trip, Morley heard upsetting news. The rebels still held Laguna, Guatemalan troops occupied Plancha, and two men had been killed in the area between those two towns. The trouble was that the news was two weeks old, and there was no way to learn of the present situation. Members of the expedition thought of alternate routes to El Cayo, but each one presented dangers. Vay decided to wait another day at Triunfo, confident that his *chiclero* friend Lencho Paredes would arrive with knowledge of the most recent developments.

The next day, Sunday, May 14, Morley made a fateful decision at Triunfo. Two mule trains arrived, one led by Paredes and another by Ladislao Romero. What Vay learned from Paredes was of little consequence compared with his dealings with Romero. Strangely there is no entry in the diary for this day, though he gave elaborate details on all of the other days from April 25 through May 16.

Romero was a Mexican chicle contractor, at the time employed by a British subject in El Cayo. "Romero approached me at Triunfo that afternoon (May 14th)," Morley later explained, "and told me that a mutual friend, no less than the revolutionary chief himself, whom I had known slightly at El Cayo, sent me his best wishes and the message that if I cared to return to El Cayo through Laguna I would not be molested in any way."[6] Romero carried a passport issued by Flores and a similar document from British Honduras permitting him to enter and leave the Colony. But he lacked a passport from Guatemalan authorities. Happily, Morley possessed credentials from that side—a letter from the Guatemalan minister of foreign affairs, another from the governor of the Petén, and his own American passport. "By traveling with Romero," he reasoned, "we would be safe if we encountered any of the revolutionists, and so far as any [Guatemalan] government troops were concerned, we naturally anticipated no danger from that source. Moreover, by joining forces with this other mule-train we increased our number from 9 to 18, a greater number than any picket of the revolutionists which we would be likely to encounter."[7] He placed his major reliance on

[6] *Morleyana,* 27.
[7] *Morleyana,* 28.

the official documents he and Romero had in their possession; and the flaw in this strategy was his failure to remember that he was in a country where persons shoot first and ask questions later.

The next day, after they had reached Dos Aguadas at two-thirty, Vay turned his attention once more to Maya ruins. He and Arthur spent the remaining daylight hours examining an area of mounds, stelae (unfortunately plain or eroded), and altars. They climbed the highest mound, encountering a ruined structure halfway up, and from the top enjoyed a distant view of the countryside. Arthur exclaimed that he could see an extensive ruin in the distance, and so it was. There against the horizon Vay discerned the structures and mounds of a city over a half-mile in length, and he identified it as Nakum. Then Arthur brought binoculars from camp, and the city seemed to lie almost at their feet. Outlined against the low sun, it appeared like a mysterious mirage of towers and pyramids, a dreamlike city. Later Vay confirmed that it was Nakum. If these two men could see a city like Nakum that seemed so fantastic and unreal, it is easy to understand how nineteenth-century explorers talked of a hidden Maya city that they had seen only from a distance.

After leaving Triunfo, the expedition took a circuitous route to avoid Laguna. The final day's journey, from the Río Holmul to El Cayo, would cover thirty miles and pass through the area between the revolutionary and the government forces. In the morning the party split; Morley, Carpenter, Lafleur, Andrew and Marius Silas, and Romero set out by way of Chunvis, and the pack mules took the Bullet Tree Falls trail. On reaching Chunvis, Morley inquired carefully about the wisdom of following that road into British Honduras, and all reports were favorable. Everything appeared quiet, and the regular chicle train was making daily trips from there to the Colony without interruption. It was only ten miles from Chunvis to the border, and Romero, saying he was familiar with the trail, agreed to act as guide. So the six men set out, with Romero heading the file, and Morley, as leader of the expedition, in second place.

At two-thirty, when they were within a quarter-mile of the

British boundary, there was a sudden, brief rain shower. Morley removed his glasses to wipe off the raindrops, and in so doing, they accidentally slipped from his hands to the ground. As he dismounted to retrieve the spectacles, Lafleur passed by him.

"I am going up next to the guide, Morley, to talk to him," Lafleur remarked as he moved forward.[8]

Andrew Silas also passed by Vay. This accidental rearrangement of the file kept Romero in first place, but put Lafleur in second position and Morley fourth.

As the party entered a clearing in the brush a few minutes later, ten to fifteen rifle shots rang out from both sides of the bush ahead. At the first shot Romero fell from his mount and twisted about, badly wounded, on the ground. At once Lafleur sprang from his horse and loaded his Winchester carbine; at that moment a shot from the bush put his right arm out of commission, and he soon fell to the ground. Andrew left his horse and ran back on the trail. Morley also fell back a short distance to talk with Carpenter, who had dismounted.

"What are they doing?" Vay asked, bewildered.

"They are shooting at us," was Arthur's reply.

"I am going to shoot," Arthur declared.

"Mr. Morley," interrupted Marius, who was with them, "I only have four cartridges; we'd better go back."[9]

Powder haze obscured the view of the opening where Romero and Lafleur lay in the low growth. No one could be seen in the ambush. Morley assumed, of course, that the attackers were revolutionaries.

"Arthur, we must get back," Vay cried, as he realized the danger of their situation. "Back! Back! Back! For God's sake, everybody back!"[10] They retreated along the trail and down a slope, where they were no longer targets for the attackers.

Carpenter announced that he would return through the bush to help Lafleur, if he were still alive. Vay was confident that the

---

[8] *Morleyana*, 31.
[9] *Morleyana*, 33.
[10] *Morleyana*, 33.

doctor was dead, and he ordered Carpenter to retreat to Chunvis. But Arthur refused, and proceeded cautiously through the bush toward the area of the two fallen bodies, while Morley, Marius, and Andrew took the trail to Chunvis. Shortly they heard two shots.

"They've got Carpenter, or that is the end of the poor doctor," exclaimed Morley.[11]

After two hours they reached Chunvis, joined the five muleteers and *chicleros*, and hastily set out for British Honduras. When night came on, they traveled with the aid of a lantern, but the discovery of footprints on the trail alarmed the Silas boys, and the party decided to sleep in a corozo palm swamp. *Garrapatas* and a shower put sleep out of the question, and by four-thirty in the morning they were on their way again. After three hours they crossed into the Colony, threw their hats into the air as a sign of relief, and proceeded to the village of Benque Viejo. Then for the first time Vay began to realize that the assailants had been Guatemalan troops and not revolutionaries. He could learn nothing, however, about Carpenter; so he pushed on to El Cayo, where he found his companion recovering from a harrowing adventure.

On the previous afternoon after Morley and the Silas boys had left for Chunvis, Carpenter returned to the scene of the firing, accidentally exposing himself to the view of the attackers in ambush, and quickly became a hunted man. Once when he eluded his pursuers, hiding in the bush from where he could see the motionless bodies of Lafleur and Romero, he concluded that they were dead. Then he attempted to get out of the danger zone, only to find pursuers in front and in back of him; and for a time he and they carried on a bizarre game of hide-and-seek until he escaped by making a large circle through the bush, coming out near Buena Vista in British territory, where he was safe. At the village he reported the attack, and was provided with a horse and escort to El Cayo, where he presented the whole affair to the district commander and telegraphed to the American consul in

11 *Morleyana*, 34.

Belize for aid. He also sent guides to Chunvis to escort Morley safely to the Colony, but by the time they arrived Vay and his companions were spending a sleepless night in the tick-infested bush. At the same time Carpenter took a native, and the two made their way to the scene of the attack to recover Lafleur's body; when Arthur discovered that armed men still guarded the trail, he gave up the attempt and returned to El Cayo fifteen minutes before Morley arrived there in search of him.

At once Vay set to work on the unpleasant task of recovering and burying Lafleur's body. This he did with dispatch and propriety, arranging a multitude of details, beginning with a strong letter to the local Guatemalan military officials and concluding with the burial services in the El Cayo cemetery at ten o'clock at night.

Through the whole affair he displayed remarkable self-control. On leaving the cemetery, he telegraphed Woodward of the tragedy. The next day he secured all of the property of the expedition that the Guatemalan military commander was willing to return, although he never received a satisfactory reason for the attack that squared with the facts. Later Vay claimed that the assailants were a band of drunken Petenero soldiers. On the twenty-second he wrote a long report of the affair to Woodward that is a model of clear narrative and specific detail; and a week later he concluded the second installment of the recital. The expedition was at an end for the season, and he and Carpenter left El Cayo for Belize.

The tragedy preyed on Vay's mind like a frightful nightmare. On the way to Belize he stopped off to visit "Red" Frazer for several days. At night Frazer heard Morley talking in his sleep, rehearsing the gruesome events.

"I'll never come back to that damned forest," he shouted from his bed. "I'm going straight to Texas where you can go a thousand miles and never see a tree. Never again in the Petén bush."[12]

By the time he reached Belize he had not recovered from the shock. His friend, Robert Boatman, mahogany exporter and agent

12 J. Eric S. Thompson to the author.

for his remittances from the Carnegie Institution, was alarmed and informed Holmes in Washington to take measures to divert Vay's mind from the tragedy.

One more task remained. When Vay reached New Orleans, he made a trip to Opelousas, Louisiana, to extend condolences to Lafleur's brother, also a physician.

On June 9, Morley and Carpenter reached Washington and gave a firsthand report to Woodward. The Carnegie Institution laid the matter before the United States State Department, which in turn made representations to the Guatemalan government. While the negotiations were under way, the Carnegie officials, desirous of acting with utmost propriety, forbade Vay to speak to the press about the matter.

The negotiations ended in a stalemate, and the United States never received satisfaction or compensation in the matter. Guatemala defended the attack on several grounds. The Americans, it claimed, had been ordered to halt and failed to do so; this Vay steadfastly denied. Guatemala charged that Romero was an accomplice of the revolutionaries, as documents on his body proved; Morley argued that he had been in the employ of a British citizen in El Cayo when he met him. Guatemala asserted further that Morley had taken out-of-the-way trails instead of traveling over well-known routes. And finally Guatemala produced an affidavit of Dr. Beto Boburg[13] of Flores to the effect that Boburg had strongly advised Morley against entering the Petén during the disorders.

The expedition of 1916 had interesting effects. As a matter of course, more archaeological information was garnered about Tulum and Copán. Also Morley was correct in considering the discovery of Uaxactún a great achievement; not only did it pro-

[13] Dr. Beto Boburg, a native of Liverpool, England, was government physician for the Department of the Petén. He was related in some way, probably through his wife, to Don Clodiveo, *jefe politico*. Morley first met Boburg in 1914 and through his influence secured a letter of recommendation from Don Clovideo. Apparently Boburg's statement of 1916, used by the Guatemalan government to support its position, did not affect the friendship of the two men. Vay recorded an evening spent with the doctor and his wife in 1921, and he reported meeting him in Flores as late as 1944.

vide glyphs dates for him, but future annual expeditions also mined valuable data about Maya civilization from its ruins. The murder of Lafleur, on the other hand, could have had unfortunate effects on Vay's explorations, because Carnegie officials, shocked by the event, appeared determined to secure satisfaction before allowing him to take future trips to Guatemala. That nation never admitted responsibility in the affair, so for the time being his scientific investigations there appeared to be halted. But by April, 1917, the United States entered World War I, and that changed the whole situation. Carnegie officials, eager to co-operate with the United States government, willingly sent Vay off on another expedition.

VI

Secret Agent

VAY'S response to World War I was instinctive and total. He supported the Allied cause without question, and when the United States became involved he was eager to make his contribution. There was no doubt in his mind that American civilization was superior to any other, a feeling reinforced by his experiences in Latin America. Like many other citizens, he also had good reason to value his nation because of the personal advantages he enjoyed—a good education, pleasant society, and a satisfying profession. It is also possible that he absorbed some of the current Anglo-Saxonism popular at that time. Finally, his maternal grandfather was a Belgian, which surely struck home when the Germans attacked that small, unprotected country.

Before the United States entered the war, Vay was prepared to help as soon as the hour struck. Seven or eight archaeologists, who had traveled widely in Latin America and had influential friends scattered over that area, decided to pool their efforts and offer their services to the government. An agreement was reached by which they would work for Navy Intelligence, the most active branch of secret service at the time, in the guise of scientists engaged in their professional research. They were told to stand by until the United States formally entered the conflict.

Vay was one of the group, and on the declaration of war on June 6, the plan went into operation and he received a commission as ensign that day. Technically, he was attached to the Naval Coast Defense Reserve of the Navy Yard, Washington, D.C. He served two years, retiring in March, 1919, as a lieutenant, junior grade. Three other men received similar commissions, but suddenly Secretary of Navy Daniels refused to grant more commissions for that purpose, and the remainder of the men in the group carried out their duties as private citizens.

The full story of the secret operations of these scientists for the Navy is not known. Obviously, the government did not publish information on the subject, and the participants, who were sworn to secrecy, often interpreted their oath as a lifetime commitment. One of the ensigns never breathed a word about his undercover work to his wife in later years; another eventually regretted the role he had played and avoided discussion of the subject. Morley did his best to maintain his vow by excluding details of the secret activity from his diary and by saying little about the special mission after the conflict was over. Several of his assignments, however, are known. He examined the Gulf coast of Honduras and Nicaragua to discover possible hideouts of enemy submarines; and his voyage to Cozumel and eastern Yucatán in 1918 was doubtless for the same purpose. Less extensive was his reconnaissance of potential enemy naval activity in the Gulf of Fonseca. So far, nothing is known of the purpose of his sudden missions to Costa Rica, El Salvador, Guatemala, and Panama.

Some of his friends were in the same work. Joe Spinden, one of the four ensigns, traveled with John Held, the artist, to Guatemala, where Held became Morley's assistant, and Spinden went on to Honduras to stimulate the output of mahogany for airplane propellers. Vay encountered Spinden later in San Salvador, Ampala, and Bluefields. Two of his other friends in the secret service were Sam Lothrop, who worked on an unknown mission in Costa Rica, and Arthur Carpenter, who forwarded dyewoods from Santo Domingo to a New York firm producing cloth for military uniforms. Central America must have swarmed with special agents;

in December, 1917, it was rumored that fourteen United States secret service men were operating simultaneously in Guatemala City alone.

Sometimes these men became victims of misunderstandings if they did not know each other personally, as was the case of Arthur Carpenter and J. J. Perdomo. Vay described Perdomo, whose mission is not known, as a friend of Spinden in Panama, and Vay and Perdomo had one exchange of letters. Then Perdomo showed up unexpectedly in Puerto Cortés, where his peculiar traits made him suspect. At this point Carpenter had a long conversation with the stranger; but he failed to make his identity clear to Perdomo, and Vay blamed Carpenter for being too mysterious himself. If that was Carpenter's trouble, he suffered for it, because Americans now suspected him of being a German spy and refused to extend him financial credit. His situation became so serious that Vay, although he was convinced of his friend's innocence but disgusted with his love of sensation, advised him to return to the States to rehabilitate his reputation.

It is interesting to speculate on how many persons were familiar with Morley's secret work. Of course, John Held, his assistant, and members of the American legations where he posted his dispatches knew what he was doing. Boaz Long, minister to El Salvador, Walter Thurston, chargé d'affaires and special agent of the United States State Department in Guatemala City, and Jack Belt, secretary of legation in Tegucigalpa, co-operated fully with him. Captain Wood of the *Lilly Elena* could not have been in the dark about the ultimate use of the soundings he took at harbors and the information about the coast he elicited from friendly natives for Vay's reports. Dick Kelvin, hard-boiled chicle company employee, surely realized the purpose of Vay's voyage, when he informed him about details of the Mosquito Coast. Certainly the officials of the United Fruit Company at Rincón knew what was up when they generously placed all of their maps at his disposal. In Guatemala City, Morley called on Jack Armstrong, the British consul, plainly told him of his mission, and asked for the co-operation of British consular officers.

Officials of the Carnegie Institution knew about Vay's special work, but they were discreet enough not to disclose it in the written records. Doubtless they were motivated by the same patriotic sentiments that stirred Vay, because they suddenly changed their attitude when the nation entered the war. Early in 1917 the C.I.W officials had decided not to send him on archaeological expeditions until the Lafleur case had been settled. But then came the declaration of war and Morley was soon off to Central America on archaeological work, with the usual credentials issued by President Woodward. There was no conflict between the two assignments, though intelligence work took priority; the surprising fact is that Vay did accomplish some scientific work between stints for the secret service. Also, the C.I.W. saw to it that he did not suffer financially, for they paid him the difference between his $1,700 a year as ensign and his regular salary. It is amusing to note that Morley and the C.I.W. never quite agreed on how he was employed in these war years. The official *Year Book* of the Institution suggested that he was on regular archaeological expeditions; but in his *Inscriptions of Copán*, published in 1920, Morley stated that there were no Central American expeditions of the C.I.W. in those years, though he admitted he had visited some of the Central American countries.

Despite claims by friends that Morley could not keep secrets, he did a pretty good job in playing the double role. Only twice was he aware that he was under suspicion. Down the Mosquito Coast a resident American at first considered him a detective and refused to talk about the Patuca River; then for some reason the man lost his reticence the following day and confidentially explained everything. A far more serious situation developed at Trujillo, where a local official, amazed that Vay and John Held, who had plenty of money to spend, were registered only as crew members of the *Lilly Elena*, wired the minister of war, who in turn asked the local governor to investigate. In the meantime Vay was off on the trip to Bluefields, but on his return some weeks later Trujillo was alive with rumors. Thereupon he had an interview with the governor, displayed his credentials and a letter from President Bertrand, and satisfied that official.

Most of his secret service work was drab routine, with none of the flair of cloak-and-dagger adventure. He took the preparation of reports seriously, and was careful to safeguard the information he compiled. When possible, he typed the reports and sent them by diplomatic pouch at the nearest American legation. After the voyage around eastern Yucatán, he settled down in Mérida and used an unoccupied country house on the outskirts of the city. Every morning a car, supplied with cigarettes and food for lunch, took him to the house and called for him at four in the afternoon. Quiet, unwatched, and free from interruption, he drew up his reports and then burned the original notes. Sometimes he collected information beyond his assignment, like the account of the shipbuilding industry of Roatán and Bonacca, or the sample of dyewood he picked up on an inlet of the Mosquito Coast.

The idealism of the war effort sustained his thought and action. In a newspaper article in Honduras he characterized the conflict as the great battle for civilization, the assurance of democracy for the world, and the triumph of right over force and of justice over Teutonic furor. About the same time he wrote to a friend that he yearned to be back in the States, where the American spirit flowered with new vitality and rose to heights of idealism probably never again to occur in his generation.

The Stars and Stripes symbolized the strong patriotism that he felt. The happiest moment he experienced in 1917 doubtless occurred one Friday night in May in the village of Copán. As he sat on the edge of the town plaza, he realized that an official was announcing Honduras' declaration of war on Germany. Thrilled and excited, Vay raised an American flag at his quarters and happily greeted the rejoicing citizens. Some months later on the trip down the Nicaraguan coast he proudly flew the American flag in addition to that of Nicaragua, until a legal-minded customs official threatened to fine him twenty-five dollars for displaying a foreign banner.

His deep commitment to the war and its ideals bred strong

feelings in his soul. He commonly referred to a German as a Hun, a word charged with hatred that later generations cannot appreciate. It is surprising to find the kindly disposed Vay filled with disgust on learning that a Guatemalan beauty, betrothed to a German, was being thrown away on a Hun who was an ugly little pig. A few days later when an earthquake collapsed a wall of the German legation, disclosing the interior of a room with Christmas tree and dinner tables, he hoped that the Hun could see the kind of destruction he had wreaked upon France and Belgium.

He made the most of every opportunity to strengthen the Allied cause and to defeat Germany. At Rincón he encouraged several men working for the fruit company to enlist in military service. The telegraph operator was in a dither over whether to keep his job or to enlist and lose his seniority rights. An Englishman, long ago banished by his family to Honduras for youthful indiscretions, did not know how to go about enlisting in the British army at that late date without being called a slacker. Vay urged both men to get into the service.

He also had his eyes open for enemy sympathizers. Richard Lehmann at Cape Gracias mouthed pro-Ally sentiments, but Vay considered him a slippery character who would side with Germany in a showdown; and he felt relieved when the British consul assured him that he was keeping an eye on the suspicious man. In Bluefields a Prussian owned the hotel and restaurant that Vay used; after a long argument with the German, Vay fumed at the man's warped, twisted reasoning in defense of the fatherland.

Even in international policy Morley attempted to give advice. He pressed the British minister in Guatemala to apply the black list rigidly against natives who traded with the enemy. When the minister countered that such practice only irritated and alienated the natives, Vay retorted violently that the natives should be sacrificed. At the same time he considered Guatemala the keystone of the whole Allied cause in Central America, and proposed that the United States must convince President Cabrera that the interests of the two nations were identical. So long as

Guatemala remained friendly to the United States, Vay contended, German connivance in Central America and Mexico would have little effect.

If peace, law, and order in international affairs were the elements for preserving civilization, he believed that Latin America must bow to the inevitable. Just as the Allies sought to punish Germany for violating those fundamental rights, so would nations—presumably the United States in particular—find it necessary to intervene to put down internal disturbances that caused the loss of foreign lives and property in Latin-American nations. (In a thoughtless moment he even found himself defending the notorious dictator Estrada Cabrera, because he did a good job in maintaining law and order.) If those nations failed to quash uprisings by their own efforts, they must expect that someone would do it for them, despite bruised pride and affronts to national sovereignty.

He was defensive, however, when faced with criticism of his own nation. On learning of confusion and mismanagement in Washington during the first six months of the war, he dismissed those deficiencies as not unexpected in a great, tolerant democracy unaccustomed to war. Several times when he heard of economic exploitation by an American firm in Honduras, the news caught him unprepared; he could do nothing but repeat the altruistic motives of his nation toward its southern neighbors. Soon he realized that platitudes were useless in the face of the cold facts. Lee Christmas startled him with stories of American pressure on the internal policy of Honduras and of proposed loans that would have enriched an American secretary of state. For the moment Vay was agape at such revelations.

He was also aware of his nation's bad reputation in Central America, and he made efforts to repair it by a show of unselfish action. After the earthquake in San Salvador he and John Held pitched in to help Boaz Long, the United States minister, to aid the stricken inhabitants. He realized that pro-German feeling had spread in that country because of earlier American blunders, and he hoped to counteract the enemy propaganda by altruistic work that would prove American interest was not entirely of the dollar-diplomacy variety.

There is no evidence that he felt uneasy over the dual role of archaeologist and secret service agent. But a fellow anthropologist disliked the whole business. A month after the war ended Franz Boas published a short, trenchant article, "Spies as Scientists," in the *Nation*. He denounced the four ensigns, without naming them, for masquerading as archaeologists when they were serving as spies, and he predicted that in the future American scientists working in foreign countries would be under justifiable suspicion. We have no idea what Morley thought of the charge.

Vay's anti-German feeling was strong and lasting. In 1923 it was still on the surface of his consciousness. When he learned in Mexico City that a former classmate at Pennsylvania Military Academy had spent much time in Germany and was about to return as Mexican consul at Hamburg, Vay suspected his friend of having been pro-German during the war. A day later when Morley dined at the home of Claude Dawson, United States consul general in Mexico City, he bristled on discovering that he was to sit at the same table with a German baron and his wife. On another occasion, as he waited in a railroad station, he saw a little German boy weeping over the departure of his father. Vay sympathized with the youngster's grief and admitted that it was the first time in a decade that he had had a kindly feeling for a German.

Morley acted in a dual capacity during 1917 and the early part of 1918. Although the relation between the two commitments will probably never be clear, it appears that he followed his professional work until he received orders to make a special investigation for the Navy. As it turned out, most of his time during the year was devoted to the war effort.

He had an unusual opportunity to associate with an interesting and talented young man when he teamed up with John Held, Jr., in 1917–18. Just twenty-eight and not yet the celebrity he was soon to become, Held deserted New York at the right time in his career. He had finished the hard days and nights of making a living at commercial art and experimenting on the side to find his natural artistic expression, but he had not yet entered on a career too profitable to abandon. His interest in the art of past ages drove him to examine the culture from which those artistic forms sprang, and so he decided to study the Maya ruins at firsthand.

Held had been reared in a Mormon household devoted to the arts. His father came from Switzerland to train as an art teacher, but he gave up that goal to become a copper-plate engraver, a manufacturer of fountain pens, the founder of a successful band in Salt Lake City, and the husband of a professional actress. The boy sketched, painted, played musical instruments, learned the printing trade, and produced his first woodcut at the age of nine. After high school, his first full-time job was that of sports cartoonist on a Salt Lake City newspaper. He soon became acquainted with the society editor and married her. At twenty-one he was off to the greener pastures of New York City, where he did all kinds of work in commercial art.

Held and Morley came together through mutual friends. Herbert J. Spinden was assistant curator at the American Museum of Natural History and knew Mahonri Young, the sculptor, who constructed Hopi and Apache models at the museum for the exhibition of artifacts. Held also knew Young, who had given him a few lessons in art, the only formal training that the future cartoonist ever had. In 1916, Young and Held went to New Mexico where they met Morley and Spinden.

When the United States declared war in April, 1917, Held and Spinden were recruited to work for Navy Intelligence in Central America. They proceeded to Guatemala City to meet Morley, and a few days later the three men, joined by an engineer, went to Copán. Spinden and the engineer soon left for points south, and Held and Morley thereafter traveled and worked together for many months.

They made ideal companions. They were held together by three bonds—a sense of humor, interest in the ancient Mayas, and patriotic wartime work for their nation. Otherwise, they differed completely. John spoke sparingly and to the point; Vay was voluble and effusive. John communed with himself and expressed his feelings in sketching and painting; the extrovert Morley had to be with people to be happy, and his expression came through the spoken and written word. John loved physical exertion, like swimming and hunting, but Vay evaded all unnecessary exercise like a plague.

As the first object of the expedition in 1917, Morley chose a trip to Copán, favorite hunting ground for date glyphs. The party he headed included John Held, Jr., the artist, R. W. Hebard, engineer, and Joe Spinden, archaeologist. Held accompanied Morley as his artist; and Hebard, a railroad builder for Minor C. Keith, industrial developer of Central America, tagged along to have a sight of Copán on his way to Costa Rica. When Hebard recalled his experience in later years, it was not the ruins that remained vividly in his memory so much as Vay's dynamic drive, sense of humor, and intense dedication to Maya study.

Hebard and Held, beholding Copán for the first time, reacted somewhat differently. Gazing at the sight, Held was quiet and thoughtful, though obviously impressed, and he let his imagination reconstruct the scene of former times. Hebard delighted Vay with his exclamations of wonder and amazement; naturally the engineering skill of the ancients attracted him; and then Vay excitedly dragged him through the small tunnel that came out of the wall high above the river. After lunch on the second day, Hebard and Spinden left for Santa Ana and San Salvador.

The first night in the village, asleep in the quarters assigned to the Americans in the municipal building facing the main plaza, Vay discovered a new aspect of life in Copán. At three o'clock in the morning an explosion rent the air, followed by a blare of music, a prolonged drum call to arms, and more music. Sleep was impossible, as dogs, frogs, birds, cows, and roosters joined in the cacophony. His first thought was of revolution. Then he learned that the natives were assembling to do battle against a scourge of nature. Grasshoppers had devoured the whole area, destroying the young corn, beans, and even the tobacco plants.

In a seven-day crusade the natives, garbed in dirty cotton shirts and pantaloons, straw hats and sandals, and armed with machetes and flails, sallied out before daylight to kill the grasshoppers while they slept, which was considered a more effective method than battling them in the air during the daytime. Just what the several hundred peasants did all day long, standing like sentinels on the neighboring hills, was not clear. If noise could kill, observed Vay, the Indians would have accomplished their mission in short order, for they battled with music, bugles, and revolver shots. On returning late in the day, the valiant fighters boasted of their progress against the enemy, but Morley saw as many grasshoppers in the air as ever. One afternoon the natives brought a reinforcement in the form of a *santo*, decorated with paper flowers and tinsel. Old women in black *rebozos*, supporting the crude litter holding the image, carried it to the fields, a picturesque suggestion of the Middle Ages. On the last day of the crusade, Vay went up to the cliffs above the village, where he saw dead grasshoppers on the ground, but he also saw many still flying about.

His friendship with the villagers and his custom of rewarding them for preserving and bringing newly found stones to his attention vastly advanced his archaeological work. On every visit he looked forward to finds made during the past year, and he was usually pleased with what had been saved for him. One native, on digging a well in his backyard, came upon a fragment of Stela 24 (A.D. 210), which had been used as the base of Stela 7 (A.D. 340), an interesting case of the ancients' reuse of older stones. This year a new altar stone (A.D. 505) and fragments of Stela 5 discovered in a field far from the other pieces of that stone were brought to his attention. Two years before, he had poked about and partly dismantled four hundred feet of stone wall, hoping to locate those fragments embedded in the modern structure; now they turned up in a field. On this visit the schoolteacher also told him of a fragment on one side of the plaza; and on digging it up, he found it was a piece missing since Maudslay's visit in 1885. That piece and Stela 24 gave the earliest and latest Initial Series at the site. He planned to place both of them in the town hall for safekeeping, which is the first suggestion of the small museum he began at Copán.

John and Vay spent their time photographing and copying the new inscriptions. The drawing was necessary because they could not rely on their camera. When John used a new tank developer they had brought with them, he was able to secure only two satisfactory pictures from the first four he processed. Vay blamed the heat and lack of experience with the new method for the poor results. He recorded, however, two days later that all of the films came out satisfactorily.

The last day at any site, especially at Copán, kept Morley busy with the unfinished business, leave-taking, paying bills, and preparing for the next lap of the journey. The unfinished piece of business was his trip to the quarries. Two boys led him to the vertical cliffs in the foothills where the ancients had cut out their stones. Although no squared pieces were in evidence, he believed that the place appeared artificially worked, and on looking at the main plaza of the ruins directly below, he could understand how the blocks were moved down the easy descent. Then he completed arrangements for a guide to take him to the new sites he planned to visit in the days that followed. At four in the afternoon, he performed the ritual of a farewell to the ruins. He and John stopped for a moment before Owens' grave, looked at some familiar stelae, and then entered the court of the Hieroglyphic Stairway, a place of utter confusion with two-thirds of the carved stones jumbled together at the base where an earthquake had catapulted them years before. With deep respect for these ancient remains and with regret at leaving them, he turned from the scene.

After a shower and dinner he settled his accounts with the town officials, a ritual in which the characters played their parts with relish. He looked up Don Tobías, the *alcalde*, who in turn summoned Don Jacobo, the treasurer, and the three went into a huddle over the table in the town hall. Don Tobías donned his gold spectacles and Don Jacobo brought out the book of municipal regulations. Vay sat there in soiled khaki field clothes and a young beard on his face, while a dirty urchin of four or five wandered in from the plaza as a curious bystander. In the room the flickering lantern threw unsteady shadows against the white-washed walls. Gravely, one of the officials read the rule that levied a fee of ten dollars a visit on each stranger going to the ruins. Then the other official offered the consideration that Vay was a *scientífico*, not a mere *turista*. And finally, with Don Jacobo wisely nodding his head, they agreed on twenty-five dollars. At that Vay added a gift of ten dollars toward furnishing the new church. Then they adjourned to Don Rafael's store, where he exchanged gold for silver and paid his debts.

As a final sign of goodwill, he and John went to their room at the other end of the plaza and held open house for the villagers, who swarmed in and out, poking about curiously among their possessions. By ten o'clock the two men, wearied by the noise and confusion and odor of liquor, gently urged the crowd out, closed the door, and turned in for the night.

During the next few days, Vay and John moved northward into the Valley of the Chamelecón and found two new sites. At Río Amarillo, the inscriptions on two altars were glyphs Vay could not decipher, although the style suggested the Great Period. At Los Higos he found among the twenty-five mounds a stela with a huge human figure, bearing the date of A.D. 510. Adding this information to that from other sites, he was convinced he had determined the southern boundary of ancient Maya civilization, and that Copán was the mother city that colonized these lesser centers.

Then in June an intelligence assignment took him and John to San Salvador a week after a destructive earthquake had wrecked the city. Vay was particularly eager to reach the city as soon as possible, because he knew that Spinden was there and had failed to answer his telegram inquiring about his safety. When they landed at the Pacific port of Acajutla and got up in the morning for customs inspection, John nonchalantly met the officials in his lavendar pajamas. The Americans expected to travel the sixty-three miles to El Salvador by train, but the railroad was out of commission for a stretch of nine miles and they had to cover that distance by mule. It was dangerous business: great cracks appeared unexpectedly in their path, landslides had torn away parts of the road, and overhanging cliffs of rock threatened to fall at any moment. At night they holed up in an abandoned cart shed for protection against the rain. The following morning they came to the rail terminus and soon reached the city.

Vay was appalled at the plight of the natives and the destruction of property in El Salvador. Adobe and wooden buildings— perhaps 95 per cent of all habitations in the city—were destroyed or damaged beyond use. Structures of cement blocks were completely shattered, but reinforced concrete edifices survived intact. A third of the city's 60,000 people had fled, and many of those who remained lived in flimsy, temporary shacks. The onset of the rainy season aggravated the lack of housing and threatened to spread disease.

It happened that Boaz Long, Vay's old friend, was at the time United States minister to San Salvador.[1] Since the secretary of legation was on leave and the minister overworked, Vay and John volunteered to help him, doing some of the desk work and maintaining the water supply and sewage disposal for the legation, since municipal services had been interrupted.

Morley relished this work. In fact, the day after he arrived he sent a message to the United States secretary of state, recommending that $5,000 should be sent to Long for relief work and citing the good feeling that such aid would create toward the United States. The telegram still has an air of mystery about it. Why Vay, and not the minister, sent it is not clear; and the Mr. Vioch, to whom it was to be forwarded in New York, could not be found.

Near the end of June, Morley went on to Guatemala for twenty days and then returned to San Salvador for about a week. It was during one of these sojourns in the stricken capital that he and Spinden were induced to write an article about the recent catastrophe for a newspaper. The public blamed the disaster on the

[1] Long, nine years older than Morley, had been in the commission business for fourteen years before entering service for the United States State Department. Vay first met him in Mexico in 1907.

damming of Lake Ilopango to secure a source of water power. Since President Meléndez had permitted that project, he was vaguely held responsible for the ensuing disaster. So the visiting scientists were importuned to issue a statement.

Morley and Spinden, disclaiming geology as their field of competence, nevertheless produced an article intended to satisfy everyone. They incorporated much ethnological data about Indian beliefs concerning such catastrophes, and then ventured gingerly into some scientific aspects of the calamity. Yes, the lava had destroyed the coffee crop of that year, but it would fertilize the land and produce an extra-large crop the next year. The earthquake they attributed briefly to "vast and uncontrollable subterranean agencies," a statement obviously intended to absolve the president from blame. Long explained the sequel of the publication:

"The President and his cabinet were delighted, and their reaction, of course, pleased the authors, who, early one morning, came around to the Legation to celebrate. Shortly after their arrival, however, a runner announced that two coffee growers were coming to kill the authors of the article. Morley and Spinden were rushed to the third story, and I received the callers, who, heavily armed, somewhat violently demanded to know where Morley and Spinden were—damning their article and asserting it was a crime to mislead innocent farmers with such unreasonable prophesies. They were disagreeably insistent, but through a combination of devices, the indignant farmers were eventually persuaded that the headquarters of Morley in Guatemala, and Spinden in Honduras, would be better places to search than the American Legation for the supposed authors.

" 'Supposed, hell!' they replied. 'We know the ropes around here, and have positive evidence that Morley and Spinden did the writing.'

"So I invited them for a drink at a downtown club and said, 'Now we will go out and collect someone who can tell what really caused the earthquake and whether it would doubly fertilize crops for 1918.'

"While we were patching wounded feelings at the club, Morley and Spinden were understood to have departed from the city. Strangely enough, the scientists were right: next year's crop was magnificent, and the irate farmers eventually full of apologies."[2]

Where Morley fled is not known, but he showed up next in Honduras in a role that was congenial to him. For more than two weeks he did spadework cultivating cordial relations with government officials in regard to future archaeological work at Copán. First he approached Mariano Vásquez, minister of foreign affairs, presented letters to him from Woodward, explaining the work he had done at Copán and the fact that his book on inscriptions of that site would soon be published. Vásquez was sympathetic and twice took Vay for interviews with President Bertrand, who was likewise friendly. When Vásquez suggested that Morley should prepare an article on the subject for the government newspaper, he jumped at the opportunity to make his views known.

The article, appearing in Spanish, was peppered with the complimentary effusiveness that Vay adopted when addressing a Latin-American audience. After giving an extensive description of Copán and referring to his recent work there, he carefully explained the aims of the Carnegie Institution of Washington. The Institution had no intention of asking for artifacts; its sole object was the scientific study of the remains for archaeological knowledge. Then he pleaded for the appointment of a custodian to protect the monuments of Copán against future vandalism, predicted a great economic development for Honduras after the war ended, and finished with a graceful tribute to President Bertrand.

When Vay sent a clipping of the article to Woodward, he circled with pencil those paragraphs about the Institution's disinterest in acquiring artifacts. As recently as April, Woodward had instructed him to emphasize such a policy. It might be added that there is no evidence that this article stirred up any such furor as resulted from the article he published in San Salvador.

Morley and Held next set off on a sea jaunt down the Caribbean coast of Honduras and Nicaragua. They no longer aimed to find Maya glyphs or monuments; they were ordered by Navy Intelli-

[2] *Morleyana*, 119–20.

gence to examine the coastal waters in order to determine whether enemy submarines could penetrate that littoral. Now the two men were busy with maps, soundings, and channels at the entrances of harbors and lagoons. Of course, the official annual report of the Carnegie Institution said nothing about this activity of its staff members.

In preparation for the twelve-hundred mile voyage, Morley charted the *Lilly Elena* at $275 a month. The charge included a three-man crew and their maintenance. On the other hand, Vay had to bear all clearance charges and buy the gasoline, which cost almost seventy-five cents a gallon. On closing the deal, he gave the specifications of the boat; it was thirty-five feet long, eleven feet across, displaced three and one-half feet of water, and had an eighteen-horsepower engine. Its captain, Dournoft Wood, was a fortunate choice, for he was completely familiar with the route they would take. Charles Osgood was the engineer, and Campbell, a Jamaican, the cook.

In the daily record of the trip, Morley revealed nothing about the facts he collected and transmitted to his superiors in Intelligence. The most interesting experiences of the thirty-nine days on the *Lilly Elena* concerned people he met. At the various ports of call he had little to say about those shack affairs, as he characterized most of the villages except Trujillo and Bluefields. Though he rarely associated with the natives, he looked up white men, especially Americans, out of sheer curiosity or sometimes for the convenience of an overnight stay on land.

In finding accommodations in civilized quarters on land, because he disliked the discomfort and seasickness of the boat, he was only moderately successful. At Rincón, the United Fruit Company town near Trujillo, H. D. Scott, an official of the company, gave him and John an unoccupied house with modern conveniences and sometimes had them in for meals. At the next stop, Santa Rosa Aguán, Charles Osgood secured attractive accommodations in the home of his relatives, the Kirkconnels. At the next two ports of call, Vay hunted up Americans and stayed with them, but in both cases he discovered that they had married natives and lived in bamboo shacks with poor furnishings and little privacy. Thereafter the *Lilly Elena* provided sleeping quarters until the travelers reached Bluefields, the southern end of the journey. There they stayed at Peterson's Hotel in rooms with bath, an unexpected luxury in that remote place. On the return trip, Prinzapolka was the overnight stay, where they stopped with a friend until they returned to the Scotts' at Rincón.

At various stops on the voyage, Vay encountered old and new friends, a source of great interest, since he loved people for the personalities they revealed. One interesting man was Dick Kelvin, whom he had met at Trujillo and encountered again at Tansín Island, the seat of a chicle company commissary. Kelvin had charge of over eighty tough *chicleros*, who had been mistreated by a contractor and were in a bad frame of mind; moreover, all of them had received sizable advances of pay, and it was up to Kelvin to see that they did not get away. As Dick secured some extra ammunition from Osgood, he explained casually that when that was used up he would resort to a club. Morley could hardly believe the nerve of the man, as he saw him depart into the bush to control his rowdy *chicleros*.

Several days later Vay met another man who commanded his admiration but for entirely different reasons. He was an English Moravian missionary by the name of Taylor, teaching native children in his modest church at Cape Gracias. Vay found him conducting two classes simultaneously, one in English and one in Miskito. But Honduras also required Spanish, and so three languages were bandied about in the classroom. Taylor considered the children intelligent, especially in reading, but somewhat slow in grasping mathematics. He reminded Morley of his friend Father Versavel[3] on the edge of the Petén, who was also laboring heroically and unselfishly for the improvement of mankind.

He encountered another schoolteacher in the village at the mouth of Great River, the only white man in the native settlement. Cooper, then in his fifties, had taught school in Bonacca,

[3] Arthur Versavel, S.J., was in charge of the Catholic mission at Benque Viejo, B.H. By 1914 Vay already knew him.

but had lost his job because he drank too much. He moved down to Great River, resumed his profession, and conquered his alcoholism; but he detested the infamous hole he was in and declared that he would leave as soon as he collected forty-five dollars in back pay. Vay invited him to spend an evening on the *Lilly Elena,* where he enjoyed the music of the phonograph and devoured a newspaper Morley gladly gave him. It seems that Dournoft Wood knew that Cooper had something of a romance with a widow in Bonacca. The captain pictured her as still waiting for him and encouraged him to write to her. The lonely Cooper did so, and gave the envelope to Wood for delivery to the lady, remarking that one of these days he might just take a trip to Bonacca.

Two incidents on the trip down the coast also intrigued Vay—treasure hunters at Brangmans Bluff and a circus at Prinzapolka. The Navy chart indicated a wreck near the bluff, and by the time Vay arrived there he had already heard the long story of an old Spanish ship, attacked by English pirates; the vessel was scuttled, and a treasure chest was buried somewhere on the coast. A map showing the location of the valuables circulated in the area. When Vay reached the bluff, he was startled to see a dozen men digging on the shore. Bitten by curiosity, he signaled the dory of those men and was taken to their operations. With no idea of the kind of characters he was visiting, he wore only a revolver and deliberately went alone, believing that they would hesitate to attack a single man while his companions waited in a nearby boat. On landing, he asked for the man in charge, a Mr. Bordas, and inquired about the progress of the work. Bordas admitted that they had not found the chest so far; at that moment they were puzzled because they could not locate the coconut tree indicated on the chart as one clue to the hiding place. Then Vay, wishing them good luck, put off in the dory, with his back to the men. Shortly a tremendous explosion shook the place, and Vay, thinking he had been shot at, turned about so violently that he almost capsized the dory. It was a charge of dynamite, planted by the men to open up a spot on the shore, and before he had reached the *Lilly Elena* several more blasts went off. He never did learn whether the treasure-hunters were successful.

More amusing and more to his taste was the circus he saw in Prinzapolka the next day. The *Lilly Elena*, anchored in the harbor, was scheduled to stay only one night at the town. When a member of the company came aboard to advertise the circus, the Americans were disappointed to learn that there was no show that night. So Vay paid ten dollars for a special performance for the six members of his party, additional admissions to go to the circus company. At eight, the men from the *Lilly Elena* were in the best seats, and the Ayala family began to go through their stunts. Mr. Ayala was an acrobat and trapeze artist, his son played a fairly good clown, and the Ayala children entertained with songs and dances. Vay and his companions enjoyed the affair tremendously, convinced that they had more than their money's worth as well as a delightful respite from montonous travel afloat.

Bluefields, southern terminus of the voyage, presented a fairly good appearance by Mosquito Coast standards. At the harbor the customhouse had an enterprising air about it, and a number of boats were waiting to enter. The town stretched a mile along the edge of a bluff, with buildings made of sawed lumber painted white and capped with sheet-iron roofing, not particularly esthetic but modern and substantial as compared with the native shacks and huts common along the coast. At Bluefields the amenities of civilization included Peterson's Hotel, Borden's ice-cream parlor that specialized in oyster cocktails, the Tropical Club, a good dentist, an ice house, thirty Chinese stores, and cement sidewalks along the main street.

Vay spent his days here chatting with Joe Spinden and writing lengthy reports. He and Joe exchanged gossip and discussed their findings for Navy Intelligence; in fact, Joe urged him to proceed down to the Canal Zone, but Vay considered the trip too long for the *Lilly Elena*. During rainy days Vay worked on lengthy reports for his superiors in Intelligence, and in the evenings read magazines and played bridge in the hotel lobby.

During these adventures, Morley and Held got along well together. Their jokes and quips at each other's expense indicated the strength of their mutual respect and friendship. On a visit to the Coopers in Roatán, when they danced with the girls of the household, Vay speeded up the phonograph just to see the breathless John wilting, as he tried to follow the increased tempo. John had his revenge; months later in Belize when they danced again with some young women, Held quietly told his partner that Vay was an atrocious dancer. Three years later when Vay happened to dance with the girl, she exclaimed with surprise that he was not so bad after all, and the story was out. All told, Vay got in more than his share of innings, as he teased John incessantly about his sleeping at the drop of a hat and his insatiable interest in shooting wildlife.

Vay was amused with John's hunting adventures, because the results were so small in proportion to the inconvenience and discomfort they caused. One night in San Pedro Sula, Held went with a friend to shoot deer, and returned after Morley went to bed. Next morning Vay rose early, saw no bloody carcasses around and then packed up the camera and film John had on hand to photograph the spoils. Down the Mosquito Coast, John tried his luck several times, usually returning with an empty bag. Once he came back with so many *garrapatas* that no one would share a bed with him that night; another time he returned from hunting doves empty-handed with the explanation that they were flying high, which made Morley arch an eyebrow; on a third occasion he came back in a rage because he had been led on a wild-goose chase into a region swarming with mosquitoes, covered with sand and tall pampas grass, and entirely devoid of the least trace of deer; the spoils from that adventure were no more than a few coconuts he shot from a tree. In fact, he had good luck only once, when he brought back nine blue-winged teal; even Vay conceded that was a good bag.

If John complained loudly of the bootless results of a hunting trip, he gave little hint of important emotions he felt. When the *Lilly Elena* crossed the first bar of a river, Vay reported that he and John were terrified; Vay probably felt that John shared his own fear. The third time they crossed a bar, John was driven below by rain; when he did emerge, it was because of stifling heat and odors, not from fear.

Vay never joked about John's art work. One afternoon at Sicri Point, the two men rushed to the beach to see a magnificent display of colors in the sky over the calm sea. John hurried to capture it in watercolors and Vay to record it in words, but both despaired of doing the sight justice before the sun suddenly dropped behind coconut trees. When John sketched the faces of crew members of the *Lilly Elena*, Vay pronounced them excellent.

Held's major contribution on the voyage was map-making. At Rincón, Vay put him to copying maps provided by the United Fruit Company in preparation for the voyage, and during the trip he continued to prepare maps to supplement Morley's reports.

One of these maps created a storm between the two men. During the stay at Bluefields, Vay directed John to prepare a map. Unfortunately, the only available paper did not take ink satisfactorily, but John went to work and did the best he could, apparently losing interest as he discovered the poor results. Vay was always a stickler for neat performance, and he was disappointed by what he saw. As he discussed the matter, John nonchalantly remarked that the map was good enough. Those words ignited smouldering anger in Vay; he exploded with a volley of accusations of carelessness. John snatched the map and ripped it to pieces, for he always revolted at carrying out an assignment that appeared unreasonable or senseless. In time both men cooled off. Vay became contrite for having lost his temper, and before the end of the day friendly relations were restored. Vay solved the problem by hiring a local artist to make the map for twenty dollars. Only one other blowup occurred over an unimportant matter some months earlier in Tegucigalpa. The fact that these two men worked and lived together for a year in Middle America and had only two disagreements is sufficient tribute to their remarkably tolerant dispositions.

After eleven days Vay and John left Bluefields for the return trip up the coast, but before they pulled out, Morley arranged for a farewell get-together aboard the *Rama,* a mail steamer in the harbor. He and his friends gathered on deck, he ordered cold beer, and then played some new records on the phonograph, a Harry Lauder, selections from the 1917 *Follies,* some blues, and a jazz piece, the latest thing. Conviviality and good spirits prevailed. Then came the time to leave. He and his men went to the *Lilly Elena,* while his friends lined the wharf, shouting goodbye and waving their hands in the air. Those on the boat did the same, and Vay put the new jazz record on the machine. The thumping syncopation mixed with whistles and horns of other boats in the harbor, and amidst the noise the boat moved out to sea. It was the kind of exit he enjoyed.

But he also felt a current of sadness permeating the noisy farewell. It seemed that he was always saying goodbye to a good friend like Joe Spinden; he admired his ability, treasured his friendship, and even got to like his contentiousness. But why the inevitable farewell? Perhaps, he mused, as the music ceased and the wharf disappeared from view, that is just the price of being an itinerant archaeologist.

In six days they doubled back to Trujillo, and except for engine trouble near the end of the trip, only one incident of note took place. It happened one afternoon in Cape Gracias, where the circus was still operating. As Vay was on his way to the performance and had almost reached the tent, a drunken native pointed a revolver at him and announced that he was about to shoot him. Unarmed and eight feet away from the man, Vay decided to resort to sweet persuasion. He engaged the man in conversation, suggesting they talk things over before he pulled the trigger, all the time moving toward his assailant. When Vay was close enough to place his arm on the man's shoulder, he sensed that the native had lost his resolve to shoot, so he advised him to put down the weapon and he led him into the crowd before the circus. Scarcely had Vay entered the tent when he heard a shot behind him. The man had pointed the weapon in the air, but the noise frightened women and children for half an hour. This was not the only time Vay talked himself out of a tight spot.

Time and experience work wonders, and so it was with Vay when he entered Trujillo Bay at dawn on October 17. The last few days of the voyage it was touch and go with the *Lilly Elena*, which had had its hull damaged on being pulled over a bar; but with the aid of wind and current she made port. As the rising sun threw streaks of light on the bluff, white houses and red roofs emerged from the darkness, and the old cathedral's twin towers loomed above like sentinels. The scene held him motionless for a moment. All of the shoddiness and neglect of the town, which he knew only too well, lay in the shadows; but now the buildings, old and new, stood forth brilliantly in the morning light and formed a charming picture. Perhaps the six weeks' absence had something to do with the appealing sight before his eyes.

Back in Trujillo, he awaited orders for further cruises in the *Lilly Elena*. He stayed a week with the Scotts across the bay in Rincón and then went to Roatán to have his boat repaired. There Bob Cooper welcomed him with a gathering of fifty people, certainly a reception after Vay's heart. On leaving Roatán for La Ceiba on the mainland, normally a brief passage, the *Lilly Elena* ran into a violent storm at sea, the worst in twenty years in those parts, and took quick refuge at Hog Islands. After landing there, Vay and John saw one vessel pounded to pieces on the reef and another making a narrow escape. Only after a week did the storm subside sufficiently for the crew to take the *Lilly Elena* back to Roatán for a new mainsail. Vay and John remained on the island. For unknown reasons the *Lilly Elena* did not show up at the appointed time, and the two men were stranded.

Although they stayed on Hog Islands nineteen days, they were hardly Robinson Crusoes, as Morley pretended. The Bushes, a white family who lived there, gave them the use of their dining-room, a small structure made of driftwood and covered with a tin roof. But food, at least a variety of it, was hard to come by, because the storm had caught everyone in low supply. Vay and John subsisted on beans at every meal, with bread, tea, and guava jelly as the only variation in their diet.

The enforced leisure drove each man to find something to do or die of boredom, as Vay observed. He completed writing a review of Spinden's *Ancient Civilizations of Mexico* for the *American Anthropologist*, wrote letters to friends, worked over his scientific notes, and finally and reluctantly toted up his financial accounts. This last chore was a nightmare because he often forgot to list expenditures that could go on his expense account, and in the end he had to pay such items from his own pocket. An earlier accounting cost him $200, and so this time he felt fortunate when he discovered that he was out of pocket no more than $100.

John painted for days on end, and when Vay had time to study the pictures with care, his appreciation rose to enthusiasm. He marveled how the artist caught the exact color of waves and water and conveyed the menace and cruelty of the sea. For a period John used his pencil to sketch islanders in characteristic poses—one man squatting, another chopping wood, and a third at his boat—and chickens and pigs and other details of daily life. Again Vay poured out praise for the result, explaining how apparently crude and sketchy strokes gave a striking, sharp impression of the subject. He observed, probably correctly, that John threw himself into this artistic frenzy rather than curse the heat and bugs, the inevitable beans at every meal, and the failure of a boat to show up and take them to the mainland.

John also like to work with his hands. One day he replaced the uneven kitchen floor for Mrs. Bush. That night Vay found him singing, obviously happy and contented with the accomplishment of his task.

The *Lilly Elena* did not appear, and John and Vay found transportation on another vessel to La Ceiba. Morley's mail contained instructions for future work, but he did not confide those orders to his diary. One must assume that some of his traveling was for Navy Intelligence; he went to Guatemala City, was in and out of Puerto Barrios and Puerto Cortés, up Lake Izabal and at Quiriguá, and then returned to Guatemala City.

In the meantime, John Held was working at his own devices. He turned to his earlier medium of cartoons and began to develop the style that eventually made him famous. As early as November, Morley found him working diligently on new ideas for humorous sketches based on the contemporary scene. Vay thought him very clever at this form of sophisticated humor that would later appeal to the smart taste of New York.

For reading matter John preferred American magazines, especially the *Saturday Evening Post,* which he eagerly seized on in any out-of-the-way coastal town. Vay claimed that John had an unerring scent for the periodical. He explained how he had slept on a bed four nights unaware that a dozen issues of the *Post* were stuffed behind it, and as soon as John entered the room, he found them and proceeded to devour the contents. Morley never realized that the *Post* was one of the major sources of John's knowledge of the spirit of the time in the United States and gave him ideas for his cartoons.

Leaving Held at Quiriguá on December 24, Vay traveled on to Guatemala City with the understanding that John would follow in two days. Before John could carry out the plan, an earthquake changed everything.

Morley celebrated Christmas day in fine style with two dinners, one at the Clarks in the early afternoon and another at the Roaches that night. He left early, at ten-fifteen, to gain some lost sleep. It was cold in the street, and he headed for the American Club for a nightcap.

"Suddenly and without previous warning the ground lurched up under my feet and began to shake violently. An arc light overhead went out, flashed on, off, and on again. Wires short-circuited, sputtered and spit. The buildings on both sides rocked back and forth. My first thought was of the wires, and I darted into the nearest doorway to escape electrocution. Plaster and even brick began to rain down here and I ran back into the street to escape falling walls."[4] Then it occurred to him that the large open cen-

---

[4] Morley, "The Guatemala Earthquake," *American Museum Journal,* Vol. 18

tral square, the Plaza de Armas, was the safest place, and he began to run, pausing only to speak with six excited men rushing pell-mell from the American Club.

The plaza was fast filling with people. It was cold. The moon shone halfheartedly, and the sky had a peculiar dusty appearance. "Slight tremors followed one after another almost without cessation. One felt instinctively that it was not over and all braced themselves for the next shock." It came at eleven-thirty, when "the ground lifted a second time under our feet, jerked back and forth, and all but upset us."[5] Buildings fell, and the air filled with adobe dust. There was little hysteria or disorder among the natives. Indian women fell to their knees, telling their rosaries, whispering *"María Santíssima,"* etc. One end of the portal of the National Palace crumpled noisily; all electric lights went out, at least removing the fear of live wires.

Everyone waited for the next shock. Morley accidentally encountered his dentist, Dr. Johnson, who went to his office and found an overcoat for him. The two men turned down Seventh Avenue, when someone called Vay's name. It was Rafael Aparício, who invited him to join his family. Inside the building, Vay found eight adults and children huddled in the automobile in the patio and a dozen native servants crouching on the ground. For want of another place to stay, he spent the night there. At two-thirty the third shock occurred. The ground rose, the car swayed drunkenly, and everything seemed to rock as he heard walls crashing nearby. Later he fell asleep on the runningboard of the car and did not wake until dawn.

In the morning, he went to see what had happened to his room in the Imperial Hotel. The clerk and the bellboy refused to go upstairs, so he went alone. His room was a shambles, plaster strewn everywhere, and three feet of bricks tumbled on his bed. Next he set out to find the Roaches and the Clarks, and came upon them sleeping on mattresses in the street. Although the

---

(1918), 202, 206, published by The American Museum of Natural History; quotations from this article are used by permission of the publisher.

[5] Morley, "The Guatemala Earthquake," 206, 208.

tremors continued, the Clarks and their servants ventured back into the house to prepare breakfast from the leftovers of Christmas dinner.

Realizing that they could not stay in the street indefinitely, Clark found a solution. As the manager of the railroad company, he had a private coach in the station yard, and four couples and Vay and Clark's son moved their belongings there and occupied it. As it proved to be too small for ten persons, they added a baggage car, which they converted into a kitchen and dining-room.

Then Vay walked about the city to survey the damage. He noticed that the homes of the poor suffered the most; also he found the bullring demolished, the railroad station damaged, the penitentiary destroyed and five hundred prisoners at large. On the fashionable Reforma, grandiose but poorly constructed buildings were in ruins as were the gaudy, insubstantial private villas. In the city, the ancient Recolección church suffered grievously.

By the twenty-seventh, temporary shacks were going up in the plaza; bootblacks, barbers, and cantinas found business thriving. People began to enter their homes to pull out furniture, and the streets were choked with these personal belongings. People also began to leave the city. The following day there was a wild rush of humanity to board the outgoing trains; when the railroad-yard gates were closed so as to admit the people in more orderly fashion, the crowd broke down the barrier and rushed in.

The government declared martial law and generally maintained good order. There was little looting. Free distribution of corn and beans was instituted to feed the poor, and emergency hospitals went into operation. Another problem was dealt with quickly and rigorously. "Hundreds of recently buried corpses were thrown from their vaults in the cemeteries and a pestilence there-from was imminent. The government again acted with gratifying promptitude, however, and vast funeral pyres lighted the sky on that and succeeding nights. It is estimated that more than four thousand bodies were then disposed of."[6]

[6] Morley, "The Guatemala Earthquake," 210.

Vay spent much of his time at the American legation, helping Walter Thurston,[7] chargé d'affaires, who had to shoulder all the work in the absence of the minister. On the afternoon of the twenty-ninth, as Vay worked in one of the rooms of the legation, another shock occurred, and he ran into the patio as the safest place. Later he learned that this quake was as destructive as the earlier ones; moreover, it depressed the people, who had assumed that the peak of the violence had passed. Then in the afternoon of the next day came still another shock. From the thirtieth on, he slept at the legation.

In aiding Thurston with numerous details, Vay became involved in an official visit to the president. Commodore Brumby, of the U.S.S. *Cincinnati,* was ordered to offer aid to stricken Guatemala. Because of other commitments, Thurston asked Vay to meet the commodore and his aides, to introduce them to Generals Ovalle and Alvarado, who had been sent by the president to accompany Brumby, and finally to take the whole party to La Palma, the presidential residence on the edge of the city. The obsolescent limousine failed to make the last grade in the road, and Vay and the rest of the party had to puff up the steep ascent to the building, where they were greeted with much ceremony.

Vay was uncertain of his place among the dignitaries, but that problem was solved when he was shepherded along with the rest of the party. They were ushered through a maze of courts and gardens, penetrating farther into the complex residence. At last they reached a tent that served as the office of President Manuel Cabrera Estrada during the days of earthquake. All were ushered to his presence and seated on benches, an interpreter sitting beside the president.

Morley had an opportunity to study Cabrera during the interview, which consisted mainly of an exchange of courtesies. Short in build, perhaps sixty years old, the president appeared to be

---

[7] Thurston became clerk of the legation in Guatemala in March, 1917, at the age of twenty-two. In later years he held various foreign service posts, including ambassadorships to several Latin-American countries.

weary. Sharp black eyes were the most prominent feature of his heavily lined face. He had a habit of reclining in his chair with his eyes closed during the translation of conversations; and Vay was struck with the fact that he refused to look a person straight in the eye. Familiar with all of the current stories about the dictator, Vay believed that one could see cruelty and love of power in his appearance and attitude.

After the interview Morley took Brumby to the American legation to meet Thurston. When the chargé became annoyed because the commodore did not come in, as protocol required, Vay took the blame and calmed the anger of his friend. After Brumby composed a telegram requesting certain medicines for the stricken city, Vay accompanied him and Thurston after dark to the wireless station, a little shack surrounded by barbed wire on the edge of the city. Then the commodore left for his vessel.

Vay and Thurston had returned to the legation, had a late dinner, and were prepared to sleep on mattresses spread through the corridors when another quake, lasting for eleven minutes, jolted the place. Everyone ran for the patio, as the sound of crashing walls resounded in the neighborhood. In fact, "the city was rocked to its very foundations by the most tremendous shock of all. The earth lifted up as though pushed by some vast subterranean agency seeking outlet, held a moment thus, and then in terrific jerks and twitchings, settled back .... And the destruction which it accomplished was more than that of all the others combined."[8]

So far, three hundred persons had lost their lives in the series of quakes. Now the citizens were demoralized and filled with terror. And Morley left at the first opportunity; as soon as the railroad was open to the north coast, he took the first train out of the city on January 8. He joined Held, proceeded to Belize, and prepared for the trip up the Yucatán coast.

Vay's four-month trip of 1918 involved exploration by sea and land from Belize along the east coast of Yucatán north and west as far as Campeche and then to inland sites including Palenque.

8 Morley, "The Guatemala Earthquake," 210.

Morley and Held joined Gann in Belize, where they had the use of the governor's official yacht, the *Patricia*, to go up to Corozal. To while away the time on this first leg of the trip, Vay attempted to oblige a Mexican passenger by rendering English proverbs into Spanish, a valiant effort with hilarious results.

There was little to hold them at Corozal. Vay met a Mr. Schofield, who apparently owned everything in sight there, including the boat *Corozal*, which had given Vay a bad time four years earlier. Since the residents of the town spoke Spanish and English interchangeably, Vay did not need to use his notoriously bad Spanish.

Here Vay and John boarded the *Lilian Y* that he chartered for the long voyage ahead. It was a sloop of twenty-two tons with a thirty-six-horsepower engine. Already all of the equipment for the expedition—and it must have been mountainous, for he never traveled light—had been stowed away by Muddy Esquivel, Gann's faithful servant, an Irish-Yucatecan who could speak Maya. In addition to Morley, Held, and Gann, the boat carried Captain Usher and five native hands.

Hubert and George, two members of the crew, left marked impressions on the Americans. Hubert, the cook, was a last-minute acquisition, employed on the unusual recommendation that he had no jail record in Belize. But Hubert lacked a picture on his passport, and Held made a hasty profile sketch for the purpose. Everyone was pleased with the drawing except Hubert, who claimed that it gave him an excessive lip. More likable was George, a giant Negro from the Bay Islands, cheerful, willing to work, and always ready to sing, though his weak tenor voice seemed ludicrous, coming from such a powerful frame. Held also preserved his countenance in several sketches.

The first stop was Payo Obispo, capital of Quintana Roo, where social activities detained them for several days. Governor Solís, a diminutive fellow for the high office he held, was happy to receive them as a break in the monotony of that outpost. The individualistic and independent Gann avoided the festivities by remaining on board, while Vay and John enjoyed dinners and dances at the governor's house, and John added to the happy spirit by drawing a striking caricature of Solís. In the midst of the conviviality, there was an exchange of speeches on Mexican-American friendship, with Vay threading his way through that thicket with his usual tact. He explained that the United States felt kindly toward Mexico. He admitted that a few Americans wanted to seize the oil wells, but he assured his audience that President Wilson would not be misled on that score. There was a fiesta and dancing in which Vay participated, always conscious of the way his hosts outdid themselves in courtesy. After several days of this sociability, two of the governor's staff, still showing the effects of conviviality, accompanied Vay and John overland to join the *Lilian Y* and Gann at Xcalac. As usual, Vay got what he wanted, a letter from the governor recommending the exploring party to all persons in Quintana Roo.

At Espíritu Santo Bay, they had to wade through several hundred feet of muddy ooze to reach shore. Morley began to navigate the dubious stretch with Muddy. Muddy, whose feet had been calloused from exposure, had no trouble moving over the sharp rocks under the ooze, but Morley floundered about like a clown, as he stepped from one razor-edged stone to another. Gann and Held, watching from the boat, roared with amusement.

During this trip, Morley was collecting nautical data for Navy Intelligence, while he ostensibly carried on archaeological exploration. He sought facts about the coastal waters from anyone who might know and had a remarkable ability for pumping an informant dry. Gann saw him question a local pilot for a whole day, until the native was completely exhausted.

Morley and Gann disliked the rolling boat and slept on shore whenever possible, though the results were not always happy. At Ascención Bay, after cots for the two men had been set up on the shore, someone discovered tiger and raccoon tracks. The two men determined to stay, however, and slept with hurricane lamps surrounding their cots, a stiff wind flapping the mosquito curtains, and firearms beside them. To encourage Gann's peace of mind, Vay recited all the stories he had ever heard of tigers eating human beings. By six in the morning the explorers were up and off with no sign of a tiger during the night.

Their first discovery was the site of Chacmool, a moderate-sized site which they named for a statue of that type found in one of the temples. All told, Chacmool added little to archaeological knowledge.

At this stage of the trip, Morley looked forward to visiting Tulum. He wanted to examine again the dated stela which had drawn him to the site several times before. The reading derived in 1916 when Morley and Gann had dug up the pieces was obviously too early to fit in with the buildings at Tulum. Some months after that Gann sent a schooner to bring the reburied pieces away, but the boat went down in a hurricane, presumably with the stela aboard. However, Gann reasoned that there was still a chance that the stela had not been transferred to the boat before it sank and that it was still hidden somewhere on the beach at Tulum.

After the party had established themselves at the site, Held took a shovel to the sandy shore and began to dig. When he found two of the fragments, everyone set to the task, and by nightfall all but one piece had been recovered. Gann's intuition had been correct; the boat he sent had never landed at Tulum, and the violent hurricane had scattered the pieces about in the sand. After a long search the missing fragment was found, and the whole inscription read A.D. 699. Once more they buried the fragments and marked the spot. The other results of this visit were relatively unimportant; more structures inside the walls of Tulum were discovered, and Held made some watercolors of the foaming waves and rocky coast.

Ten miles north of Tulum they put in at Playa Carmen to buy provisions, only to discover that the natives would not accept their money. The Indians here did not use money. Vay proposed the idea of bartering his supply of sugar for the chickens, eggs, and vegetables he wanted, and the plan worked. The rate of exchange was a small calabash of sugar and a one-inch slice of soap for eighteen fresh eggs or a chicken.

The *Lilian Y* proceeded along the coast, stopping at Puerto Morelos, Cancuén, and Mugeres islands, and then rounded Cape Catoche. Here and there Morley and Gann found ruins, though nothing remarkable and, all in all, in the same Tulum style. On the northern coast of Yucatán the archaeological results were also thin. At Silán there was a mound fifty feet high and four hundred feet long, but its facing stones, some of them carved, had been built into the local church and municipal building.

They stopped at Progreso, where Gann and Morley left the boat to explore other points of the peninsula, while John sailed on down to Campeche. Forgetting that Yucatán had a new prohibition law, Vay continued to carry with him half a dozen bottles of claret, never thinking to use them. At one point, Muddy, who took care of the luggage, was jailed because of the liquor and had to sit in a cell until he was rescued the next morning.

Also, Yucatán had gone Socialist since Morley's last visit in 1913, and the new regime did not strike his fancy. Henequen was selling at nineteen cents a pound as compared with five cents on his former trip, and the money flowing in from its sale boosted the cost of living. The government derived income entirely from a monopoly on the export of the fiber. Likewise, the peons had been freed, and Morley complained that they worked only half the time and that henequen was rotting on the stock because of the shortage of labor. Gann, on the other hand, seemed to be more fascinated with than critical of the new regime that released the Indians from semibondage, closed the churches, and produced prosperity.

Morley managed to have an interview with the governor by using Juan Martínez y Hernández, the only Maya scholar of the region he respected, as the intermediary. Carlos Castro Morales, an admitted Socialist, was a striking character who had become governor after twenty-three years as a master mechanic on the railroad. Tremendous in physical size, he had a deep voice, wore gold spectacles, fancied salt-peter-saturated cigarettes, and proclaimed himself a freethinker. Gann perked up at the man's excellent command of the Maya language and his well-grounded knowledge of the archaeology of the country. At their request the governor generously gave the visitors a letter recommending them to all local authorities in carrying on their research.

The rest of their travels was largely a repetition of visits to sites Vay had already seen, but they were new to Gann. The exception was Holactún, which provided a small harvest of date glyphs. Then they visited Chichén Itzá, Kabah, and Uxmal. By this time Held had rejoined the team. So the four men, Vay, Gann, Held, and Muddy, traveled in a Ford, chauffeured by Pablo Pantoja, a native who became Morley's driver in the future. Actually, they walked most of the way between Kabah and Uxmal, because the car was loaded down with impedimenta and the road was almost impassable. They had to lug rocks from the path of the car and push the vehicle up the stony slopes. They were either courageous or foolhardy to attempt the trip with a Ford, for even today the journey by jeep is no pleasure jaunt.

They were fortunate in visiting these sites under satisfactory conditions. At Kabah they slept in the open, untroubled by mosquitoes or ticks. The place lacked water, however, and they secured a small amount of the precious liquid from an Indian who brought it a distance of three miles at four dollars a trip. At Uxmal they took up quarters on the terrace of the House of the Governor for three days, and again they enjoyed a pest-free existence, though earlier travelers had always complained of the unhealthy state of the place.

They made a happy discovery at Uxmal. Until their arrival, no one had found hieroglyphs by which the ruins could be dated. In poking around through the ruins, Morley and Gann came upon several glyphs that indicated the thirteenth century, and so they were able to correct the tradition of hoary antiquity that earlier explorers had attributed to the site. Held was now pressed into service. In order to secure copies of paintings and glyphs on capstones in several rooms of the Monjas, they erected a tottery scaffold, and Held, lying on his back on the weak framework fifteen feet above the ground, tried to reproduce the inscriptions.

They returned to Mérida, satisfied with the results of their work.

Gann went up to Progreso and took the *Lilian Y* back to Belize. At the end of the expedition they could chalk up the discovery of several new sites, a knowledge of the Cauac sign, and the recording of thirteen new dates.

Morley and Held remained for six weeks to complete other tasks. They took a flying trip to investigate the ruins of Santa Rosa Xlabpak. When they returned to Mérida, they were laid up with malaria. The Jameses let Vay use their *quinta* on the outskirts of the city where he spent day after day writing up his intelligence reports of the trip around the Yucatán coast. He also gave a public lecture at the School of Fine Arts, probably his first appearance in this role in Mexico. Alfredo Barrera Vásquez, an art student at the time, was employed to prepare large drawings to illustrate the address. This was the beginning of a friendship that culminated years later in a collaboration on an account of some of the Books of Chilam Balam. In connection with the lecture, Held also exhibited his paintings in an adjacent room, and later drew caricatures of some members of the audience.

On leaving Mérida in May, they made their first visit to Palenque, and, after a few days there, went down the Usumacinta to Frontera where they took ship for New Orleans. After a year of traveling together by mule and boat, and working on Maya archaeology and Navy Intelligence, Vay and John ended their association. The collaboration was over, and each man, still in the early stage of his career, went his own way toward prominence, one in caricaturing the youthful spirit of America in the 1920's and the other in broadening the horizon of knowledge in Maya archaeology.

VII

In the Petén

DURING the years from 1919 through 1922 Morley spent most of the field seasons in the Petén, still on the quest for date inscriptions. Two brief trips to Copán were the only exceptions. After retiring from service in the Navy early in 1919, he made an expedition to Central America. He visited Costa Rica and Guatemala to examine public and private archaeological collections in order to study Maya influence in those areas. Aside from ceramics, however, he found practically no trace of ancient Mayas in those countries.

He spent some weeks in Quiriguá and completed the excavation of two temples at that site. If the results were scant, because few artifacts were found, he had good reason to note two other things: the heat of the place was excessive, going up to 104 and 105 degrees, and there was a twenty-five-minute earth tremor on May 21.

Then on Saturday, May 31, he proceeded to Copán where he had a fine reception. A mile from the village, Juan Ramón Cueva and Rafael Villamil were on hand to greet him. In town he called on Doña Julia, who gave him an *abrazo* to show her joy. That night the local band played in his honor, and Vay had his servant Nicolas hand out cigarettes after the first number and *copitas* of Medoc wine after the second. Then he learned what was up. On Monday night the leaders of the municipality met in solemn session and elected him a citizen of the town. Although the action was brief and businesslike, Morley was deeply touched.

Before he left Copán he set up a small museum to house carved stones from the ruins. In a room in the *cabildo,* he placed two dozen pieces that formed the nucleus of the present museum at Copán.

By June 6 he was in Guatemala City. Doubtless he timed his arrival carefully, for the Roaches had a big party and dance to celebrate his thirty-sixth birthday.

In 1920 he had to stay on in Washington to complete final proof for the *Inscriptions of Copán,* and he did not arrive in British Honduras until May. He and Guthe headed for the Petén, going first to Benque Viejo, where he dined with Father Versavel, his old friend. Then he went on to Flores to prepare for an expedition to the north. But he had trouble finding a guide. The first man he approached was drunk and begged off because he was about to be married; the second fellow claimed he had to do guard duty, although he was good enough to supply some geographical facts. Finally, the third man signed up at the rate of twenty-five dollars for every new site he located, and he claimed that he knew five.

Then Morley suffered an injury to his foot, and he had trouble getting back to Benque Viejo. He had to be lifted on and off his mule; and he attempted to ride with his foot on the pommel, while a native led the animal. Back in Benque Viejo he went to the mission.

Vay had high esteem for Father Versavel as a friend and as a noble man performing great humanitarian work. He had known him for at least six years and received a royal welcome and in turn did a favor when he could; this time he brought a bottle of Scotch for his friend. He considered the Belgian missionary an unselfish, altruistic, heroic soul toiling at the hopeless task of cultivating Christianity in stony soil. Good-for-nothing *chicleros* swarmed over the town, squandering their advance pay on women and liquor, degrading the morals of the inhabitants, and setting a bad example for the conscientious native farmers. When Versavel explained on one occasion that a change in the price of chicle might turn Benque Viejo into a ghost town, Vay was not sorry as he contemplated the evil effects of the rascally *chicleros* on the whole area.

Father Versavel, however, seemed to bear up under his fruitless task. Despite his serious nature, he had a sense of humor. He wrote a play called *The Dogs* for the villagers to perform. When Vay translated it into English, he was amused at the sly thrusts made at local customs and the witty atmosphere of the piece.

At the same time, Versavel helped Vay with his project of advertising rewards for *chicleros* who brought him information of new ruins. In searching for chicle trees, these men knew the whole Petén region, and sometimes they gave valuable help in locating ancient sites with carved stelae and other monuments. Versavel put Vay's announcement into good Spanish and agreed to receive such reports from *chicleros* coming to Benque Viejo.

The one copy of Vay's announcement that has come to light asked *chicleros* to remember places where there were ruins with stones carved with figures or letters. Morley offered twenty-five dollars to each person who would guide him to a site he did not know. Preliminary information was to be left with Father Versavel in Benque Viejo, Edward Enright in El Cayo, or P. W. Schufeldt in Laguna Perdida. These three towns were jumping-off places for trips into the Petén as well as places where *chicleros* congregated when not working. If the Spanish version of the announcement was written by the priest, that accounts for the inclusion of several words not commonly used in that region.

Morley and Father Versaval meant much to each other. Vay brought humor, liveliness, and a dynamic interest in the Mayas to the kindly father, and Versavel in turn inspired Vay with his devoted Christian struggle against insuperable odds.

During the field season of 1920, Morley visited only two sites. Petipet had nine stelae but none with a date. The only consolation was the tenth stela that had a fine figure of a priest. Then his guide led him to Xultún, where he found two Initial Series and seven sculptured monuments of the sixth and seventh centuries.

It was at Petipet that the beans exploded. Vay had carefully

Marshall Saville who represented the Museum of the American Indian, Heye Foundation, in Yucatán in February, 1923. Courtesy Mrs.
Elinor Vail.

Chichén Itzá, as seen from the air. Courtesy University Museum of
the University of Pennsylvania.

Morley and his sister Elinor used this part of Las Monjas at Chichén Itzá
for their sleeping quarters in March, 1923. Courtesy Mrs. Elinor Vail.

Staff of Chichén Itzá project, 1924. Left to right: J. O. Kilmartin, A. Munroe Amsden, Earl Morris, Ann Morris, and Morley. Courtesy J. O. Kilmartin.

Work begins at Chichén Itzá, May 19, 1924. Morley, in center wearing his characteristic tall sombrero, gives instructions to native laborers at the Thousand Columns. These are only part of the sixty-nine *mozos* who began work that day. Courtesy J. O. Kilmartin.

Las Monjas, the "Nunnery," at Chichén Itzá. Courtesy Peabody Museum, Harvard University.

Temple of the Warriors, Chichén Itzá, after reconstruction. Courtesy Peabody Museum, Harvard University.

The Ball Court, Chichén Itzá, looking toward the south temple. It was here that Morley installed his phonograph and gave his famous moonlight concerts. Courtesy George F. Andrews

instructed Chico, a native assistant, to punch a hole in the container of beans before placing the can on the fire. Chico forgot, the can exploded, showering beans everywhere, and Chico saved his eyes only by involuntarily throwing his hands over them. In later years, Vay enjoyed relating the incident, but he changed the character and added a punch line: the cook was a German, who after suffering from the explosion, stoutly declared, "The directions didn't say to punch a hole in the can! That comes from not following directions." Vay's conclusion: "That incident explains why the Germans lost the First World War."[1]

Carl Guthe, a graduate student at Harvard who accompanied Vay on this expedition, gave some sidelights about the trip. Riding a mule through the monotonous and tedious jungle of Guatemala at the rate of three miles an hour wearied both men. At one point Vay half turned on his mount and called to Guthe, "If these mules just had a little more sense, they would be riding us instead of us riding them."[2]

The *chiclero* guided them to the new site of Xultún, where Vay flustered with excitement as he searched for glyphs and then settled down to the task of copying them. Carl described his intense application: "During these days Morley worked like a Trojan from early morning until late afternoon. All the monuments had to be located and some of them had to be raised or turned over, by our Indian guides. The carved inscriptions were carefully scrubbed. Sometimes it was necessary to clear a space around the monuments by cutting down shrubs and trees. Once the stage was set, Morley would spend many hours transferring his inscriptions to his Lefax notebook as an accurate scale drawing in miniature. Sometimes it was necessary to verify the details of what he saw by the touch of his fingers. Wetting the surface might bring out other details. Again, he would return to the monument after a few hours in order to see whether the passage of the sun had thrown new shadows in the hieroglyphs which might bring out further details.

[1] *Morleyana,* 235.
[2] *Morleyana,* 67.

Because of his care and patience, I marvelled at the speed with which his exquisite drawings were completed."[3]

In 1921 the members of the five months' expedition into the Petén were Morley as leader, Carl Guthe, O. G. Ricketson, A. K. Rutherford, and William Gates. After a brief stay at Belize, Vay moved on to Guatemala. There he renewed his friendship with Jack Armstrong, who was now in private business, the Roaches, and Don Clodiveo Berges, who had moved his family there from Flores.

By early February he was in El Cayo, ready to lead an expedition to Uaxactún. Ricketson and Rutherford accompanied him; Chico and Muddy went along as assistants, and ten pack mules carried the impedimenta, including the phonograph. The daily schedule called for breakfast at seven, dinner at four-thirty, tea at eight, and to bed soon after nine.

Scarcely had he started on the trip when he had to put down an incipient rebellion. Hearing from Rutherford that the native guides and muleteers complained about the food, Vay strode at once to their campfire and made his position clear. He would serve sufficient food but no luxuries like jams, hot biscuits, and soups. When they said it was the insufficient quantity that annoyed them, he promised that they would have enough to eat.

Several days later, Ricketson, acting as a physician for the natives, encountered a fifteen-year-old girl subject to epileptic fits. Unable to cope with the case, he discussed it with other members of the party. Muddy helpfully volunteered the information that his wife and her two sisters had been similarly afflicted, but were cured by marriage. So Ricketson soberly offered that prescription. If Muddy could volunteer advice, he could also on occasion be officious. Once he berated the cook for using too much lard and started a squabble, so Vay told Muddy to keep out of that department. When the expedition returned to El Cayo, Muddy succumbed to the joys of white rum for several nights, a common lapse that Gann and Vay had early learned to overlook.

Guthe and Gates joined the expedition at El Cayo on March 9.

[3] *Morleyana*, 67–68.

William E. Gates, now fifty-seven, had made his money in the printing business and retired some years earlier to study Maya history and linguistics and to collect important documents on those subjects. When Morley wrote his *Inscriptions of Copán,* he invited Gates to contribute a paper on linguistics for the volume, and that scholar also prepared the index for the book. In 1920, it was Gates who was responsible for the formation of the Maya Society and became its president. But Gates had a peculiar temperament that brought him into conflict with everyone with whom he worked. And at times he could be crude; before going on the expedition of this year, Gates appeared in high laced boots in Washington at the dignified C. I. W. for a conference with Woodward and Morley. Vay was annoyed at this breach of good taste.

Three months later, on the expedition in the northern Petén, Morley had more experiences with Gates. At Naranjo when someone found an inscribed stela, Gates was annoyed that he had not discovered it. But he felt better a few days later at Tikal when he came upon the base of Stela 6 with half a dozen clear glyphs on it. As they were about to investigate the new site of Uoluntún, the traveling exhausted Gates by eleven in the morning, and Vay confided to his diary the man should never have undertaken the trip. Gates and Rutherford had been getting on each other's nerves. The storm broke on April 10, but Vay was so embarrassed over the triviality of the affair that he decided not to record it. He attributed the blow-up to bush nerves, that is, the accumulated irritations from insect bites, sleeplessness, fighting the bush as one traveled, and long days without food.

When the party reached Flores and Vay went to examine the new ruins of Ixlú nearby, Gates preferred to rest rather than see the site. That night the members of the party had a convivial evening with Boburg and his wife in Flores. Next morning Gates boiled over with disgust at the goings-on of the preceding night. Again Vay attributed the incident to bush nerves. Apparently Gates recovered his equilibrium in the days that followed, because he was a perfect gentleman on a grand Sunday picnic to the ruins of Ixlú. At an elaborate turkey feast, he toasted the governor of Flores, who was present on the excursion. And when Gates went for an interview with the governor the following day, he surprised the members of the expedition with his attire of tweed suit and high stiff collar that he had somehow brought in his luggage. Then Gates left the expedition, and by the next year he was director of antiquities for Guatemala.

So far during the Petén trip, Vay could chalk up two new sites, Uoluntún and Ixlú, and visits to Tikal and El Naranjo. He found seventeen new Initial Series and a total of thirty new dates. In addition, Guthe carried on excavations at Tayasal for six weeks.

While Carl continued his digging, Morley planned to finish the expedition by going down the Usumacinta to Piedras Negras and then out to Frontera on the Mexican coast. Morley had written to P. W. Schufeldt, of the American Chicle Company, for help with transportation. At Laguna Perdida, Schufeldt greeted the five staff members and gave them comfortable quarters. This was his first meeting with Vay, and he was amazed at his spontaneous friendliness and lively conversation.

The chicle company representative presented an important archaeological fact that went against everything Morley believed. Schufeldt took him out into a large field of sprouting corn and showed him evidence of innumerable house mounds and low dividing walls; obviously the ancients had carefully used every bit of land. And this was not a ceremonial site, because the nearest ruins were twenty miles away. Vay found it difficult to accept the idea of a large rural population at a distance from ceremonial cities; but a decade later he assigned young Robert Wauchope to excavate house mounds in the neighborhood of Uaxactún.

Vay visited Piedras Negras and went on down the Usumacinta to Frontera where he received his mail with interesting information on two subjects. One letter came from Pennsylvania Military Academy, announcing that he would receive an honorary Ph.D. And the other letter dangled the possibility of an attractive appointment. In March, when he had learned that Senator Albert Fall of New Mexico had been named secretary of the interior, Vay was excited. Would he now secure the appointment he hoped to

get? Vay wrote a reminder to the secretary, only to receive a routine answer that his letter would be read. But on reaching Frontera, a letter from a friend in Santa Fe urged Vay to accept the
appointment as minister to Guatemala, if it were offered. In his
diary he acted as if all of this were a great mystery. It was no
mystery at all; he had angled to get that appointment—and failed.
It was one of those disappointments that he did not mention in
the future.

In 1922, Vay started off as usual soon after the first of the year.
In New Orleans he noted that some persons were beginning to
take an interest in the old French architecture, which pleased him,
for it brought to mind the crusade he had led a decade earlier in
Santa Fe for the preservation of the old style. Sam Lothrop joined
him in New Orleans, and on shipboard he met Victor Cutter, of
the United Fruit Company, and M. D. Bromberg, of the American Chicle Company. Cutter proposed that Vay should write a
brochure on Quiriguá that the United Fruit Company would publish. Apparently the proposal was never carried out.

In Guatemala City, Morley visited the Roaches, got in touch
with Adrián Recinos, had dinner with the Schufeldts, and called
on Jack Armstrong and Don Clodiveo Berges, former *jefe* of
Flores. At the moment, Vay's passion ran to buying antiques, and
he secured a number of pieces that later became part of the collection he presented to the Museum of New Mexico. He also visited
the mounds on the Arvelo *finca* in Kaminaljuyú, but failed to
suspect the wealth of archaeological material they contained.

At Quiriguá, Dr. McPhail favored him with a clean, modern
room in quarters at the hospital. And once more Vay marveled at
the civilized living he could enjoy there—shower bath, electric
lights, iced tea, and starched clothes—as compared with the rough
life in the bush that lay ahead of him.

Then he went to Belize to prepare for an expedition to eastern
Yucatán. Sickness cut Gann out of the party, but he sent his servant Muddy. Morley chartered the *Esperanza*, an old but recently
rebuilt motorboat, at eight dollars a day. Although it had a 36-
horsepower engine, Vay had no gift for selecting ships, and in the

middle of the voyage the vessel had to fall back upon its sails. Morley, Lothrop, and Ricketson were assisted by nine servants and the crew, representing a mélange of nationalities.

Tulum was his major objective, and the stay there was far more pleasant than on previous visits. The party landed easily, camped in the Castillo, placed the phonograph on the terrace in front of their rooms, and played everything from Liszt to jazz. Muddy, who could speak Maya, became the interpreter between the Americans and the local natives. A blue wooden cross and candle drippings indicated that Indians had been worshiping in one of the rooms of the Castillo; and Vay warned everyone not to touch a thing in the shrine.

One morning the archaeologists faced a delegation of local Mayas who came to seek the protection of England. After much handshaking, Vay distributed cognac among his unexpected guests, and soon learned through Muddy the unusual mission. The white visitors were welcome if they were Englishmen. No one said otherwise; and the Americans soon found they had a curious situation on their hands. Years ago, said the natives, Queen Victoria had promised to take them under English protection, but nothing had been done and the Mayas were perturbed over the delay. At this point Muddy came to the rescue by explaining that Victoria had died and a young boy had come to the throne; now that he was grown up, perhaps some attention would be given to the natives. That seemed satisfactory, and the guests left.

A week later another delegation of Indians, each one armed with a gun, appeared. Morley carefully sought out the chiefs and greeted them personally. This time the natives feared that the white men were felling trees to build a settlement for the Mexicans, and with remarkable understatement the Mayas said they would not like that. At once Vay, speaking through Muddy, explained that they came only to measure and photograph the ruins. Then why did they cut down trees, demanded the natives. To make better pictures. Did these white men have permission of the governor of British Honduras? Of course, they did. And Vay now asked permission of the Indians themselves, adding that if they objected, the whites would go away. This put the question squarely up to the natives, and a tense period followed for Morley and his party. He watched Muddy, who easily sensed the attitude of the visitors, and noticed that the servant was uneasy. Finally, the chief and Juan Vega, the Indians' interpreter, recommended that their followers adopt a policy of friendship.

At that moment Vay had cognac and cigarettes passed around, and the phonograph was started.[4] He took pictures of his guests, plied them with more cigarettes, and the crisis was past. Vega assured Morley that all was well; the chiefs said goodbye; there was more handshaking and expressions of good will, and Vay sent a gift of quinine for the sick wife of one of the chiefs.

The following day a group of twenty Indians showed up, saying they wanted to hear the phonograph. Actually, they went to pray in the shrine in the Castillo. The thoughtful Muddy sent up three candles for their religious ceremonies. Afterwards Vay took their pictures and gave them medicine.

After making modest archaeological finds at Tulum and examining ruins at Tancar and Xelhá, the party returned to Belize.

Six weeks later Vay made a trip into the Petén with a number of *chicleros* who promised to lead him to new sites. The results were varied, with more disappointment than success. Several of the men talked about ruins only to get a free trip into the back-country in order to scout for the best chicle prospects for the coming season. When four of the *chicleros* proved to be liars by failing to find the stelae they promised, Vay gave them three days' pay to get out of the bush. On the positive side, he discovered Naachtún, with eleven stelae and seven Initial Series, the major event of those weeks in the Petén. In the meantime, Ricketson went to Naranjo, where he mapped the site and recorded its thirty-six sculptured stelae and the Hieroglyphic Stairway.

Summarizing the whole season's gains, Vay tallied up five new sites, twenty-nine new monuments, twelve new Initial Series, and nineteen new deciphered dates.

---

[4] This incident was probably the origin of the anecdote related by Gregory Mason, *South of Yesterday* (New York, Holt & Co., 1940), 74.

VIII

Writings and Lectures—1

MORLEY'S publication record during the first fifteen years of his career is substantial. It is almost exclusively devoted to Maya civilization, and it is remarkable for popular treatment as well as for scholarly contribution. Of the two dozen articles, some fourteen can be regarded as scholarly and the remaining ten as popular in nature. One of the books, *The Introduction to the Study of Maya Hieroglyphs*, a technical manual, was certainly not designed for popular appeal, though it aimed to instruct laymen in the intricacies of glyph decipherment. His reports in the *Year Book of the Carnegie Institution of Washington*, beginning a few years after his appointment, summarized the contributions of the annual expeditions he led or supervised in Central America; those reports provide the best continuous record of his work in the field. One surprise is a piece of historical fiction that illustrates his flair for popularization. Finally, he reviewed three books in this period and wrote several newspaper articles and an obituary.

As an ambitious young man, Morley first published serious articles before putting his hand to more popular presentations. In fact, his initial appearance in print, which is usually omitted in bibliographies, occurred in 1907, when he had just entered graduate work. William H. Holmes, artist, archaeologist, and head of the Bureau of American Ethnology at the Smithsonian Institution, wrote an article on the Tuxtla statuette, which he believed to bear the oldest Maya date, and asked several scholars to comment on the glyphs that appear on that curious duck-billed figure. A lengthy statement by Morley was included in the article alongside comments by Cyrus Thomas, Charles C. Willoughby, and Charles Bowditch, men highly respected in the field. Morley concluded that the object undoubtedly belonged to the eighth cycle. A generation later, scholars like J. Eric S. Thompson considered the statuette as Olmec and the glyphs non-Maya. But that does not change the fact that Vay, with his usual good luck, made his bow to the scholarly world in distinguished company.

In several articles he discussed other subjects than the Mayas. The results of his excavation in the Southwest during several summers appear in three reports on Cannonball Ruin, Puyé, and McElmo Canyon. His account of the Guatemala earthquakes of 1917–18 came from firsthand experience. Having seen the city destroyed before his eyes, he presented the story with photographs to emphasize the calamity; but even in this account he suppressed many of his personal adventures, preferring to picture the total catastrophe with a plea for aid for the stricken populace.

His first complete article on the ancient Mayas got him into trouble. During the early months of graduate study at Harvard, he began to examine a report on the inscriptions at Naranjo, written by Teobert Maler in 1905. Charles Bowditch had financed several expeditions by Maler to the Petén; and after the reports appeared in print, Bowditch published an analysis and commentary on the findings. The report of 1905 was available at the Peabody Museum, though it was not printed until three years later. In the meantime, Vay mined Maler's data for his article on "Inscriptions of Naranjo," that appeared at the end of 1909. He showed that the site had passed through five periods of alternating activity and calm, and that the earliest period of Naranjo coincided with the first age of Copán. In a note he indicated that the article represented research in partial fulfillment of the requirements for the doctorate at Harvard.

The article had curious effects on his career, as J. Eric S. Thompson has revealed, because of one omission. Bowditch assumed that because of his patronage and previous practice he had first use of Maler's report. In publishing the article, Vay intruded on Bowditch's preserve without obtaining permission from that gentleman. When Morley first began to study the Maler report, he was doing graduate work in some capacity under Bowditch and held the fellowship in Central-American study subsidized by Bowditch. The puzzling question is why Vay, who always valued friendly personal relations so highly, should have failed to secure his mentor's consent to use the Maler material. There is a story that even when he was about to send off the manuscript, his friend Spinden advised him to secure clearance from Bowditch, and he failed to do so. As a result, Bowditch became angry at the young man's brashness, and converted Putnam, curator of the Peabody Museum, to the same point of view. This ill-feeling apparently explains why Morley never received a Ph.D. from Harvard; it is also the reason why Bowditch's book on Maya glyphs that appeared in 1910 omitted mention of Morley and his article; and most important, it explains why Peabody Museum leaders put forth Tozzer for the position that Vay was attempting to secure with the C. I.W. a few years later.

In this early period, Morley also tackled the thorny problem of Maya chronology. At the 1909 meeting of the Archaeological Institute of America he announced a system of correlation between the Maya and Christian calendars, and the following year he addressed the American Anthropological Society on the significance of three of the Books of Chilam Balam in supplying data to support his correlation. Both papers were printed, and Morley's system, later reflected by Spinden, became known as the Morley-Spinden system, which placed all dates some 260 years earlier than the correlation devised by J. T. Goodman and later improved by Juan Martínez and J. Eric S. Thompson.

By 1915 he had also worked out the chronological pattern of the rise and fall of Maya civilization, which he explained to the International Congress of Americanists in Washington. At the same meeting he also presented his theory that stelae were erected at regular intervals in order to mark the passage of 1,800-day periods called *hotúns.*

In the field of decipherment, he made a contribution in 1916 in a paper that set forth his conclusion that the Supplementary Series of glyphs were a lunar count just as the Initial Series constituted a diurnal count. J. Eric S. Thompson has noted how the material in this article provided the data by which J. Edward Teeple, the chemical engineer who turned to glyphic study, solved the riddle of the lunar count in 1925.

Several book reviews and an obituary round out the record of Vay's smaller serious works in this period. George B. Gordon's *Book of Chilam Balam* gained a favorable though not enthusiastic review from Vay, and one might wonder whether Gordon's cool reception of the young man a few years earlier had some bearing on the tone of the review. The other books he evaluated were by his close friend Herbert J. Spinden. Correctly, Vay estimated the *Study of Maya Art* as a brilliant attempt to establish Maya chronology by an analysis of artistic style. He disagreed only with Spinden's results in the case of Palenque, where Vay said the method failed to produce agreement with evidence from the inscriptions. Several years later he favorably evaluated his friend's *Ancient Civilizations of Mexico and Central America,* with but two reservations. He and Spinden did not see eye-to-eye on the theory that stelae were erected at regular intervals. More significant, perhaps, was Vay's claim that the author should have discussed the interrelation of the different cultures in Mexico and Central America. This is an interesting observation, because three decades later Vay left himself open to a similar charge.

It was appropriate that he was asked to write the obituary of J. Thompson Goodman, one of the founders of Maya glyphic research. Morley met him once, in September, 1916, at lunch at the faculty club at Berkeley, California. J. Alden Mason, the third person at the table, remembered how the two men "argued hotly, but no blood was spilled."[1] Goodman insisted that all glyphs had an arithmetical content, a point Morley could not accept.

[1] *Morleyana,* 151.

In addition to the scholarly articles, he also produced in this early period two books, each significant in its own way. One was a manual for beginners and the other a masterly compilation of date glyphs for the advanced scholar.

An Introduction to the Study of Maya Hieroglyphs was a remarkable performance in view of the author's relative youth and his short professional experience. He was twenty-eight years old when he wrote the text in the last six months of 1911, and had had only four years of firsthand experience with the subject. He aimed to provide a simple guide that would lead the layman into the mysteries of deciphering glyph dates. The self-confidence of the author in undertaking the task was fully justified by the volume he produced.

Almost four years passed before the *Introduction* appeared in print. Though the text was completed in 1911, delays held up publication until the end of 1915. Vay spent much time collecting the illustrations, revising the manuscript, and reading proof. All told, he enjoyed favorable conditions in producing the volume. He was paid for the manuscript, he had almost unlimited freedom in the matter of illustrations, and he worked for a patient and sympathetic editor, F. W. Hodge, who later claimed that it was he who had originally suggested the idea of the book to Vay.

Hodge chose Alfred M. Tozzer to give the manuscript a critical reading. Vay's former teacher turned in a favorable report, declaring that the volume was "worthy of bearing the imprint of the Smithsonian," that it was "a good piece of work . . . needed by students of the Maya culture," and that he was "glad to pass favorably" on it. Then he noted a few criticisms. He believed that Vay was "a little too dogmatic" in the early part of the book, he felt that Bowditch's volume was given insufficient recognition, and he advised more subheadings and a bibliography.[2]

Morley took the criticism in stride, though maintaining his independence as a scholar. If the charge of dogmatism meant that he differed from Bowditch's interpretation, he insisted on the right to his own conclusions that resulted from his study on the subject.

[2] Tozzer to Hodge, Feb. 24, 1913, in J. Eric S. Thompson's possession.

But the point that he had not adequately recognized Bowditch's book struck home, and he rewrote the preface with fulsome praise for the venerable gentleman. Was Vay attempting to be eminently fair or did he perhaps see an opportunity to mend broken fences? Surely he was conscious of Bowditch's feeling toward him, for when he wanted permission to use some illustrations from his volume, it was Hodge, not Morley, who carried on the correspondence. In the end, the *Introduction* was published too late to affect Bowditch's attitude when Vay's name was discussed by the Carnegie Institution.

E. L. Hewett, Morley's employer until 1914, unfortunately displayed his worst traits in connection with the *Introduction*. When Vay was assembling the illustrations, Hewett borrowed a collection of pictures of Chichén Itzá and failed to return them. Then Hewett insisted that the School of American Archaeology share credit with the Smithsonian Institution on the ground that Vay had gained his knowledge as an employee of the school. Hodge, of course, refused to accept Hewett's contention.

Morley intended the *Introduction* as a textbook to instruct the neophyte in the decipherment of glyphs. Years later when he presented a copy to a young man, he explained that he wrote it so that a boy of sixteen with average ability could comprehend it, and added that if the reader mastered ten to twenty pages at a time and carried out the calculations that were required, he would be able to read the glyphs.

His second book was the more important *Inscriptions of Copán*. As early as 1910 he had decided to compile a corpus of Maya glyphs. His immediate interest, of course, was in the date glyphs that he could decipher; and he spent many seasons in the field to uncover every inscription that could be found. Although other tasks interrupted the ambitious project, he persisted until he published the record for Copán and later for the Petén region.

The project went forward slowly. As a fellow of the School of American Archaeology, he announced that he would begin the book as soon as he completed the study of the orientation of Maya buildings. Only after turning in final copy for the *Introduction* in 1913 did he begin to write up the inscriptions. The contemplated volume, which he referred to as "Maya Chronology," was planned so as to devote one chapter to the inscriptions of each important site. He worked several days devising an appropriate formula for presenting the information about each inscription, but hardly had he conquered that problem when he became dissatisfied with the material for study. Quickly he discovered that the photographs of inscriptions were not satisfactory, especially when every line did not stand out clearly. He concluded that he must examine the originals himself and soon took off on a five-and-one-half-month expedition through the Petén in 1914. His scholarly instinct, which insisted on working directly with the original sources, was not only sound, but in the end produced more data and more accurate transcription than if he had relied on the findings of others.

Fortunately, he was able to continue the project under far more favorable conditions after he joined the staff of the C. I. W. Woodward saw the scientific value of the project and told him to go ahead with it until work could be started at Chichén Itzá.

Hardly had he settled down in Santa Fe in August, 1914, when Hewett walked into his office and coolly claimed that the projected volume belonged to the School of American Archaeology because Vay had collected the data while employed by that organization. Vay turned on his exasperating former employer with a barrage of argument undermining that absurd position. He reminded him that the bulk of the data had been collected during the expedition earlier that year, an expedition Hewett had done everything to discourage, and the school had paid only one-fifth of the cost of the trip. Moreover, Vay pointed out, it would take him two years to digest and write up the material, and the school was in no position to pay him for that service. He reminded Hewett also that his arrangement to work on Maya chronology for the C.I.W. had been made with Hewett's full knowledge. As a compromise, Morley offered to write four or five reports on his work as Fellow, but Hewett would not accept this substitute. As Vay privately predicted, Hewett eventually settled for a note in the preface acknowledging the school's participation in the earlier stages of the work.

Year after year, the project went on. Each winter Vay was in the field collecting and verifying data, and each summer and fall he wrote up his findings at the Peabody Museum. The C.I.W. gave him full freedom in choosing the sites to visit, and it set no deadline for completion of the work.

Because he uncovered a large number of new inscriptions at Copán in 1915, the original plan of the book took a new turn. The projected chapter for Copán, a site that provided almost 40 per cent of all known dates, swelled into a volume of its own. And so the original "Maya Chronology" became *The Inscriptions of Copán*, with later volumes to cover the other areas. By the fall of 1915 he had made considerable progress; two chapters were completed and illustrations for the volume had been sent to the C.I.W.

As he worked over the material, he was convinced that the inscriptions dealt mainly with chronological and astronomical information. He concluded that the hope of learning about wars, conquests, and rulers from glyphic sources must be abandoned. Also he firmly held to his theory that the Mayas erected stelae at regular intervals to mark the passage of time. He was so certain on this point that he claimed he could predict the date of the next monument to be discovered at Quiriguá.

In the last stage of work on the volume Morley relied on Carl Guthe, the graduate student of Maya hieroglyphs who shared an office with him at the Peabody Museum. Vay regarded the young man's ability so highly that he recommended him as the person most qualified to finish the job in case anything happened to the author during his service for Navy Intelligence. In the early months of 1920, Vay made a frantic effort to complete the book, and he employed Guthe to see him over the final hurdle; for weeks the two men wrestled with proof sheets at the Cosmos Club in Washington.

It is an impressive volume in every way. The descriptions of the glyphs extends over 460 pages, while eleven appendices and the index swell the book to 643 pages; thirty-three plates and ninety-one figures provide illustrative material. For the frontispiece, he used the panorama of Copán drawn by W. H. Holmes.

The content of the book goes far beyond the limits of the title. Not only does the author give a full history of the archaeological work at the site, but he also includes essays that pertain to the whole Maya area. In one of those discourses he presents the case for the correlation of the Maya and Christian calendars that he first put forth in 1909. Ironically, the inscriptions in the text contain data that scholars later used to refute his position. Vay was so convinced of his hypothesis that he was blind to facts that did not square with it.[3]

There is an interesting sequel to its publication. Vay loved the people of Copán, and they in turn responded to his friendly, vibrant personality, as was attested by their electing him a citizen of the municipality in 1919. It is not surprising that when he returned the following year he bore a copy of *The Inscriptions of Copán*, attractively bound in leather, which he formally presented to the village officials. Alfred Kidder adds the final touch: "When I first went to Copán the *alcalde* showed it to me. 'A very fine volume, this of *el Doctor*,' he said. 'We take great care of it. It weighs nearly two *kilos*.' "[4]

As a writer and speaker, Morley had remarkable gifts for conveying the wonder of ancient Maya civilization to the general public. Moreover, he enjoyed this activity tremendously. He was quickly in rapport with an audience. He was a born teacher, able to explain his subject step by step, an evangelist trumpeting the glories of the Mayas, and to some extent an actor with a flair for the dramatic and an ability to hold an audience. Instinctively, he knew what would appeal to the uninformed listener, because he responded to the same appeal himself. Nor did he look down upon this form of writing and lecturing; he took the task of pop-

---

[3] Reviewers correctly praised him for providing a great storehouse of material on Maya date glyphs. Philip Means was entirely favorable; T. A. Joyce and Hermann Beyer took exception to a few small points; only Beyer questioned some of the decipherments. At the time of its publication, it was the first book to present all inscriptions of a single site.

[4] *Morleyana*, 100.

ularization seriously and worked hard to achieve the effect he desired.

His first articles of this genre, describing the sites of Chichén Itzá, Uxmal, and Copán, appeared in the *Bulletin of the Pan American Union*. Many of the earmarks of his method are evident in these early accounts. More than half of the space is devoted to illustrative material—a map, a bird's-eye view of the site, and clear, meaningful photographs. Every illustration had a caption with additional information on the subject. Already he had the habit of indulging in superlatives, though he kept the practice within reasonable bounds.

Three field seasons at Quiriguá provided material for several articles for the interested general reader. The account in *El Palacio* is too brief to do more than whet the appetite. On the other hand, the articles in the *Scientific American* and the *National Geographic Magazine* are in the nature of reports on the excavations presented for the layman.

In 1917 and 1918 he wrote two articles featuring personal experience. One describes the expedition to Tulum and the other the Guatemala earthquakes. Although he began to unbend somewhat by relating adventures that happened to him, he carefully avoided use of the first person.

He produced one piece of fiction, for Elsie E. Parsons' *American Indian Life*. On finishing the manuscript in Guatemala in January, 1921, he appeared not completely satisfied with it. "How Holon Chan Became the True Man of His People" is an imaginative reconstruction of the investment of a seventeen-year-old with the insignia of leadership at Tikal in A.D. 531. Rather than a story, it is a fictionalized incident with no conventional plot but with a large amount of the life and times of the Mayas squeezed into every page.

In the same year he published another popular article of a very different nature in the *National Geographic Magazine*. This time he treated Maya hieroglyphs, setting the tone with the title, "The Foremost Intellectual Achievement of Ancient America." Wisely, he refrained from entering too deeply into the subject, impressing the reader mainly with the mathematical and astronomical knowledge of the Mayas. As usual, there are many good illustrations, but not all of them are closely integrated with the text. If the article was intended to do no more than stimulate interest in the subject, it was well designed for the purpose.

The public lecture gave him even greater freedom than the printed page in appealing directly to individuals. This was true despite several potential handicaps. He lacked the commanding presence that a physically large man enjoys on the public platform; Vay was short in stature and slender in build. Also, his subject was narrowly specialized, such as usually appeals only to a small circle of scholars in the same or an allied field; and his topic had no immediate relevance to present conditions or contemporary problems. His appeal came from his personality far more than from the subject; it is true that Maya civilization has inherent interest, but only a man with his peculiar qualities could exploit that interest.

He slipped into public speaking easily and naturally at the start of his career. As early as 1908 he addressed students and visitors in the summer camp at Frijoles, and during the subsequent years of his association with the School of American Archaeology he made one or more appearances in its summer sessions. For example, in 1912 he gave a lecture series and four Sunday night addresses for the summer school. With rare exceptions his subject was always the Mayas. After he began annual expeditions to Mexico and Central America, he emphasized the discoveries he had made, usually as a climax to a general discussion of the Mayas.

During these early years he did not speak as much as in the following decades, although he perfected the method of achieving the effect he sought. In every instance he utilized the visual approach as much as possible. For an address in 1914 he used Carlos Vierra's paintings of Chichén Itza and Uxmal in their glory, Mrs. Jean B. Smith's sketches of ancient Maya ceremonies, and also figurines, pottery, stone and metal objects, and facsimile reproductions of pages of the codices. As soon as he collected photographs, he used slides and color transparencies when they became available. And at times he drew figures on large sheets of paper as the audience listened to him.

The aim of his platform delivery appears in an incident recalled by his friend Jack Armstrong. Morley promised to give a lecture in Guatemala City in January, 1921, on results of recent Maya research, and he asked Jack to introduce him. Unfortunately, Armstrong's knowledge of Maya civilization was less than fragmentary, resulting in dull, dry remarks that scarcely mentioned Morley's achievements, and, more important in Vay's view, omitted all reference to the rewards that awaited archaeologists. After the address the two men evened scores with each other, as Morley referred to the uninspired introduction and Armstrong countered with a criticism of Vay's atrocious Spanish.

The nature of his audiences varied greatly. He addressed such diverse groups as the Archaeological Society of New Mexico, a women's club in Washington, the National Geographic Society in the same city, the International Congress of Americanists, a group at the University of Pennsylvania, and audiences in Toronto, New Haven, Providence, and Hartford. One December night in 1916 in New Haven he had only seven listeners, but among them were Simeon E. Baldwin, outstanding jurist and former governor of Connecticut, Hiram Bingham, discoverer of Macchu Picchu, and George Grant MacCurdy, well-known anthropologist, and Vay felt extremely gratified at the quality of the audience.

In these early years his favorite approach was to refer to the Mayas as the Greeks of the New World. The words occur so often in his lectures and articles that it is a wonder that he did not tire of them. They happened to suit his purpose precisely. By implication the Toltecs and Aztecs were the Romans who did no more than crudely copy the culture of the Mayas. Just as the Greeks were the source of European civilization, so were the Mayas the cultural innovators and intellectual superiors of all other indigenous American peoples. And that was exactly Morley's gospel of his beloved Mayas.

IX

The Great Year—1923

THE year 1923 marked the second high point in Morley's professional career. The first occurred in 1914 with his appointment to the staff of the Carnegie Institution. In 1923 he negotiated arrangements to begin the long-delayed project at Chichén Itzá that eventually developed into an elaborate multidisciplinary investigation of pre-Columbian culture in the Maya area.

For a decade he had explored the whole area of that ancient civilization, discovering new sites and re-examining old ones to collect date inscriptions in order to chart the rise and fall of that culture. With the inauguration of the new project he shifted his emphasis to excavation and restoration of Chichén Itzá, to excavation alone at Uaxactún, and to the exploration of new or little-known sites. Also, he encouraged other specialists to use Chichén Itzá as the base of their operations.

As he carried out the preparatory negotiations that led to the signing of the contract between the Mexican government and the Carnegie Institution, the habit of cultivating friends everywhere over the years paid handsome dividends, and in these delicate negotiations he naturally and casually combined social and professional activity so astutely that it is impossible to separate them.

By 1923, officials of the Carnegie Institution believed that conditions in Mexico were favorable for inaugurating the long-delayed project of excavating Chichén Itzá. It had been a decade since the plan had been adopted, and during that time a new president had taken office at the Institution. John C. Merriam, a paleontologist at the University of California, became head of the Institution in 1920. Naturally, he wanted to see Chichén Itzá before undertaking the project; so he sent Morley ahead to arrange for the visit in the middle of February. William B. Parsons, who had favored archaeological work since 1909 and had vigorously supported the appointment of Morley to the Carnegie staff, was a trustee of the Institution and the appropriate person to accompany Merriam.

Morley reached Mérida on February 7 in time to enjoy the festivities of the carnival season while completing arrangements for the entertainment of Merriam and Parsons. Vay's future plans, of course, depended on the success of this visit, for only if these men were favorably impressed would he be able to carry out his great ambition. There was also the other side of the shield, not to be overlooked; the local officials in Yucatán must likewise be sympathetic to the idea, because their wishes could have considerable bearing on the action of the central government. If everything went well, then the final step would be the negotiation of a concession between the government of Mexico and the Carnegie Institution.

Morley clearly understood the role he had to play in each one of these stages. It was his job to keep the wheels well greased so that every part of the machinery would move smoothly. He could not have been cast in a happier role, for he enjoyed the challenge of pleasing people and putting them in good spirits. How well he succeeded in his task appears in the results; the concession was signed in the late summer.

On arriving in Mérida at this time, he commenced a round of activity that lasted for weeks. He looked forward to meeting old friends: Gaylord Marsh, United States consul at Progreso, and Don Felipe Cantón, the Cámeras, Don Rafael Regil, and others he had known on his last visit a decade earlier. Doubtless his closest friends were Mr. and Mrs. William James, who had befriended him on his first visit in 1907, and David Goff, Mrs. James's nephew, who was the same age as Vay.

Joe Spinden and Marshall Saville accompanied Morley to Mérida as representatives of American archaeological societies. Joe, completely familiar with the city, went his own way most of the time. Saville, on the other hand, was constantly with Vay, had a room beside his in the Gran Hotel, and went with him to many of the functions. The fifty-four-year-old Saville, dignified and impressive in appearance, had a gift of wit and anecdotal conversation that he somehow failed to use to best advantage during the visit; and apparently the pace of affairs in the city was too fast for his leisurely habits, for he disappeared from social events at the earliest possible moment and went to bed. Vay also found him a habitual complainer about the smallest things. Just before the important meeting of the local archaeological society, at which Saville was to be made an honorary member, he sulked in his room, declaring that everything had been mismanaged and that he was fed up with it all; Vay coaxed him with soft words and dragged the reluctant man off to the meeting. Something always seemed to go wrong. If Marshall was impressed by his first visit to Chichén Itzá and enjoyed the jaunt to the ruins of Aké, he came back from the cave of Loltún severely abraded by the horseback ride. When the visitors completed their mission and left on the twenty-seventh, Vay returned to his room and wrote half-humorously that he would miss Saville's grouching about his health and the state of the country.

The carnival season, which conveniently occurred during Vay's first week in the city, provided social opportunities galore. What Saville and Spinden did during those days and nights, Vay did not have the time or interest to explain because he was too occupied with his own comings and goings. He paid particular attention to some of the attractive young women of Mérida, not perhaps with any serious intentions in mind, although he was longing for a resumption of domestic life, but for the amusement and diversion he found in the company of these Yucatecan girls.

At this time Morley was deeply in love with a young woman in

Washington. The fact that she was fifteen years younger made no difference. During his months in Mexico, they exchanged letters, and sometimes as he read her messages he felt a great wave of homesickness for Washington. It was not remarkable, then, that whenever he met Latin-American girls, he inevitably compared them with her, always to her advantage. Friends who knew her and Vay believed it would be a good match.

His affection for the young lady did not prevent him from enjoying the company of Mérida's beauties in those early weeks of 1923. The second day he was in town he encountered three houris, as he called them, at a tea at the Jameses'. Margarita had the advantage of speaking English; Isolina was an excellent dancer; and Cholé, who also spoke English, was a trained singer. All were beautiful, slender in build, which he noted as unusual in Latin America, and attractive to men.

Cholé made a strong bid, too strong in fact, to attract him. From the first meeting it was abundantly evident that she liked him; she took the initiative in inviting him to meet her at some of the carnival balls; and at other social events he was suddenly aware that she was beside him. She even attempted to join his party that was going to Chichén Itzá for several days. Only a week after their first meeting, she chided him for giving too much attention to Isolina, who was sitting on the other side of him at a dinner; considerate Vay had spoken in Spanish so as to bring Isolina into the conversation. Then at the end of another week Cholé asked him point-blank if he would ever marry a Yucatecan; and he gave a quick and decided no, explaining that there was too much difference between a North American and a Yucatecan to expect a happy marriage. Despite that showdown he called on her several times. Once, when he was tired from a day of strenuous activity, he found the conversation boring and soon left; on another occasion he danced two numbers with her at her home and watched a beautiful moon rise in the tropical sky, but he felt no particular attraction to her. Rather, he pitied her for being too pretentious about her ability to sing and too eager to attract him.

The two other local girls gained even less attention from him. Isolina was attractive, but she was a poor conversationalist. He liked to dance with her—she was the best dancer among the girls —and at one social event he found her alluring in a gorgeous white gown; but that was almost the end of it. Just before leaving Méri-da, he let himself in for a session of taking photographs of her modeling various dresses, and he had to confess that she was lovely. When he later showed her the pictures, she liked all of them except those in which she wore the native *huipil*. Another attractive girl was Adrianna, perhaps twenty years old, and very beautiful. At a carnival ball, he suddenly became aware of her in a stunning red and silver evening gown. At the moment she was alone, so he boldly introduced himself in English—he had overheard her use that language—explained his business in Mérida, and asked for a dance. She accepted, and soon he learned that she had just returned from six years in New York. He had three dances with her and one at the ball the following night, but thereafter he did not mention her name.

Margarita, on the other hand, interested him, doubtless because she was clever and not easy to win. Not only was she attractive and full of life, but she was also a born flirt, coquettish, sophisticated, and exceedingly smart. She played an elusive game, such as pleading ill when he called to take her out or not showing up at a social affair where he expected her. Twice she sent him notes, purportedly from a mysterious person, proposing meetings; quickly he identified the author and played along with the game for the amusement it provided. Several afternoons he called at her home for tea, and was happy to discover that she had more ideas than most Latin-American girls. When he returned to the city in midsummer, he saw her again; once she even proposed walking with him in the streets at night, but this he knew would endanger her reputation and he refused to agree; however, he continued to call on her at her home. During the field season of the following year when he asked her to do some typing for him, she was only too happy to help and refused to accept the usual pay for the task. Thereafter, he never mentioned her.

Not only was he aware of the attractive girls in Mérida but also of changes that had taken place in that city since his visits of 1907 and 1913. At the *mestiza* balls he deplored the modern dresses that were replacing the distinctive, colorful *huipil*. He was pleased, however, to find that the aristocrats no longer flaunted costly dresses, jewels, and feathers at their formal dances. That small upper crust of society he admitted was delightful to associate with; the men and women were charming, cultured, informed, and well bred. But when he heard them complain about the new order— high taxes, their dwindling estates, the freeing of the peons—he observed that they failed to realize that for centuries their wealth and power had come from the enslavement of the Indian; they were Bourbons who could learn nothing and forget nothing. To him it was only too evident that Yucatán had entered a new age, and the symbol of the new order was Felipe Carrillo Puerto, whom the good old families cursed as a threat to their wealth and prestige.

Of the friends Morley made in Mérida in 1923, Governor Carrillo was the most stimulating. This was noteworthy indeed, because Vay came to the city completely out of sympathy with the socialistic regime then in power. He called it Red and Bolshevistic, he noted the presence of local soviets everywhere, and he shuddered on seeing the red flag flying from public buildings. He also considered it significant that the governor refused to use the state palace and instead had his offices at the League of Resistance, center of all of the workers' unions. But during his first day in the city, Vay had an interview with Carrillo and came away completely captivated by the man. As the weeks passed by, Vay found him increasingly friendly.

Felipe Carrillo possessed a rare combination of ability, leadership, and personal vitality. Coming from humble origins in Motul, he followed the hard life of a worker on a hacienda, until he advanced into a modest trucking business of his own. Sensitive to the depressed condition of the peons, he became a Socialist, called for reform, landed in jail, and escaped with a price on his head. When the revolution came to Yucatán, he was a natural local leader of the new order. Among other things, he translated the

Mexican constitution into Maya for the Indian natives. In 1921 he won a landslide victory as governor and carried with him the election of a Socialist legislature. The new regime set to work to bring Yucatán into the twentieth century with a vast program of reform to improve the conditions of the lower classes. Construction of schools, roads, and public works went into high gear; marriage and divorce laws were liberalized; birth control information was distributed; wages and hours of peons were brought within reason and enforced; and a graduated property tax drew money from the wealthy. The major source of income, to finance these reforms, however, came from the state monopoly on the export of henequen fiber.

Despite his strong reservations about this Socialist regime, Morley found Carrillo irresistible. The governor was about forty years old, physically large, exuding self-confidence and command; he had gray eyes, wore bone-rimmed glasses, and brimmed over with genial vitality. He carried on business informally on a roof terrace, with only a few chairs for visitors, and saw dozens upon dozens of all kinds of citizens who came with their petitions and complaints. Despite the apparent disorder and makeshift arrangement, each applicant had his word with the governor, who at the same time grappled with the larger issues of state. On one visit Vay found him enthusiastic about introducing baseball for Yucatecan boys; teams had been organized in more than 70 per cent of the state, and he had just ordered $20,000 worth of equipment.

Although Carrillo claimed descent from the Mayas, he had the appearance and bearing of a Spanish aristocrat. What is more, he was the conventional gentleman when occasion required. He dressed in clothes of the finest quality, lived in a house on the fashionable Paseo de Montejo, entertained graciously at formal parties and dances, had a private railroad car where he served sumptuous meals while traveling, and presided at formal state functions with dignity and urbanity.

In the beginning of the friendship, it was Carrillo's knowledge of Maya history and his love for the Maya people that attracted Morley. When Vay spoke of archaeology, Felipe not only knew what he was talking about, but contributed stories of discoveries in different parts of the state. When Carnegie Institution officials proposed excavations at Chichén Itzá, he happily welcomed the idea as a way to let the world know about the glorious civilization that once flourished in the land of his ancestors.

Morley noted several instances of Carrillo's deep interest in the Maya past and present. After visiting the cave of Loltún, the party stopped at the village of Oxkutzcab, where Vay looked up a descendant of the Xius, ruling family of ancient Uxmal. When he asked Felipe if he wished to meet the lady, he received a curt no, with the remark that the Xius had betrayed the Mayas by joining the Spaniards; and Vay had to admit the truth of the statement. Another incident occurred a few weeks later in Mérida, where several Fox movie cameramen had been sent to get documentary pictures of Mexico. They were in a quandary. The central government opposed any scenes that would give an unfavorable picture of Mexico, while Carrillo told them to photograph the peasants, the poorest class in the land. Vay also learned that Carrillo did not draw class lines rigidly where the needy were involved, for the governor was very fond of Rafael Regil, scion of old, wealthy, Yucatecan families, who maintained a school and free kitchen for the underprivileged of Mérida.

Morley and Carrillo hit it off well together. After visiting Chichén Itzá, Vay wired him congratulations on the new road to Dzitas, phrasing the message in Maya and referring to the governor as *halach uinik Yucatan* (chief of Yucatán), all of which pleased Don Felipe immensely. In a public lecture he had the presence of mind to correct a mistake he made in the use of a Maya word, which brought applause from the governor. Then he drew several birthday dates in glyphs, including Carrillo's, which the audience appreciated as a graceful compliment to their leader. After the performance, Don Felipe came backstage, gave Morley a double *abrazo*, and told him how magnificently he had carried off the performance. In the days that followed, Carrillo invited him to many affairs. He had him as a companion on automobile drives about the city and as a guest on his railroad car; he took him on trips to Aké and Izamal, and also to Motul, his birthplace, where the governor's mother unpretentiously served a meal with her own hands. Vay was Carrillo's guest at Sunday afternoon bullfights; by this time Vay took the spectacles in stride, coolly noting the good and poor parts of the performance. He was amused as they sat together at one of these exhibitions when Don Felipe leaned over and remarked that people who relish such a spectacle must be savage; but Vay observed that the man thoroughly enjoyed it.

Less than a month after first meeting the governor, Morley was listening to a recital of his love life. It appears that Don Felipe, the able administrator, was not too succesful in handling the women in his life. After a period of marriage, a girl came between him and his wife. He and his inamorata got along well in Mexico City, but in Mérida she became jealous of his public activity, and earlier in the year they had parted and she had returned to Mexico City. Then Mrs. Alma Reed, correspondent for *The New York Times*, appeared on the scene on February 15 along with other tourists, and he quickly fell madly in love with her. All of this Vay could understand, because she had a good mind, wore stylish clothes well, and was a beautiful woman by Yucatecan standards. One Sunday several weeks after this conversation, Don Felipe proudly showed Vay colored photographs of Alma in a *mestiza* dress, and Vay had to agree that she was attractive. After a few weeks in Mérida she left with the visiting dignitaries, but rumor had it that she would return and marry the governor. Felipe's first marriage posed no problem in view of the easy divorce laws in Yucatán— three months' residence and no questions. With rare prescience, however, Vay doubted that the marriage would take place, and events proved that he was right.

Five months later, after Vay had completed some preliminary work at Chichén Itzá, the governor took him and Gann in his car to Progreso to board a boat going to Vera Cruz. Gann was struck by the silent, distraught attitude of the usually lively governor. While waiting for the passengers to arrive by lighter from the vessel, Carrillo took Morley aside and asked his advice. The *Esperanza*, that Vay was about to board, was bringing Don Felipe's wife and child; in addition, he had his mistress in Mérida whom he no longer cared for; and of course he was still madly infatuated by Alma Reed. What should he do? If Vay gave any advice, he did not record it; instead, he merely observed in his diary that it is bad enough for a man to choose between two women, but in this case poor Felipe had to face three.

Merriam and Parsons arrived on February 15 and were hurried about from one event to another for thirteen days. Several striking facts emerge from this round of activities. One was the expansive and extensive manner of entertainment the Yucatecans indulged in to display their hospitality. The other and perhaps more amazing fact is the way Morley, Merriam, and Parsons withstood the rigorous schedule of dinners, ceremonial meetings, and trips into the country. Since Vay had arrived before his guests, he had gone through a preliminary week of social events; even though he flagged a bit just before Merriam and Parsons left, he continued to meet the various engagements that did not end until March 1. Merriam and Parsons, who were older than Vay and not endowed with his nervous energy, must have found the pace grueling, but they bore up manfully, doubtless because of their sense of duty. They knew that part of their task was to please the Yucatecans, and they carried out the self-imposed assignment perfectly.

The governor sent his private coach with Vay and some aristocrats from Mérida to Progreso to meet Merriam and Parsons when their boat arrived. There Vay greeted the guests, as well as his sister Elinor and her friend Jean Hiland, and escorted all of them back to the city in the special railroad car. Then began the round of ceremonials and entertainments that lasted almost two weeks.

Merriam and Parsons were received in Mérida in grand style. At the railroad station, the state band played American college airs, and a welcoming delegation, including the governor's brother, the city council, and the highest military official, greeted them. After perfunctory introductions Vay whisked the two men off, already two hours late, to an outdoor luncheon provided by the city council at Centenario Park. That night Governor Carrillo presided at an elaborate banquet with more than one hundred guests in the spacious lobby of the Peón Contreras Theater, where the Americans were welcomed with speeches in Spanish, English, and Maya. Carrillo gave an excellent address in Maya, certainly appropriate for the occasion, asking the Carnegie Institution to inform the world of the glories of that ancient civilization.

Next it was Merriam's turn, and he was also in good form, as he replied felicitously in slow, distinct English, which many in the audience understood. After acknowledging that it would be a privilege for the C.I.W. to carry out excavations and add to the knowledge of the prehistoric people, he championed the need of going about the work in the most scientific fashion.

Then Vay arose unexpectedly and added an impish touch. Calling himself a fellow Yucateco, a remark that brought down the house, he also offered greetings to the visiting dignitaries. Only he could have gotten away with this humorous impudence, as the intonation of his voice and the mock seriousness of his countenance left no doubt of the joke he injected to lighten the solemnity of the occasion.

The affair ended with dance numbers. Since there were only seven ladies present, there was no problem of overcrowding. The state band provided admirable music and the two-hundred-foot sweep of marble floor made the foyer a majestic ballroom. Vay took several turns with Isolina and Cholé, and then as midnight struck he escorted Elinor and Jean back to the hotel.

A ceremony was also the highlight of the second day for Merriam and Parsons. After making a formal call on the governor at his office, they were taken on an automobile tour of the city and then to an afternoon tea held in their honor by Mr. and Mrs. James. Rushing from that event, Vay escorted them to a formal dinner at the home of the governor's brother, Benjamin Carrillo. From there they hurried to the Peón Contreras Theater again. This time the large lobby had been converted into an auditorium, with a dais at one end, for a meeting of the new Archaeological Association of Yucatán. Since Merriam, Parsons, Morley, Saville, and Spinden were to be made honorary members, they were seated on the platform; that is, all but Spinden, who had been away on a trip to Uxmal and wandered in late, dressed in an unpressed, light-colored suit. He was rushed posthaste to the platform just in time to receive the honor. Merriam and Parsons made gracious remarks, the state band offered some musical numbers, and the affair came to a happy end. But Vay had not finished the long day; he and friends went to a local restaurant, where they talked and ate until after midnight, disregarding the strenuous schedule that lay ahead.

The trip to Uxmal on Saturday the seventeenth was a fifteen-hour excursion. At the ruins Vay gasped as he saw Merriam scamper up the steep stairs of the Pyramid of the Dwarf and wander enthusiastically about the high ledge, examining everything in sight. Among the rubble the eager visitor found a carved head and was soon at work with a pocketknife picking away the rubble that surrounded it. Hardly had Vay discovered that Merriam had a surer step than he or Parsons than he suffered from a new anxiety; Merriam was so interested that it seemed that he would never satisfy his curiosity and come down to continue the tour. After an hour and a half atop the pyramid, he descended, and the party looked at other structures. As they walked among the ruins, Parsons, the engineer, had an eye for structural details of the buildings, and he suggested that he could detect the beginnings of the true arch. Then they met José Reygadas, government inspector of monuments, who happened to be on the site that day with photographers, who took pictures of the Americans. On they plodded, visiting the Monjas, the House of the Governor, and the House of the Pigeons. On the way back to Mérida they passed through a heavy rainstorm, and everyone suffered from heat, humidity, and weariness. But Vay was delighted: it was evident that Merriam was impressed and enthusiastic.

Sunday the eighteenth was a day of relative leisure, though not without ceremonies for the guests. Merriam gave Alma Reed an interview for a newspaper article. Morley prepared for the forthcoming trip to Chichén Itzá, visited a friend's country home, and had tea with Margarita. At night the University of the Southeast held a convocation to welcome the Americans. The affair began auspiciously with an excellent address in English, followed by a formal speech of greeting by the director. The next item, however, a discourse on Maya architecture, turned into an exasperating bore. The slides were poor, and the speaker read rapidly from a manuscript for an hour and a half. Don Felipe Cantón, sitting next to Vay, whispered that the man was reading a whole book, and so it seemed. Elinor came to Vay and asked to be excused, but he forbade such a discourtesy. At last the program ended with several musical numbers. One was "The Rosary," sung in English as a compliment to the visitors, but Vay claimed he did not recognize the words. Happily the last number was splendidly performed by a soprano with male chorus and organ accompaniment. On leaving the university, Morley and his party attended a *mestiza* ball, also held in their honor, which featured native dances. Well after midnight, as he escorted Elinor and Jean back to the hotel, he made it clear that they were in a foreign land where the freer practices of the United States did not apply; wearily they agreed they would behave themselves.

From Monday through Thursday, February 19 to 22, Vay had Merriam and Parsons in tow at Chichén Itzá, showing them the site of the future work of the Carnegie Institution. This was, of course, the major purpose of their visit to Yucatán. Edward Thompson provided quarters in the Casa Principal, which he managed to put into usable shape, although it had been ravaged by discontented natives two years earlier.

Every morning and afternoon Morley guided his guests through a different part of the vast assemblage of ruins. They climbed a wall of the Ball Court, and they mounted the staircase of the imposing Castillo; then he took them down to the intriguing Sacred Cenote. Merriam was so awed by the mysterious spot that he would not allow the Ford to pull up to its banks; he had the car stopped three hundred feet away and they walked to the edge of the pool. Next day they visited the Monjas and the Group of the Thousand Columns and the Caracol. In crawling through the tortuous inner passage of the Caracol, the rotund Parsons got stuck; after much puffing, however, he managed to emerge on top of the building. At the High Priest's Grave, Thompson related the story of his burrowing down into the core of the pyramid and coming upon the crypt. Then they visited "Old Chichén" with its numerous and curious ruins. At the end of the third day Merriam asked to see the Sacred Cenote again, and once more he stopped the Ford some distance from the pool in order to avoid committing a sacrilege.

Before they left for Mérida on the last day, in the true Morley spirit they paid a farewell visit to the Ball Court and the Castillo. By this time Vay knew that his two chiefs, as he called them, were thoroughly impressed by what they had seen, although he was eager to hear them say so. Indirectly he broached the subject to Parsons. Parsons assured him that Merriam was on fire with the whole idea and would pass on his enthusiasm to the trustees. After returning to Mérida on Thursday afternoon, Merriam and Parsons longed for a rest; Morley, however, went on to the Jameses' to dance and hear native songs. Then he learned with some envy that during his absence Saville had bought a fine old Maya bowl with attractive decorations.

Although the two Carnegie officials had covered the high point of their visit, they stayed on in the city a few days beyond schedule because of the late arrival of their boat. This change of plan in no way diminished the social activities. Although Merriam suffered from abnormal swelling of the *garrapatas* bites on his legs and could easily have pleaded to be excused, he bravely went through all of the events. On Friday, Vay took the two men to see the archaeological collection and fine private library of Rafael Regil; next came a visit to the state museum; and the day ended with a formal dinner at the home of one of the aristocrats living on the Paseo de Montejo.

There was one more big event in the offing, a visit to the cave of Loltún on Saturday. The governor generously invited a party, including all of the guests and Vay's sister Elinor, Jean Hiland, and Alma Reed, to accompany him in his private coach. An ample breakfast was served en route, although the Americans had already eaten before leaving Mérida. At Oxkutzcab they left the train and took horses to the cave. When they reached the entrance of the cavern, local people joined the party, swelling the number to about seventy. A sixteen-year-old local Maya claimed that he could guide them. Each person carried a lighted candle, and they filed into the dark passages and over narrow, slippery ledges above steep precipices. At one place they had to crawl on all fours. On halting in one cavern to await the directions of the guide, they were almost suffocated by the candle smoke and intense heat. It was soon evident that the guide was lost; individuals wandered about shouting that they had found an opening here or a way out there, and others cried out in fear. Confusion increased, and the expedition turned into a nightmare. At that point the governor took charge, issued stern commands, restored order, and had them led out of the cave without tragedy or accident. Vay considered it a miraculous deliverance.

The members of the party returned to Oxkutzcab by horse, had some beer, and then entrained for the return trip. Nerves calmed down and good spirits returned as the guests found that dinner was being served on the train. It was soon evident that the governor did nothing in a niggling way. They were faced with a banquet of seven meat courses, great quantities of vegetables and tortillas, an egg course, seven kinds of drinks, and four different desserts. Vay, who always loved good food, gave up after the third meat course and passed the others by. Everyone was satiated.

At Acanceh they made a brief stop so that Vay could show Merriam and Parsons what remained of the wall carvings in one of the ruins. He had seen them in their prime in 1907, and although they had deteriorated since then, they were still worth examination.

When they reached Mérida at seven o'clock, everyone was too exhausted to attend a ball held in honor of Alma Reed by the journalists of the city. Morley, however, thought that someone from his group must make an appearance, and so, tired as he was, he attended as representative of the visiting Americans.

On Sunday the round of activities continued unabated. The governor gave a formal luncheon, again with fabulous quantities of food and drink; and Merriam and Carrillo exchanged graceful compliments. Three hours later, the visitors had to face another dinner as guests of the Jameses.

By Monday the twenty-fifth Vay was suffering from a heavy cold he had contracted at the cave; and though it slowed his pace, it did not stop him. He decided to forgo the trip to the ruins of Aké that had been arranged for Merriam, Parsons, and Saville; instead, he danced with some of the young Yucatecan women and missed a country club party for Jean Hiland only because of a flat tire on the car he was using. That night he had dinner with Merriam, Parsons, Saville, and Thompson, and as might be expected, archaeology was the topic of conversation.

At last the guests left on Tuesday. Morley escorted the Carnegie officials on a tour of farewell calls. At some homes they were offered a *copita*, the sign of hospitality, that consisted of a stiff drink of raw cognac. Parsons evaded the compliment, but Merriam and Vay accepted and felt the results. On the way to Progreso, Morley had a long conversation with Merriam about the Chichén Itzá project, writing down details that his chief told him to keep in mind when discussing the plan with Mexican authorities. After seeing his guests off to their boat, he took time out for tea with Consul Marsh and his wife, who were old friends, and then returned to Mérida by train. His room in the Gran seemed lonely after the weeks of hectic activity, and he was also very weary.

He was tired but supremely gratified. Now he knew that Merriam was convinced of the wisdom of the project and was enthusiastic to carry it out. Before parting, he had told Vay that now was the time to press for the concession.

Morley stayed on in Yucatán for a month. The first thing he did was to feel out José Reygadas on the chances of a long-term concession. Reygadas admitted that there would be criticism from the anti-American press in Mexico City, but he believed that the Carnegie's policy of not taking artifacts from the country would be the trump card in favor of the concession.

Before leaving for Chichén Itzá, Morley gave a public lecture on Maya civilization at the Peón Contreras Theater on the night of March 1. By nine o'clock the auditorium was crowded, with the governor and the elite of the city in the audience. The state band provided music. And Vay was in top form. He spoke in Spanish— that is, in his peculiar brand of Spanish—with flattering remarks about the audience and the governor, which Latin Americans expected on such an occasion. He showed slides and then drew glyphs; and he closed with the wish that he had Maya blood in his veins. Backstage, friends crowded about, telling him how successful the performance was, and Carrillo gave him a double *abrazo*.

When he returned to his room in the Gran, away from the sympathetic audience and cheering friends, the exhilaration of triumph ebbed. He was exhausted, worn out from thinking and speaking in Spanish; and he was also debilitated from a nagging tropical ailment. Then he remembered Merriam's advice about taking care of himself; in fact, both of his chiefs were worried about his reckless use of physical energy. What does it matter, Vay thought. If he could write one or two more books and finish a little other work on the Mayas, he would be satisfied; after all, one person more or less in the world does not count for much. This kind of ruminating was not normal for him. Physically and emotionally exhausted, he had the good sense to turn off the light and go to bed.

To relax from the hectic pace he had followed, he took his sister to Chichén Itzá to show her the place where he would work in the future. During the ten-day visit, they stayed at the Casa Principal as paying guests and enjoyed a leisurely inspection of the ruins. He and Thompson examined the Thousand Columns, where the first excavations were to begin; Vay and Elinor descended the shaft of the High Priest's Grave and explored the crypt, though they came up without finding anything; after dinner at night they climbed the steps of the Monjas to see the moon rise in the clear sky. The archaeological surprise of the visit was his discovery of a column of glyphs at the Caracol.

Morley was never completely comfortable with the new Socialist regime in Yucatán. One day on the road to Dzitas, he met Gallo in a pleasant reunion after sixteen years. Back in 1907 during his first visit to Chichén, Gallo was the intelligent, attractive boy who helped him to measure the structures. When Vay learned that Gallo was now president of the Socialist League of Pisté and the important man in that village, he stated those facts in his diary without enthusiasm. Some days later when he visited Motul, Vay described that village as being very socialistic, which implied no recommendation from him.

On returning to Mérida, he gave attention largely to public relations. Twice within a few days he lectured to local audiences. On March 23, his subject was the sacred cities of the Mayas, illustrated with a hundred slides. After the intermission he followed his usual custom of drawing glyphs; this time, however, he ended the performance with a sentence in Maya, composed by Carrillo for the purpose; and this final touch brought down the house. A few days later he addressed the Socialist League of Mérida, doubtless as a favor to the governor. If Morley was somewhat reluctant about speaking before this group, he did not admit it. What really annoyed him was the presence of two American journalists, Morris D. Erwin from a Cincinnati newspaper and Ernest Gruening, editor of *The Nation*; both appeared to Vay to be overzealous in championing the leftist regime in Yucatán.

At the same time he made use of newspapers to call public attention to the ruins and to pave the way for his future work in that region. The interview he gave to the *Revista de Mérida* was for local consumption, but the article he prepared at the invitation of the Associated Press received wider coverage. In that account he declared that the Maya civilization was the most advanced of any pre-Columbian culture in the Western Hemisphere, and that the ruins dated back to the fourth and fifth centuries A.D. He could not resist a reference to the maidens who had been hurled into the Sacred Cenote at Chichén Itzá. It is amusing to notice that the report that appeared in the Mexico City *Excelsior* had Morley dating the ruins before Christ and declaring that they were unsurpassed in the whole world. The full interview, as it appeared in the *New York Herald* and *The New York Times*, represented him more accurately by quoting directly from his account.

His plans called for permission to begin work simultaneously at

Chichén Itzá and Uaxactún. To carry out his double aim, he had to secure concessions in Guatemala as well as in Mexico. Although he concentrated most of his efforts on the Yucatán project, he made a visit to Guatemala in April and May to get a five-year contract in that country.

William Gates, of all persons, became the fly in the ointment in Guatemala. As we have seen, Gates had been a friend of Vay; he had contributed a chapter to the *Inscriptions of the Petén* in 1920 and had accompanied him on a field expedition to the Petén in the following year. After Gates left the expedition, he was appointed director of archaeology and director of the museum of the Republic of Guatemala. At the beginning of 1922, the year Gates assumed his posts, Morley arrived in Guatemala City, inquired about excavating, and concluded that there would be no trouble in operating under the Carnegie concession of 1920. He even visited President Orellana and received a letter of recommendation to the *jefe político* of the Petén. Some time later in the year Gates spent a few weeks in Guatemala to inaugurate his program. He drew up plans for a new museum of archaeology to be constructed adjacent to the Temple of Minerva, appointed P. W. Schufeldt, a friend of Morley, as his deputy inspector in the Petén, and heard tidbits of gossip that convinced him that Morley and the Carnegie Institution had engaged in highly unethical acts in respect to the nation's archaeological treasures. Gates now became a violent and vindictive enemy.

In the meantime, members of the Maya Society in the United States became restive under Gates's presidency. They wanted to get him out of that position, and Vay, never dreaming how bitterly Gates would oppose him, counseled time and patience and urged the members to give the president another year. Apparently Morley shared the views of the other members when he characterized Gates at this time as brilliant, erratic, and bizarre, and declared that his unpredictable habits nullified whatever usefulness he might have. At this time Vay was secretary-treasurer of the organization.

By early 1923, he realized that he could not work through Gates for permission to dig at Uaxactún, so he decided to use other avenues. His good friend, Adrián Recinos, was minister of foreign affairs, and he knew that he could count on him. But when he arrived in Guatemala City in April, he discovered that Recinos had left his post two months earlier in a cabinet shake-up. Nevertheless, he hunted up Recinos and explained the situation. At once Recinos arranged for Vay to see Abraham Cabrera, minister of public education. It turned out that Cabrera and Roberto Lowenthal, the new minister of foreign relations, favored the permit. Two days later Vay learned that he had gained his goal; the concession was formally granted May 19, and the Carnegie Institution released news of it to American papers at the end of June. The announcement that appeared in *The New York Times* suggests the hand of Morley, for it noted that Gates was director of archaeology and of the museum in Guatemala. It is a good guess that Vay was trying to mollify Gates for having bypassed him in the negotiations. As far as Morley was concerned, everything went swimmingly. He flitted in and out of Quiriguá and Copán, and in Guatemala City he gave a public lecture marking the revival of the Geographical and Historical Society. It was a grand affair at the Palacio Centenario with President Orellana as the distinguished guest and an audience of 1,200 persons. Morley had secured the concession, little dreaming that he still had to reckon with Gates.

If negotiating for contracts was a necessary part of the business of archaeology, the heart of the matter was the digging. And Vay took time out to do a little excavation at his two favorite sites. He spent a week at Quiriguá and continued to marvel at the comfortable living conditions at the fruit company hospital.

Nor could he resist the temptation to spend a few days at Copán. As in the past he had quarters with Don Juan Ramón Cueva and took his meals with Doña Julia. It was like home to this man without a home. The first night a ten-piece band, exhibiting more goodwill than musical concord, greeted him on the plaza. But it made him happy and contented to know that in this little out-of-the-way village he had friends who welcomed him back as a fellow citizen. To show that he reciprocated their feelings, he gladly distributed whiskey and cigarettes; finally, he thanked them, and slipped some money into the hands of the musicians.

When he left the place several days later, he recorded his only disappointment. Back in 1920 he had placed some carved stones from the ruins in a room in the *cabildo* as the beginnings of a museum; now he found the pieces scattered about the room and used as supports for benches. But he said nothing, for he knew that friendship, time, and ultimate objectives are variables that must be held in delicate balance.

The negotiations for the Mexican concession took Vay to Mexico City on three visits during the year; all told, he spent more than nine weeks there. During his first stay he sought to mend fences and to create a favorable atmosphere for the negotiations.

He had been in the city only a few hours when he learned that there was public indignation over E. H. Thompson's smuggling ancient Maya art objects to the United States. Exactly a month earlier, *The New York Times* had announced Thompson's admission that he had dredged many artifacts—jade carvings, gold ornaments, turquoise masks, etc.—from the Sacred Cenote at Chichén Itzá, and that they were then in the Peabody Museum at Cambridge. The report emphasized the objects of gold. It was easy to read between the lines that Thompson had smuggled these valuable items out of Mexico to the United States. Archaeologists had known of this activity for years, but now for the first time it had been made public. Why he chose that precise moment, when the Carnegie Institution was seriously negotiating for a concession, to make his disclosure is a mystery. It could only arouse the Mexican public and hamper the immediate plans of the C.I.W.

At once Morley set out to take the edge off the report and calm the public by explaining the mission of the Institution. He gave a newspaper interview, and the article appeared within two days after he had heard of the trouble. *La Universal* featured the story along with a photograph of Morley on the front page. The headline, "Yucatán Was the Cradle of Maya Art, Says Dr. Morley," gave no hint of the real purpose of the article. In fact, it was only near the end of the account that he described the nature of the work carried on by the Institution. The organization was not a museum and did not work for a museum, he said; its work was only scientific, such as making sketches, taking photographs, and reconstructing fallen ruins. What effect the story had is not known, but Morley made his point that the C.I.W. did not seek to take monuments or artifacts out of the country.

Actual negotiations for the concession Vay carried on with Manuel Gamio and José Reygadas. Unfortunately, a horse had fallen on Gamio and fractured his hip so that he was confined to his home for several months. He did not want Merriam to come to the city for discussion of the concession until he could accompany him on a formal call on the president. This delayed the whole business for two months. In the meantime Morley spent much time revising Merriam's draft of the various provisions and having them typed by his stenographer. Vay soon discovered that his stenographer was making too much of his prosperity; he began drinking, and finally did not show up for work at all.

A visit to Teotihuacán provided surprises for Morley, who had not been to the site since 1909 and had not seen the recent excavations. Reygadas, who had restored the *ciudedela* in 1921–22, guided him over that huge enclosure, and Vay found it a good piece of work. Then Reygadas led him up to the Quetzalcoatl-Tlaloc pyramid wall, and he gasped with wonder and astonishment. There in front of him was the elaborately carved surface—stylized masks, rippling lines, brilliant colors—all in mint condition. It was stupendous.

Then Reygadas told him how Leopoldo Batres, long-retired inspector-general of monuments of the Díaz regime, tried to disparage the accuracy of the work of the *dirección* at the *ciudedela*, and Vay's blood boiled. Right there in Teotihuacán one could see how Batres had ruined the great Pyramid of the Sun by removing the outer covering. So Vay determined to counteract Batres' possible influence in any way he could.

The following day he gave an interview to *Excelsior* that appeared with the innocuous title, "Mexico Is the Egypt of the New World." He praised the work done by Gamio and the *dirección* at

Teotihuacán, declaring that nothing matched those ruins in the Old or the New World. He encouraged Mexico to continue the study of its ancient civilizations and its contemporary indigenous peoples. The United States, he observed, had not accomplished archaeological work as significant as that done in Mexico. At least three times in the article, the *dirección* received an accolade. Morley hoped that this praise would help to silence the few followers of Batres. But it was not the end of Vay's efforts. He wrote to Tozzer, who was preparing a book on the artifacts retrieved from the Sacred Cenote, asking him to underscore the fact that Thompson had exported those objects during the Díaz regime, thus implying that Batres, who was in office at that time, was responsible for letting the items get out of the country.

While Morley fidgeted over the delay and waited anxiously to see if Merriam would postpone his arrival, he was busy meeting people. The article in *La Universal* prompted Manuel Sánchez Marmol, an old schoolmate at Pennsylvania Military College, to call upon him. They had a grand time reminiscing, and that night Morley filled pages of his diary with recollections of his early days in Pennsylvania and Colorado.

He had also been waiting for months to meet Frans Blom, a fair-haired, blue-eyed Dane of thirty, who looked promising for archaeology. Blom came from a wealthy family in Copenhagen, grew up with considerable advantages, including a knowledge of four languages, but he left home rather than enter the business world of his father. After wandering about for some years, he turned up in Mexico as an employee of the Eagle Oil Company, trekking through the forest to find oil seepages and guiding geological parties through Chiapas, Campeche, and Tabasco. An intelligent and inquisitive fellow, he noted the customs of the Indians and the archaeological remains. After three years of this life, he succumbed to tropical fever and went to Mexico City to recuperate. He wrote to Morley in August, 1922, an account of an inscribed stela at Tortuguero, Tabasco, and enclosed a sketch of the glyphs so accurately copied that Vay could decipher the date at once.

Blom left the oil company for a job with the Dirección de Antropología, and as his first stint in the field he was sent to examine Palenque. On his return from there, he and Morley finally met, eight months after he had written the first letter to Vay.

Friday, April 6, was a red-letter day for both men. Already favorably impressed by reports of Blom's intense enthusiasm for all things Maya, Morley met him in the lobby of the Regis Hotel with great expectations. They talked about his work in Palenque. They went to lunch; Vay called it a Maya lunch and was so excited he neglected to enumerate the dishes they had. In the afternoon they went to the National Museum, where Frans showed him stones with carved figures from Ocosingo; and Vay believed he had found another Initial Series. Blom took him to his hotel and showed him his notebooks of Palenque, and Vay marveled at the neat, accurate record. His interest rose to fever pitch as Frans displayed copies of new hieroglyphs he had found at that site. Finally, Frans described eleven sculptured stelae at Toniná, and Vay's mouth watered at the news. He needed more dates from that area.

Morley decided to add him to the field staff as soon as the concession was signed. Within ten days after the first meeting, he wrote to Tozzer at Harvard to find a scholarship, so that Frans could complete his M.A. in two fall semesters and work in the field in the spring and summer.

Vay also re-established his ties with Mrs. Zelia Nuttall, the outstanding woman Americanist of the day, by frequent visits to Casa Alvarado, her home in Coyoacán. She was now in her sixties, and she continued to enjoy the charm and comfort of her luxurious home with its fine Spanish colonial furnishings—Vay noted the virgins, saints, hangings, porcelains, and silver—and the influence she carried with important people. Her receptions were famous for the noteworthy persons she assembled and the charming atmosphere of the setting. When Merriam visited the city briefly in June, she was quick to have him attend a tea that included two United States commissioners, several diplomats, and a military attaché. Vay accompanied Merriam to the event, largely in order to extricate him at the proper time for other business. On another occasion, when Vay and Gann had lunch with her, she astounded Vay by her knowledge of Mexican pre-Columbian and colonial history. She soon came to respect and like Morley, and when he made a farewell call in July she unburdened herself of some of her troubles. In turn he explained details of the concession, and she took a lively interest in the progress of the negotiations.

If Frans Blom and Mrs. Nuttall were favorite companions, he also met other friends and made new ones. There was Caligari, the Italian dealer in antiques, buying objects for his government, with whom he dined at Mrs. Nuttall's. Another collector, Emilio Misonyi, joined him and Blom at Sanborn's, and afterward Misonyi took Vay to his rooms and showed his items from Palenque and detailed maps of southern Mexico. Several times Vay talked with Hermann Beyer, a curious personality who had recently entered the field of Maya archaeology, and examined the objects he had collected.

Vay never developed a warm feeling for Alma Reed, possibly because he felt she was content to pick up just enough archaeological information from the professionals to provide copy for a newspaper story or a magazine article. When he and Gann dined at the Gamios she was also one of the guests, but Vay made no comments about her. The following day when he lunched with her at Sanborn's he was fuming inside over a hitch that had just occurred in the Carnegie negotiations. He knew her instinct for news, and he was determined not to let her question him about the concession; instead, he steered the conversation to a discussion of life and love and liberty on the hunch that all women enjoyed talking about those subjects. His strategy worked, and he came away from the meeting proud of the fact that she did not suspect his turmoil.

In addition to meeting people, he envisioned new projects. At the time of his first visit to the city, he believed he had good ideas for motion pictures based on his favorite subject, the Mayas. He had two different ideas. One was for a "big" film to be made at Chichén Itzá; it is not clear whether he had in mind a documentary or a dramatic story to be filmed against the background of the ruins. The other he called an educational film, probably patterned after his public lectures. One of the Fox movie men in Mérida gave him some slight encouragement. Two weeks later he boldly sent synopses of both projects to the head of the Fox Film Corporation. The subject, however, never appears again in his diary, and it is likely that he received no reply.

Another project that failed to materialize involved a fine pre-Columbian jade. In April a man at the museum showed him a photograph of a beautiful jade plaque that had been found near Teotihuacán, and offered it to him for $500. Gamio was suspicious and warned Vay that it could be a plot to get him into the suburbs and hold him for ransom. After all, that article in *La Universal* identified Morley as a representative of the reputedly wealthy Carnegie Institution. Gamio warned him not to go out alone at night. Vay made light of the danger, but resolved that he would be careful.

Two months later he was still intrigued by the jade, which Gamio had now authenticated. When Merriam was in the city, Morley proposed that Merriam find $250—the price had dropped —from private sources, buy the piece, and present it to the Mexican government as a gesture. But Merriam had no intention of getting into that kind of business, and when Vay later appealed to him by telegraph to carry out the plan, he received no answer.

With the groundwork laid for Merriam's conference, Vay went on to Guatemala. On his return to Mexico City on May 31, he was ready for the critical stage of the negotiations. According to plan, Merriam appeared on June 2 with the latest version of the terms of the contract as he had drawn them up on his trip south. The next day Reygadas, Merriam, and Morley went to Teotihuacán to confer with Gamio, director of Mexican archaeology. After viewing the ruins and the spectacular Quetzalcoatl pyramid in the *ciudedela*, they lunched in the grotto. Then Gamio had a table and chairs placed in the garden in front of the museum, where they conferred on the project. For three hours Merriam expounded the provisions of the concession, point by point, as Vay marveled at his sure grasp and keen insight. It turned out that there was disagreement on only a few minor points, which were settled the next day.

Merriam also carefully carried out formalities in order to strengthen the goodwill that had been established. At the Dirección de Antropología Morley introduced him to officials and also made a point of having him meet Blom. Merriam called on the minister of agriculture and the minister of foreign relations. Then on the last day of his four-day stay Merriam, flanked by Gamio, Reygadas, and Vay, made a courtesy call on President Obregón. It was a brief, happy meeting, for the president had already approved the concession. Gamio took the party to see the archaic burials he had uncovered in the Pedregal, and then Merriam hastily boarded a train to return to the United States.

Merriam had finished his part of the task, but it was far from the end of the road for Morley. He had to stay on the scene until every detail of the concession was settled; small points kept cropping up and occasional setbacks occurred, so that he did not leave the city until the end of August.

During the negotiations, Vay was on tenterhooks lest some minor point might hold up the approval of the concession. It is curious that Merriam's visit was not noted by *Excelsior* until a week after he had departed, and the notice was extremely brief. Is it possible that Gamio and other officials tried to avoid a flare-up of anti-Americanism by delaying the announcement of Merriam's visit until after he had left? Then at one stage of the negotiations Blom gave Morley temporary uneasiness by telling him of a rumor that certain officials at the museum hoped to block the concession by insisting that a member of the National University must be in attendance at Chichén Itzá and be put on the Carnegie payroll. Gamio laughed off the rumor, and he was correct.

It is interesting to speculate whether two other incidents had any bearing on the fate of the concession. On June 29 the American press carried the Carnegie Institution's announcement that it had secured a five-year concession in Guatemala. Actually, the contract had been signed six weeks earlier. Was the news of it issued at this time to hasten Mexican dealings to a favorable conclusion?

The second incident involved the Bucareli Conference then in progress in Mexico City. Among the outstanding problems between the United States and Mexico was the former's refusal to recognize the Obregón regime. The United States sent Judge John B. Payne and Charles B. Warren to meet counterparts appointed by Mexico for the purpose of resolving the problems. The commissioners' meetings, known as the Bucareli Conference, were held from May 15 to August 15. Zelia Nuttall, who knew many influential persons, told Vay that she believed the fate of the concession depended on United States recognition of Obregón. It is difficult to determine whether her speculation had any basis, because the C.I.W. concession was signed on July 6; the Bucareli Conference, continuing for five more weeks, did end by granting United States recognition.

Morley planned two expeditions for the beginning of 1924, one to Uaxactún and the other to Chichén Itzá. Late in 1923 he ran into trouble with both plans: Gates kept the situation uncertain in Guatemala, and a revolution appeared to threaten the plan for Mexico.

Some time after the Mexican contract had been signed, Vay learned that Gates was raising a furor in Guatemala. Incensed because high government officials had bypassed him when they gave the Carnegie Institution a contract to excavate, Gates had the government pass a law placing all archaeological matters in his hands. He charged Morley and Gann with smuggling artifacts out of the country and claimed further that they molested sites and exposed monuments to the mercy of the elements. He even asserted that Vay had taken stones from Quiriguá. To make matters worse, Schufeldt told him that Morley considered Gates's pompous title a joke.

It appears that when Gates was unable to control other persons, especially persons he suspected of being stronger than himself, he made desperate charges based on half-truths at best and on mere suspicion at worst. Since he spent very little time in Guatemala, his letters to Sinforo Aguilar, secretary of the museum, reveal his state of mind. Merriam and Morley, he claimed, boasted that they had secured the concession which made them responsible to no one, and that the Carnegie Institution had maneuvered to exclude all other organizations from working in Guatemala and Mexico. "I am going to fight this thing" in the United States, he vowed, "in the Maya Society, before the board of the Carnegie trustees, and all the way up to the chairman of that board, no less person than Elihu Root . . . ."[1] He even declared that Morley had published Guthe's doctoral thesis as his own work. And somehow he had decided that everyone conspired to defeat his project for a new museum in Guatemala City. Actually, the new museum that Gates planned as an addition to the Temple of Minerva stirred up so much popular protest that the government abandoned the project after spending $7,000 on it. Each letter to Aguilar rose to a higher pitch of invective. To summarize his indignation, he drew up a list of charges against Vay and the Carnegie Institution and sent the letter to President Merriam and to a member of the board of trustees.

In December, when the Maya Society held its meetings, Gates was ready for drastic action. The members, already uneasy over his accusations, were aghast when he attempted to expel Morley from the organization. That was the end of the Maya Society.

In the meantime Frans Blom went to Cambridge in September and enrolled for graduate study at Harvard. Like a good soldier, he performed his duty, but books, lectures, and museums could not hold a candle to life in the tropical bush. He also missed the exciting conversations with Vay, especially about the coming field season at Uaxactún. The weeks dragged on, his financial resources dwindled, and then at the end of December Carnegie officials informed him that it was doubtful that the Uaxactún project would get under way. Alone and discouraged on New Year's Day, he wrote to Vay, "This university makes me feel so damned blue, so

[1] Gates to Sinforo Aguilar, Oct. 15, 1923. J. Eric S. Thompson kindly provided excerpts from the Gates correspondence.

write and cheer me up. Write every day, at least I wish you would, so that I can feel in contact with happenings and yourself."

With the opening of 1924, Morley found the situation in Guatemala more confusing than ever. Gates resigned and reconsidered several times; no one knew whether he was still in office or not. Vay decided that he would attempt to go to Latin America by the end of January. But where did Blom come into the picture? "If you all go to Guatemala," he asked Vay, "will I then go exploring? Or do you want me to arrange for transportation and outfit for Guatemala?"[2] No answer. And a few days later Frans exclaimed, "Studying is all right, but, man, the sweetest music I know is the sound of the bell-mule at the head of the packtrain and the singing of the insects in the tropical night. . . . That is how I feel, the young colt in the corral, eager to get out in the great open for a canter. And you bet your soul I will be standing at the gate waiting for you to open. . . ."[3]

While Blom bombarded Vay with inquiries about Guatemala, a revolt in Mexico threw doubt on the Chichén project. In December, La Huerta in Vera Cruz proclaimed revolution against President Calles. Governor Carrillo supported the federal government in Yucatán, but the military garrison in Mérida, abetted by some large landowners, turned against him. Without an army to support him and unwilling to involve the natives in bloodshed, Carrillo fled in an attempt to reach Cuba. But a storm prevented his boat from sailing, and he was captured, court-martialed, and shot with his three brothers and other supporters. General Broca became military governor of the state and closed the ports of Yucatán.

Morley had no idea how long he must wait for affairs to quiet down in the peninsula. In the meantime his other staff members were, like Blom, inquiring eagerly about dates of departure—and he had none to give. He was almost at the end of his wits.

Finally, at the close of January, Blom received orders from Carnegie officials to join Morley for the expedition. So Vay, Frans,

[2] Blom to Morley, Jan. 1, 1924, in possession of Mrs. Frans Blom.
[3] Blom to Morley, Jan. 3, 7, 1924, in possession of Mrs. Frans Blom.

Monroe Amsden, and Oliver Ricketson went to Belize. From there Morley sent the three men on to Uaxactún, while he went to Guatemala City to clear up the matter of the permit. He hoped that while he was at that task the situation would calm down in Yucatán.

Shortly after reaching Guatemala City, he heard rumors of Gates's resignation. So he called on Aguilar, then under secretary of foreign relations, and heard the whole story. Only a week earlier the government had received another resignation from Gates, and this time, happy to be rid of him, it accepted his withdrawal from his post.

Then Vay applied to Aguilar for a permit to excavate. The under secretary appeared agreeable to the idea, and all looked well. But the usual Latin-American complications and delays developed. Morley even gave an address at the Palacio Centenario in an attempt to create goodwill, but apparently that gesture had little effect. He asked for a permit, which would not require Merriam's signature, thus to save time. But when the document was finally approved and presented to him, he learned that it was a contract that required signatures on both sides. In addition, Guatemala withheld the privilege of taking artifacts out of the country, even for study in the United States. Friends advised Vay to accept the contract as it stood, and so he did.

Blom had a good field season in 1924. With twenty-two pack mules and a gang of laborers, he reached Uaxactún by the end of February. During the next two months he cleaned the site of brush and undergrowth, built houses for the staff and native workers, developed a water supply, and sketched all of the monuments and inscriptions. His feat of the season was the accidental discovery of a group of buildings that the Mayas had designed for astronomical purposes. On the return trip through the Petén he discovered a new site and visited fourteen others.

In September he returned to Harvard to complete his graduate study. Again Morley planned to send him to Uaxactún at the end of the semester; and again the cycle of anxiety and uncertainty began its course. As early as October there was news of trouble over the concession to work in Guatemala and also a problem with the Carnegie budget. By the middle of the month Vay gave up plans for Uaxactún and told Frans that he would add him to the staff at Chichén.

Blom was tired of this part-time arrangement. He wanted a job and a salary he could count on. William Gates, after leaving his post in Guatemala, was made head of the new Institute of Middle American Research at Tulane University, and he invited Blom to join his staff. Frans explained the situation to Morley and even submitted to him a draft of the letter he planned to send to Gates. Vay was heartbroken over the news, but he restrained himself and respected his friend's right to do as he saw fit; though he counseled careful, rational appraisal of the offer, he never advised Frans not to take the job. Finally, Blom accepted the Tulane proposal; and happily it did not affect his friendship with Morley. In fact, Frans went to the expense of a trip to Washington, which he could ill afford, just to say goodbye to Vay.

And so the year and a half of close association of these two men came to an end; they remained friends but no longer as close as they had been. Each went his own way, Morley to Chichén Itzá and Blom to New Orleans and years later to San Cristóbal in the heart of Mexico. Each made his contribution to Mexican archaeology.

When Morley went to Europe in the summer of 1924 to attend the meetings of the International Congress of Americanists, he visited Blom's father in Copenhagen and encountered Gates at the scientific sessions, though one can be sure that those two men spoke little to each other.

Unfortunately, Vay suffered from sickness during much of the sojourn, beginning with an attack of colitis the third day at sea. When he reached London, Gann, who accompanied him, put him to bed for a week, prescribed a strict diet, and warned him that on his return home he must receive hospital treatment. Before he recovered his strength, exposure to chilly air at garden parties and outdoor suppers in Göteborg caused bronchitis and a fever, and he spent almost a week in his room in Paris to get over that attack. Despite his ill health, however, he enjoyed the trip abroad.

The first session of the Congress met at The Hague, but it interested him little, because there were no papers on the Mayas. Although he had been sent to the Congress at the expense of the Carnegie Institution, he was nettled because William Gates, his enemy, claimed to be an official United States delegate; and Vay understood that the American government had made no such appointments. Other archaeologists from the United States were Spinden, Saville, J. Alden Mason, and Franz Boas. But Vay associated most with Adrián Recinos, then Guatemalan minister to France, Spain, and Portugal and also his nation's delegate to the Congress; for several weeks he and Adrián traveled together from city to city.

The second session, meeting in Göteborg, was more to his taste. Thomas Joyce came from the British Museum, Walther Lehmann from Germany, and Max Uhle, the authority on South American prehistory was present. Here Morley was delighted to meet Alfred Maudslay for the first time, and found him a charming septuagenarian who entertained his associates with colorful recollections of his explorations in Middle America at the end of the last century. And Vay was more than flattered when this dean of Maya archaeologists invited him to his home in England.

On August 20, the first day of the Göteborg session, Morley arranged to give an illustrated lecture under the most favorable conditions. It was a plenary session, assuring him the largest audience; and he manipulated matters so that he would have an early place on the program before his hearers had been wearied by too many papers. Moreover, his slides had been made from recent photographs that he had prepared in Washington just a few days before leaving. In half an hour he explained the excavations at Chichén Itzá and invited the co-operation of individuals and institutions at the Maya research center that was to be set up there. He was far more excited by this presentation than by the scholarly paper on early Maya dates that he read several days later.

On the way to Göteburg he had stopped off at Copenhagen to

visit Frans Blom's family. The elder Mr. Blom gave him a royal welcome, breezed him through five museums and entertained him at dinner at his country residence. Vay was duly impressed by all of the attention from this locally prominent man, while Blom was gratified that his son was working for the highly respected Carnegie Institution.

As Morley traveled from city to city and country to country, he was always alert to the passing scene despite his illness. With his customary enthusiasm he made the usual tourist's observations in letters to friends back home. England was a great, meticulously groomed garden; in Holland lush grass and grazing cattle suggested an abundance of milk, butter, and cheese; Germany, on the other hand, was down at the heel, though its people were fat. He poured out comments that ranged from the lack of pretty girls in Holland to the failure of the Germans to speak English or French.

If he found the travel refreshingly varied, it was an incidental pleasure compared with his joy over the Maya treasures he saw. In Holland he made a side trip from The Hague to view the Leyden Plate. As he held the eight-inch jadeite plaque in his hands, he was thrilled to find it far more attractive than any of the casts of it; it bore the oldest recorded Maya date glyph, A. D. 61, according to the correlation he then employed, and was a rare object of Maya epigraphy, with remarkable artistry for such an early period. In Berlin he managed to gain access to the museum, but the objects were still crated from World War I days, and he saw nothing worth noting.

In company with Recinos and Gann, he went on to Dresden to examine the Dresden Codex. As he first peered into the glass case where it was displayed, he trembled with ecstasy at that masterpiece of Maya art and craftsmanship. All reproductions failed to capture the brilliant color, the clear black lines, and the firm drawing. If this was a product of the twelfth century, he asked himself, what heights did Maya art attain in the fifth and sixth centuries when that civilization flourished at its best?

He also planned to see the Maya items in the Trocadero and

the Bibliothèque Nationale in Paris, including the Peresianus Codex. And he arranged for a week's tour to Spain, mainly to view the Tro-Cortesianus Codex. Unfortunately, his comments on those experiences have not come to light.

X

At Chichén Itzá

EFORE the staff arrived at Chichén in 1924 for the first
season, Jerry O. Kilmartin, of the United States Geological Survey, went ahead as an advance guard. His task was
to put the place in shape, hire domestics, clear the area of the
Thousand Columns for excavation, and map the square mile that
contained the important ruins.

The day after he arrived, the Huerta revolt flared up against
President Calles. But even the overthrow of Governor Carrillo
in Yucatán did not affect Kilmartin, because he was able to carry
on his work without interference. General Broca, the new military governor, abided by the concession and even allowed the
gringo to buy the dynamite needed in his work.

Morley counted on time to solve the Mexican crisis. He spent
weeks in Guatemala negotiating a contract, then rushed back to
Washington to be on hand for Manuel Gamio's lectures, exhibition, and conference on archaeology, held by the Carnegie Institution on April 16 and 17. After the conference he attempted to
go to Yucatán, but in New Orleans he was delayed some ten
days, waiting for the first boat to sail for Progreso.

During the enforced delay he encountered some Yucatecan
exiles in the lobby of the St. Charles Hotel. Among them were
his old friends Felipe Cantón, Leopoldo Ponce, and Felipe Solís.

They stoutly denied complicity in Carrillo's murder and also whitewashed General Broca. Somewhat lamely, they claimed that certain subordinates had admitted responsibility for the deed. Whoever was to blame, Morley considered it a brutal act. Somehow the exiles seemed to protest too much.

Morley, Monroe Amsden, Earl Morris, and his wife Ann arrived at Chichén on Sunday, May 18, to start the project. Vay felt an air of anticipation tinged with sentiment. They got off to a good start as Jimmy Chan, the cook, welcomed the party with a fine meal. Then they planned how they would use the sixty-nine workers who would show up the next morning. That night Earl, Ann, and Vay drove down to the Sacred Cenote, walking the last 150 feet so as not to desecrate the spot with a modern automobile, to view the mysterious pool by moonlight. It occurred to Vay that every time he returned to Chichén it was more wonderful and more magnificent. Back at the Casa Principal, where he tried to go to sleep on the hard cot on the porch, he found it difficult to believe that the great plan was at last under way. He concluded that if a man desires a reasonable goal and works hard enough to achieve it, he will win.

The first task was to make the place suitable as the headquarters for fieldwork. Back in 1921 some local natives had ravaged the buildings, and Thompson had been unable to recover from that blow. When Vay arrived, he found the Casa Principal a pigsty, and he ordered the whole building put into good shape. The nearby church of San Isidro had lost its roof, and so he put men to work covering it. He had a bell hung in one of the openings of the belfry and ordered it to be rung at six, eleven, one, and four-thirty. Soon structures were erected to house the native workers who came from a distance. Equipment arrived by rail from Mérida to Dzitas, and from there it had to be hauled seventeen miles over a rough road to Chichén. A gasoline pump and a pressure pump were installed, a photographic laboratory was set up in the sacristy of the church, and the Casa Principal received a coat of cream-colored paint.

Accommodations for the staff were simple but adequate. Some

lived in the main house and others in the bachelors' quarters in two modest thatched-roof stone structures on the grounds near the Casa Principal. Orange trees marked the paths from one building to another; and near the main building someone erected a stone *atlante* figure from the ruins, supporting a stone *metate*, perhaps an appropriate if somewhat curious touch. During the first two weeks Vay slept in the corridor of the Casa Principal until his quarters could be properly prepared in the Monjas. Not until he brought his new wife to Chichén in 1927 was a modern residence constructed for him.

Diversion and entertainment were also simple and restricted. Vay, addicted as always to the phonograph, played the raucous "Tiger Rag" so often after dinner at night that the other members had their fill of the repetitious cacophony. When he attempted to round up a fourth for bridge, the younger men tried to dodge out of sight, because they found that that game, despite Vay's relish of it, also became extremely monotonous. After a day's work in the warm, dry season, the junior archaeologists sometimes joined natives for a swim in the *cenote* of Xtoloc. There was also the fortnightly trip to Dzitas for the payroll. At first Vay, flanked by a Winchester shotgun, was driven over the rocky road to meet the old-fashioned train that brought the 1,500 silver pesos from Mérida for payday. Soon, however, he relinquished the job to one or two of the young men, who enjoyed the trip as a welcome change from routine. By 1932 the fortnightly payroll for native labor amounted to 3,000 pesos.

Evening dinner at the Casa Principal provided the only occasion when all of the staff members came together. Dinner was good because Vay insisted on tasty dishes and had an excellent cook in Jimmy Chan. As the members of the team relaxed over the leisurely meal, Vay presided at the head of the table and provided much of the conversation. Any chance remark easily set him off on a train of reminiscences or a series of humorous anecdotes; and sometimes the conversation turned to hot arguments on a disputed point of archaeology. Generally, the atmosphere was lighthearted and gay, as befitted the end of a day's work. Since little other entertainment was available, the evening dinner became the focus for celebrations.

Music in the Ball Court provided another form of relaxation and enjoyment. Shortly after the 1924 season got under way, Vay had the phonograph taken to the Ball Court and placed in the temple at the far end, and the auditors sat on the platform five hundred feet away. The strains of Kreisler's violin, despite the thin tone, traveled perfectly down through the space between the thirty-foot-high walls. Vay was delighted, but he had to admit that for carrying quality "It Ain't Gonna Rain No More" was the best piece. He concluded the celebration of his birthday on June 7 with a concert in the Ball Court that included phonograph records and also a violin performance by Eduardo Martínez, inspector of ruins for Yucatán. Thereafter, music in the Ball Court became standard entertainment, especially for visitors. As time passed, Vay adopted the policy of playing only classical records there, because he felt that popular music did not comport with the dignity of the venerable ruins.

The living quarters were serviced by a number of domestics. By 1925 there were, in addition to the cook, three houseboys, two laundresses, and a gardener. In the early years Vay acquired Tarsisio Chang, a Korean, who quickly became *mayordomo* of the establishment. He was an able and versatile man, credited with ability in barbering, tinsmithing, watchmaking, and even some sleight-of-hand; and on an expedition Vay found him a perfect *arrerio*. The servants received respectable wages, but like any other employer Vay did not want to be cheated. After settling down at Chichén for the 1925 season, he discovered that through a miscalculation he was grossly overpaying Jimmy Chan, and he proceeded to correct the mistake. On the other hand, the fact that Jimmy occasionally got drunk on anise was almost to be expected, and Vay quietly overlooked the indiscretion.

The native laboring force that was used for archaeological excavation and repair varied in size and quality. Generally, there were fifty to one hundred men employed in the work. Just after the season began in 1925 with sixty-nine workers, the number jumped to eighty-two. But when Vay returned after a brief absence he discovered to his consternation that the foreman had gone on hiring natives until 215 were on the payroll. Vay worked on a close budget, and what was more, he could not manage that many men. The next day he called 133 of them into the yard of the Casa Principal, explained that they had been taken on by mistake, paid them off and added a gratuity, and sent them away in good humor. He realized that he might need them in the future. Gradually he reduced the work gang to forty-nine and then to thirty-three.

The natives were energetic and willing to carry out their tasks. Although they were unskilled, Earl Morris knew how to choose the most capable men for the more delicate jobs. Small in build but with strong bodies, these Indians sometimes labored in oppressive heat and stifling interiors, always without complaint. They resisted only when they were faced with unfamiliar techniques. Morris constructed a labor-saving contraption by which excavated dirt could be wheelbarrowed to a high platform and dumped into a truck. At first, the natives refused to push their vehicles to the high platform. Then the resourceful Norwegian Stromsvik angrily asked them if they were old women, and they courageously made the first trip to the platform; thereafter, there was no trouble.

During the first season Morley had few visitors to disturb his routine. Alma Reed and Pilar Carrillo showed up twice, with Susan Treadwell from the *New York Tribune* joining them on the second jaunt. Alma and Susan were sniffing about for journalistic material. Alma, garbed in an exploring outfit, smilingly posed atop the Pyramid of the High Priest, poised to descend the hole that Thompson had opened years before. Actually she refused to go down, but had her picture taken for publicity purposes. Why she, who had been so ardently in love with Governor Carrillo, joined his widow on these visits is hard to understand. The last day of the season President-elect Calles paid a visit to the site, much to Vay's gratification.

During the next season more officials appeared. Governor Iturralde of Yucatán showed up one day with an American newspaper woman, and Vay went to the trouble of dressing in white to greet him. A few days later Mariano Vallegos, *presidente municipal* of Dzitas, came to see what was going on, and he promptly fell in love with Edith Bayles, Morley's secretary. In true native style, he sent a group to serenade her at night, much to the annoyance of the staff members who wanted their rest. Merriam, Kidder, and Clark Wissler arrived in February for a ten-day stay, and were greeted with an elaborate lunch and a cake decorated with the hieroglyph 15 Zac to celebrate the occasion. This time Vay was too ill to show his guests about the grounds, and he soon left for Touro Infirmary in New Orleans.

Occasionally E. H. Thompson came, creating headaches for Vay and the C. I.W. Merriam decided to pay him $1,200 a year rent for use of the buildings and one hundred acres of land on the hacienda, which was a generous rent according to Mexican standards. It turned out that Thompson was at the end of his financial rope. He pestered Vay for advances on the rent, which Vay refused; but he gave him a personal loan of $200 just to keep him on his feet and to avoid any hitch in the plan to use his hacienda. Then the question of encumbrance on the property came up, and Thompson admitted that he had not paid taxes on Chichén or on a house in Pisté for years; in the end the C. I.W. paid $400 he owed in delinquent taxes.

Thompson's situation became critical in 1926, when the Mexican government brought suit against him for smuggling valuable objects, taken from the Sacred Cenote, out of the country to the United States. The government estimated those objects to be worth $500,000 and seized his hacienda. This action made Carnegie officials somewhat uncertain about the continued use of his property. But the government did not interfere with the Chichén project, and Thompson continued to receive his $1,200 a year, the sole income to support him and his wife.

By the end of the 1924 season, Vay decided that it was high time to remove any criticism of his own possession of objects from the Sacred Cenote. The previous year had provided warning signals. Early in 1923, Thompson had publicly admitted taking artifacts out of the country. Then in August, after Vay and Gann were safely across the Río Grande, Gann showed him a beautiful jade plaque he had brought from Mexico, neatly sewed in the back of his coat. Later Gamio in Mexico City learned of Gann's exploit and was furiously angry over the incident.

Vay owned two items from the Sacred Cenote, an anthropomorphic pendant and a little gold bell surmounted by a bird. He had bought them in 1909 on his second visit to Mexico. Now he had copies of them made, and formally presented the originals to Reygadas for the Mexican government. In his diary Vay explained his action on the basis of Merriam's action: in February, 1923, when the dignitaries visited Chichén, Merriam found a little gold bell clapper on the banks of the Sacred Cenote; though everyone in the party urged him to keep it, he turned it over to Thompson. But Vay did not add the stronger reason that Merriam later refused to hire Gann as physician at Chichén because he had broken Mexican law by smuggling out the jade plaque. Merriam insisted that all C. I. W. workers in Mexico must be above reproach.

After three years of a bachelor's existence at Chichén Itzá, Morley married. In 1926, when he bounced into Santa Fe on July 1, he called his friends the Thorntons on the phone to inform them of his arrival. At the other end of the line was a strange, rather intriguing voice, and he soon learned that it belonged to Frances Rhoads, a guest. He was eaten up with curiosity. A few days later he dined with the Thorntons and met Frances for the first time. Vay fell in love with her at once, completely captivated and knowing in his soul that this was the woman he had been waiting for. Carefully, he laid plans for marriage, including a trip to Rock Island, Illinois, to gain her father's consent.

He took her to Chichén the following March for an engagement ceremony that he had planned as a unique event. On March 19, 1907, he had first examined the Castillo, that giant pyramid that dominates Chichén, and now he chose the same day and the same place for the engagement. At sunset he helped her to climb the ninety steps of the structure, with Dr. Hewett and Jesse Nusbaum, both old-time friends, accompanying them. There on the sum-

mit against the background of Maya splendor and the fading light
of day he presented the engagement ring he had fashioned in
Mexico City according to his own design. The next day he celebrated the event with a party for the visitors and staff members
and arranged a fiesta for the native workers who were completing
his house.

In turn the staff members, who had been in on the secret for
some time, made their own contribution to the occasion. That
night after dinner everyone adjourned to the north temple of the
Ball Court, where the staff staged a pageant depicting the story of
Chichén Itzá; in the epilogue they caricatured Morley and Earl
Morris in the act of discovering and restoring the Temple of the
Warriors. Costumes, music, and lighting combined to make this
the spectacular climax of the celebration of the engagement.

Frances and Vay returned to the States and went to Rock
Island, where they were married on July 14. It was a small affair,
with only members of the family, Mrs. Thornton, and Paul Martin
present. Martin, a young archaeologist and friend of Vay, acted
as best man.

Once more Vay re-established domestic life. There was a difference in age—Frances was twenty-nine and he was forty-four—
but it did not matter; the two were deeply devoted to each other
the rest of their lives. They went to Chichén and took up residence in the new house not far from the Casa Principal. The
structure was small, comfortable, and equipped with the conveniences of modern living. In fact, it was a luxurious oasis in the
Yucatecan bush. Bachelor days were over for Vay, but he was
more than happy to resume married life. At last, he knew there
was someone to love him and care for him, a yearning that had
gone unfulfilled for more than twelve years. Whatever freedoms
he gave up in the new arrangement, he surrendered most willingly.

Frances brought a feminine touch to Chichén Itzá. She managed the servants, planned the meals for the staff, and began to
take an interest in the native children. Vay's work also engrossed
her, and she quickly became adept in photography and accompanied him on archaeological expeditions. She watched over him,

keeping him calm and reminding him to eat his food when he became too animated in talking at the dinner table. Staff members noticed no change in his friendly, frank relations with them, but they were conscious that he was no longer as free to mix with them as formerly.

Vay had a sentimental tenderness for the Mayas. When he and Karl Ruppert visited the camp of the University of Pennsylvania at Yaxchilán in 1931, Luis, one of the native workers there, greeted both men as old friends he had known at Chichén. Though Vay and Karl did not recognize him, they indicated they did. Later Vay explained that he would never let a native lose face among his fellows for such an innocuous lie.

Another illustration of Morley's reactions occurred in the same year, when Vay became angry with the worker Petuch. The Fox movie cameramen were at Chichén shooting material for a short educational picture in which Morley made comments in front of the prominent structures at the site. Stromsvik tells the story. "Some of the boys were not exactly helpful and would play tricks on Morley, like driving past where he was talking, with a truck-full of rattling tools; this made him very nervous and irritable. To be prepared to give a talk at the Caracol, he had to come down to the hacienda house to look up some references. He was driven about in the sidecar of the motorcycle, chauffeured by an overgrown Indian we called 'Petuch' (Monkey). He told Petuch that he would be ready to be taken back to the Caracol in fifteen minutes, then went into the hacienda house to find his references. In the meantime, Angelino, the head mason, came out from the *bodega* [storage room] with a tackle, urgently needed at the Mercado, then under reconstruction. Petuch thought he could easily take the gear up to the Mercado and be back at the time Morley had set. Morley heard the motorcycle roar out of the yard, rushed out on the porch, and started calling after Petuch with all his might, but, of course, he could not be heard against the roar of the open exhaust. He paced up and down the corridor, raving mad with fury. Petuch came back in about five minutes.

"Morley jumped on him; grabbed his shoulder and shook the

hulking big fellow and really boiled over in scolding the poor devil out. He ended up with 'You are fired; do you hear, fired. Get off the hacienda immediately.' Petuch slunk away to his quarters crying. Morley, feeling better, finished the Caracol speech to his liking and came back to the hacienda all smiles and satisfaction. I told him that I thought he had treated Petuch very rudely and unjustly, and that he was now lying in his hammock crying his heart out. Morley grabbed my arm and said, 'Oh, I'm so sorry, let's go and see Petuch.' Morley sat himself in the hammock beside the desolate Indian and told him about his nerves and how angry he had been at the fellows that were playing tricks on him, and that he just had to explode when Petuch didn't stop when he called out, but he (Petuch) mustn't mind, everything was all right again. Petuch got up from his hammock, all smiles and happy, feeling quite proud of having nearly had his hide burned off by the fire of Morley's tongue."[1]

When official visitors came to Chichén Itzá, the Morleys were their hosts, acting in the name of the Carnegie Institution. If it was the guest's first visit, Vay gave him a personal tour of the whole site, taking him from structure to structure and talking continuously about the Mayas in a monologue that combined information with enthusiasm and spontaneous humor. Although he had made the tour dozens of times, his remarks always had the zeal and freshness of a first performance.

He also showed new staff members over the site regardless of the work they came to perform, and one never knew when the unexpected might occur. One Sunday morning in January, 1929, he was escorting some new staff members among the ruins, including a young woman who was sent to aid the natives in public health. When the party reached the Temple of the Phalli in Old Chichén, and Morley casually mentioned that phallic rites might have been carried on in the ancient days, the young lady sidled up to him and asked sheepishly, "What is a phalli?" He was delighted to give her the information.

The important event of every day continued to be dinner at the

[1] *Morleyana,* 243-44.

Tikal, with Temple II in the foreground. Courtesy Peabody Museum, Harvard University.

The walled city of Tulum, on the eastern coast of Yucatán, which Morley risked life and limb to explore. Courtesy University Museum of the University of Pennsylvania.

Uxmal, as seen from the air. The long façade of the Governor's Palace is in the center foreground. Courtesy University Museum of the University of Pennsylvania.

Tatiana Proskouriakoff's reconstruction of Temple E–VII sub at Uaxactún. It was Morley who first made it possible for her to execute a series of drawings of buildings in the Maya area. From Tatiana Proskouriakoff, *An Album of Maya Architecture.*

Miss Proskouriakoff's drawing of the reconstruction of Chichén Itzá. From Tatiana Proskouriakoff, *An Album of Maya Architecture*.

Morley at the Temple of the Initial Series, Chichén Itzá. Courtesy J. Eric S. Thompson.

The Morleys (left) and the Eric Thompsons at Chichén Itzá in 1930.
From J. Eric S. Thompson, *Maya Archaeologist*.

Morley and John Bolles designed the costumes for a Maya fiesta at Chichén Itzá, 1931. In this picture, the Morleys are in the background. Courtesy John Bolles.

Casa Principal. Vay was an unabashed gourmand, and he saw to it that the Chinese cook provided delectable and sometimes exotic dishes. When the staff was large and there were visitors, there might be twenty or more persons at the table. Vay and Frances presided at the head "like royalty," as someone remarked.[2] One visitor remembered the archaeologists J. Alden Mason and Karl Ruppert, the linguistic specialist Manuel Andrade, and the sociologist Robert Redfield, all of them engaged in work for the C. I.W. The conversation was stimulating and unpredictable, Morley leading but not dominating the exchange of anecdotes, experiences, and witty remarks. In moments of absentmindedness or in order to illustrate a point, he drew figures on the white tablecloth. When he became so animated in discussing a subject that he neglected the food before him, Frances tugged at his sleeve and reminded him to eat. He did so quickly and dutifully, only to resume the discussion as soon as possible.

Everyone was conscious of the hawk-eye watch Frances kept on his eating. One visiting artist memorialized the habit with an imitation Maya lintel, depicting Vay seated cross-legged, a favorite posture of his, before a bowl with glyphs reading, "Vaynus eat your spinach."

He was deeply in love with Frances and did not hesitate to display his affection before his associates and guests. Between remarks he would casually lean over and give his wife an ardent kiss. Margretta Dietrich tells what happened one night: "Dr. and Mrs. Francis I. Proctor were also at the hacienda, and Dr. Proctor liked a joke. He persuaded some of us to kiss our right hand neighbor when Vay kissed Frances. Dr. Proctor led off by kissing his wife, Elizabeth kissed the astonished scientist at her right who caught on and kissed his neighbor. It wasn't necessary to go very far, for Sylvanus was quick to see the point and laughed uproariously. I do not remember that it reformed him."[3]

If it were a moonlight night and he wanted to give his guests a special treat, he ordered a phonograph concert in the Ball Court.

[2] *Morleyana*, 58.
[3] *Morleyana*, 58.

Tarsisio and the servants set up the phonograph in the north temple, where the back wall slopes forward and forms a perfect sounding board. At the opposite end of the court the servants supplied cushions and the guests sat on a raised dais among the half-ruined pillars of the south temple that extends eighty feet across the end of the Court. The acoustics were amazing, for the audience could hear perfectly the strains of Sibelius, Brahms, and Beethoven.

The total effect was indescribable. The brilliant Yucatecan sky formed a great overhead dome, the moon cast ghostly light on the stone walls and the north temple, and the calm air, rarely disturbed by a breeze, added a sense of mystery to the setting. After the performance the guests, awed by the uncanny effect, walked quietly back to the Casa Principal through the moonlight, still under the magic spell.

One of the visitors in 1931 was Leopold Stokowski, who spent four days with Morley. He brought the latest recordings of his Philadelphia Symphony Orchestra and played them in the Ball Court, at the Castillo, and at the Temple of the Warriors. One staff member believed that if Stokowski "and Morley could have found a sponsor, their plan to conduct a symphony with instruments all over the place would have gone through. We'd have loved it too."[4] Actually, Stokowski had a far more serious purpose, as he and Morley attempted to learn the acoustical secret of the Ball Court. At the time, the conductor was designing an open-air theater for concert work. He and Vay spent hours placing the phonograph in different positions in the Ball Court in order to determine the reflecting surfaces. Theoretically, the structure should have had poor acoustics, but as every visitor to Chichén knows, it possesses amazing properties of sound. After days of experiment, they failed to learn the secret, which remains one of the unsolved mysteries of ancient America. Stokowski and Morley respected and liked each other; Vay was captivated by the conductor's great personal charm, and Stokowski in turn was equally

---

[4] John S. Bolles to the author.

impressed by Vay's enthusiasm for the Mayas and his warm-heartedness.

By the early 1930's Morley was becoming selective about whom he wished to entertain, largely because of the drain on his time and energy. After young John Bolles became a staff member, he had an interesting experience in this respect. "One morning I met a pleasant Mexican couple on the train from Mérida to Dzitas," Bolles explains. "After a few beers and tortillas at stops, I finally offered them a ride to the Inn where they were to stay—two rooms run by Fernando Barbachano—and on the way, extended an invitation to dinner at the hacienda. Morley was furious—unknowns, etc., since I had failed to get their names. When they arrived I greeted them, said I was sorry I had not caught their names, and choked with laughter when I had the pleasure of introducing Miguel Covarrubias to Morley. All was forgiven!"[5]

Another visitor who delighted Morley was Nicolay Vavilov, prominent Russian plant geneticist. The scientist believed that corn originated in southern Mexico or Central America and that the *milpa* system was the only form of agriculture ever practiced by the Mayas. Vay was delighted to find such eminent confirmation of his own cherished views. A decade later Vavilov, an opponent of Lysenko, died in a concentration camp in Siberia.

On several occasions President Merriam dissuaded visitors from going to Chichén. Frans Blom called on him in February, 1927, to ask if he and Dorothy Dix, the famed lovelorn columnist, might visit the site. Blom explained that she wanted to publish popular material and suggested that such articles would stir up interest in Chichén. Merriam thought otherwise. He was horrified at the thought of Dorothy Dix's writing about Chichén, and he attempted to argue Frans out of the idea. Apparently he succeeded for the time being; however, she visited the place some years later. Even when a representative from the Milwaukee Museum asked Merriam for permission to go to Chichén to prepare for a Maya exhibit in his museum, he was advised to wait until the work there

[5] John S. Bolles to the author.

had progressed further. And wait he did. He finally got to Chichén in 1937—ten years later.

The problem of entertaining guests gave rise to the famous incident that illustrates Vay's careless pronunciation of Spanish. The story centers on the words *ocho*, eight, and *otro*, another. One day Tarsisio shepherded eight Orientals out from Mérida to work at Chichén, and he proudly appeared at Vay's office with the men:

"Do'tor Morley, here are the eight Chinese."

"Eight Chinese! What do they want?"

"Well, Do'tor Morley, you told me that as many guests were coming, we needed eight Chinese."

"No, *hombre!* I told you *otro chinos*. Not *ocho chinos, otro chinos*."

"No, Do'tor Morley, you told me *ocho chinos*."[6]

The argument continued, and Vay finally insisted on returning seven disappointed Orientals to Mérida.

More and more visitors flocked to Chichén Itzá as the years passed by. Apparently it had become the place to go, for in 1929 *The New York Times* carried an article headed, "Society Group to Sail to View Maya Ruins," and the destination, of course, was Chichén, where Morley was working. He reported to his chief that he was swamped with guests, filling six pages of a single-spaced letter describing them. One count shows that by April, 1932, he had entertained 109 so far that season, and the Institution set aside a special fund of $600 to cover the expense. By 1935 he had given up the personal tour of the ruins for all comers, treating them to a lunch or dinner and perhaps a Ball Court concert. One person who attended such a concert in the late 1930's felt that the Morleys were fastidious about whom they invited; it was doubtless sheer numbers that required them to be as selective as possible.

Even after Morley curtailed entertainment, he was carefully attentive to distinguished guests. He went out of his way to give attention to the chief of the military zone, the manager of the bank in Mérida, the under secretary of the Mexican federal treasury, and a former governor of Campeche; and especially did he

[6] *Morleyana*, 152.

cultivate the inspector and assistant inspector of monuments for Yucatán.

He made a particular effort to interest Josephus Daniels, United States ambassador to Mexico, to visit Chichén Itzá. When Vay attended a scientific meeting in Mexico City in September, 1935, he and Frances were dinner guests at the embassy, and he soon realized that the Danielses were contemplating such a trip. At once Vay informed Merriam and suggested that he send a special invitation.

Six months later Morley suddenly learned that the Danielses were almost at his doorstep. The Mérida newspaper announced that a group of notables, including Daniels, had already landed at Progreso. Fifty-two persons from the diplomatic corps in Mexico City and from the Mexican ministry of foreign relations were on a special excursion. Hurriedly Vay wired an invitation to the whole group to have tea at Chichén Itzá three days later, and he sent a personal invitation to the Danielses to stay as long as they wished. During the visit Daniels was impressed most by Morley's account of Maya architecture, as they passed from building to building, and of the astronomical knowledge of the ancients, illustrated by the star-studded Yucatecan sky above. It was Vay's ability to weave a magic spell that entranced the ambassador.

Morley also like to have his relatives visit Chichén, and at Christmas time in 1939 members of his family and of Frances' joined in a grand get-together. This was his last Christmas there; in a few months he was scheduled to move headquarters to Mérida. His daughter, her husband, and their two children were among the guests. Vay showed them over the ruins and then took them to Uxmal for a similar inspection. On Christmas night he staged a fiesta. He invited natives from Pisté and Chan Kom for the dancing and secured an eight-piece orchestra that performed only native music. Periodically, Tarsisio plied the musicians with rum to keep them in top form; eventually, the liquor took its toll, though not before everyone had had a good time.

When there were no guests to entertain and Vay could spare time from his regular duties, he and Frances looked after the

Maya natives who swarmed about the place. Without children of their own, they found the young generation particularly appealing. Frances became interested in the deficiencies of their diet, brought vitamins on the annual trip from the States, and advised the natives to eat more fruits. When Vay took a liking to a Maya boy who showed promise, he would take him to his home in Santa Fe for schooling. One such lad, after this experience, returned to Chichén Itzá to become the favorite guide of American tourists. Vay's philosophy was to help the individuals to become self-reliant. So popular was he among them that he eventually became godfather to more than a score of children, a position that carried responsibility according to the native custom.

In the later 1920's, Nina Piatt became his secretary. Her recollections throw additional light on his habits:

"He was very absent minded about little things, had great difficulty in locating items on his desk, leaving his walking stick, fountain pen, or even hat wherever he might stop on his way to work or while out of the office, and one of my almost daily tasks was to locate these articles. It soon became relatively simple, at least in Santa Fe, as some of his friends would call me and tell me he had left something.

"Much of his dictation of letters or reports was given with him pacing the floor, twirling his mustache, poking at office furniture, etc., with his walking stick, or leaning over one's shoulder to watch the stenographic writing or typewriting; interrupted with personal asides and related remarks. He loved to chew on butterscotch candy and 'candy corn' too while at his work. These so typical characteristics seemed to make him more human, and never an impersonal employer."[7]

Vay was fortunate in the choice of archaeological assistants who helped him in the early stages of the Chichén Itzá project. In the first season Earl Morris was his major assistant, the second season he added Ruppert and Ricketson, and then from 1926 the staff increased and the scholarly research spread into additional fields.

Earl Morris was a first-rate man in his personal relations and

[7] *Morleyana*, 200.

in his professional work. Born in New Mexico and educated at the University of Colorado, where he majored in psychology, he happened to meet E. L. Hewett one day on a train, succumbed to that man's persuasive charm and attractive visions of the future, and was converted to archaeology. He interrupted his college career to go into the field, and in 1912 had worked under Morley at Quiriguá, bringing his fever-ridden superior safely out of Copán. He received the A.B. in 1914 and later began graduate work at Columbia University, but gave it up in favor of fieldwork in the Southwest. By 1924 he was thirty-five years old, with a new wife—he had married Ann Axtel the preceding September—who accompanied him to Chichén Itza, where she soon demonstrated ability as an artist.

Morley and Morris got along together splendidly. Vay had seen Earl in operation as a tyro at Quiriguá; now he marveled at him as a natural-born excavator. In the field he knew what he was about, had an instinctive feel for the work, and dug swiftly and accurately; sometimes the slower-moving Maya laborers exasperated him, and he grabbed a shovel and went at the work himself. Practical in his outlook and in the solution of problems as they occurred, he considered Vay naïve and addicted to fantastic schemes, but he was fond of him and admired his fire and enthusiasm. Vay in turn usually deferred to Earl's good judgment, as was evident in the excavation of the Temple of the Warriors.

The most spectacular achievement of the early years was the work of Earl Morris, whose hunches and ability transformed a nondescript mound into a magnificent structure right in the center of Chichén.

Unusual circumstances marked the choice of the mound to be excavated. Early in February, 1925, Morley and Morris were looking forward to the visit of President Merriam, and they wanted to have something striking to show him. By arrangement with the Mexican government, the Carnegie archaeologists had agreed to work first on the Court of the Thousand Columns. But those columns, row upon row of them, all the more visible since the bush had been removed, did not provide anything new or unusual.

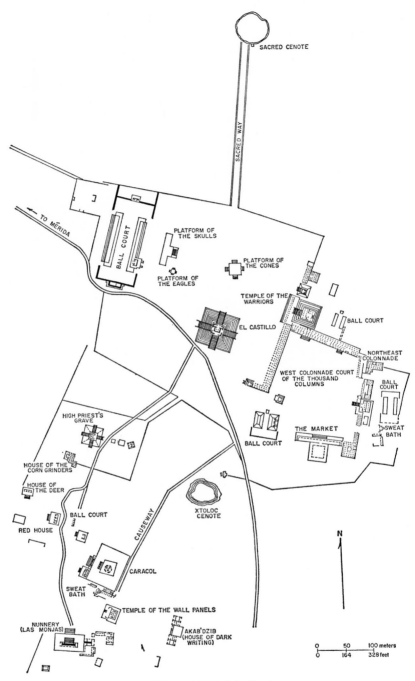

Plan of Chichén Itzá

At one end of the columns was a lofty mound covered with trees and bush; nothing had been done about it although it lay within the area open to excavation.

It was still early in the season and loads of equipment and supplies were being carried by auto from the railroad in Dzitas to Chichén. Late on Wednesday afternoon, January 28, when the last load had arrived, Morris discovered that a twelve-foot bar of tool steel had been lost somewhere along the road. That metal could be turned to too many uses to be given up, so Vay, Ann, and Earl, with the aid of two flashlights and a Coleman lantern, set out in the car during the rainy night to find it. Although the road was treacherous and they had a flat tire, they traveled straight on through to Dzitas. They found three sections of small pipe that had been lost along the road, but the steel bar eluded them, and they returned without it. Several days later a native brought it in for the small reward he would receive.

During the dreary journey Vay and Earl discussed possible sites to uncover in time for Merriam's visit. Morris spoke up for the large untouched mound.

"But, Earl, have we had enough experience to tackle such a job?" queried Vay, conscious that they had just begun the second season.

"I believe we can swing it."

"Well, old man, if you think so, go ahead," Vay agreed.[8]

Little was done about the mound for two weeks. Morley was sick and went into Mérida for nine days to consult Dr. Palma. Shortly after he returned, he went to look at the mound, which Morris had cleared of vegetation. The outlines were clear, but there was no indication of what lay underneath; Earl planned to begin excavation the following week.

On Saturday, February 14, Vay, Earl, and Ann, accompanied by a native workman, went to examine the mound in order to learn as much as possible before actual digging began. Looking up at the west end of the north side, Morris noticed a gray tree stump

---

[8] Earl Morris, *The Temple of the Warriors* (New York and London, Charles Scribner's Sons, 1930), 4; quotations from this book are used by permission of the publisher.

jutting out from its roothold in the covered stones. Ann got out her camera and began to ascend the side of the mound, with Earl following her. When he was within arm's length, he grasped the stump and pulled himself up to it; there he saw among its roots a carved stone two feet long and four inches wide. Obviously it was part of a sculptured column, and perhaps it was but one of numerous pieces, a fragment, scattered over the face of the mound. Using sticks, stones, and his hands to dislodge the dirt—he had not thought to bring a machete—he found a fine head with plumed headdress. It was cemented to another stone block below it, and he knew it was a column. With incredulous surprise, he concluded that it was the exposed part of another structure, an inner temple that had been filled in and covered when the outer temple was constructed. Morley recorded the event in his diary with restrained enthusiasm. Acknowledging that the discovery made the structure more interesting than had been expected, he realized that it also complicated Earl's work, because the inner temple had to be excavated without damaging the outer one.

Morris could not suppress his excitement. The next day, Sunday, when Morley was in Mérida for more medical treatment, Earl took a pick and dug down by the column, and at seven feet he came upon a red polished floor. That settled it; there was an older temple inside. On Monday workers began the excavation of the mound, and two days later Vay remarked that Earl was finding all kinds of things there.

Merriam, Kidder, and Wissler arrived a week later, and Morris had ready for them not a showpiece but the promise of a spectacular pyramid and temple that would emerge only after three seasons of work. Vay was too ill to meet the guests or to show them over the grounds. He agreed to return to the States for adequate medical diagnosis and treatment. But weak as he was, he would not leave without seeing the progress that had been made on the mound. He had a cot placed in the Dodge and was driven to the foot of the steep stairway that leads to the temple at the top of the mound. Then half a dozen strong natives hoisted the litter to their shoulders and bore him to the summit.

When he returned ten weeks later, now with the prospect of regaining his health, he remarked, "The old hill has looked up a bit since I saw it last. It's about time we decided what to call it."

"Temple of the Plumed Serpent it should be," Morris said offhandedly. But then he realized that the Castillo often bore that name. So as a second choice, he mentioned Temple of the Warriors.

"We could not make a better choice," concluded Vay.[9]

By the end of the 1925 season the major outlines of the Temple of the Warriors were disclosed. The structure covered two-thirds of an acre, rose thirty-seven feet, and had a majestic stairway thirty-four feet across that rose at the sharp angle of 66 degrees. On the top platform two striking columns representing feathered serpents greeted the beholder. The platform temple, sixty-nine feet on each side, had fallen in, with many stones bearing fresco pictures lying in a jumbled mass. It was necessary to assemble and copy them as soon as possible. Earl's wife Ann was hurriedly pressed into service as artist to make watercolor reproductions of the figures of priests, animals, serpents, and scenes of fighting and fishing. Educated at Smith College and then at the American School of Prehistoric Research in France, she had never sketched or painted before. Fortunately, she proved to have remarkable talent, and reproduced the figures from two hundred stones by the end of the season. Midway in her work occurred the unexpected and devastating hailstorm of April 14, which destroyed the frescoes on many stones; however, only twenty-three were lost, for she had recorded the others before the catastrophe.

Morley added Jean Charlot to the staff the following year to supplement the work of Ann Morris. Then in his late twenties, Charlot had been born in Paris, although he had Mexican ancestors on the maternal side. After service in the French army in World War I, he started his career as an artist in Mexico City and had already produced considerable work when he joined the Carnegie staff in 1926. For three years he made a detailed pictorial record of the artistic decorations of the Temple of the Warriors.

[9] Morris, *The Temple of the Warriors*, 61.

One of the archaeologists who helped in the restoration of the Temple of the Warriors was Karl Ruppert. He joined the project in 1925 and continued in Maya archaeology until his retirement in 1956. He was born and reared in the Southwest and educated at the University of Arizona, where he began to study archaeology under Byron Cummings and Neil Judd. Also an architect, thirty-three-year-old Ruppert was admirably equipped to work on the various structures at Chichén, beginning with the rebuilding of the front wall of the Temple of the Warriors, where he puzzled over the pieces of stone that had to be assembled in order to re-create the masks and panels of that façade.

Since he was shy, moody, hard to know, and self-effacing, it is not surprising that Morley gave him little notice in his diary. Ruppert did excellent work, but he disliked the social life in which Vay reveled. When his sinuses pained him, he withdrew from other people, almost to the point of rudeness. After Vay brought Frances to Chichén, for some reason Karl took a dislike to her and avoided her; at the evening dinners he took his place at the table as far from her as possible. Despite his eccentricities, Vay valued his professional performance.

When the Temple of the Warriors began to take shape in 1926, two men joined the staff who could not have differed more completely from each other. One was an English scholar and the other a Norwegian ship's carpenter. Both proved to be extremely useful in their respective fields and eventually made remarkable contributions to Maya archaeology.

The Englishman was twenty-eight-year-old J. Eric S. Thompson, trained under Professor Haddon at the University of Cambridge. After serving as a second lieutenant in the Coldstream Guards in 1918, he learned the Maya language and the decipherment of glyphs on his own. He wrote to Morley in 1925, explaining his qualifications, and at once Vay asked Oliver G. Ricketson and his wife to interview Thompson in London. Everybody was satisfied. When Thompson arrived at Chichén in January, 1926, he was conducted along the path to Old Chichén; first he heard a high-pitched voice and then met the short man under the tremendous straw hat. Vay put him to work under Earl Morris to puzzle out the scrambled pieces that formed the frieze on the Temple of the Warriors. And soon Vay made use of Thompson's knowledge of glyphs by sending him to Cobá to decipher stelae there. After several years at Chichén, Thompson became assistant curator of American archaeology at the Chicago Museum of Natural History; nine years later Vay was delighted to have him back as a permanent member of the Carnegie staff. Eventually, Thompson established a brilliant reputation for his knowledge of Maya hieroglyphs.

The man who solved many of the practical problems in restoring the Temple of the Warriors was Gustav Stromsvik, a colorful, blue-eyed Norwegian wanderer from the sea who seemed to appear from nowhere. Actually, he had deserted his ship at Progreso, went into Mérida, and heard of Americans working at Chichén.

"Well do I remember the first time I met Dr. Morley," Gustav wrote later. "It was on an afternoon during the first week of January, 1926, while he was having tea with some ladies on the porch of the hacienda house at Chichén Itzá. I barged right up to the tea table and asked if I might speak to Dr. Morley."

" 'I am Dr. Morley. What can I do for you?'

"I inquired how the chances were for a job.

" 'Well, what can you do?' said Morley.

"Having previously found out that houses were being built at Chichén Itzá and having had some experience in the building trade at sea, I promptly answered:

" 'I am a carpenter.'

"Morley jumped up and said, 'The very man we need; when can you start work?'

" 'Immediately,' I answered, 'but I have a companion, a blacksmith who also needs a job.'

"They did not need a blacksmith and I wouldn't stay unless my partner also got a job, and there we stalled. Meanwhile, the grapevine had informed Earl Morris how the situation stood, and he rushed up just as I started slowly to walk away.

" 'The carpenter we badly need,' he said, 'and the blacksmith might be turned into a plumber. Let's take them on and see how they work out.' "[10]

Stromsvik became one of the most valuable men on the project, for he was a genius at solving practical problems with amazing simplicity. Everybody liked him for his kind and even temper. Morris called him "a bit of flotsam from the sea but a nobleman at heart."[11] And everybody respected him for his mechanical ability. Morley became fond of Gustav, not only for his likable personality, but also because he could solve mechanical problems that mystified the Harvard graduate.

"From the very start I got along swimmingly with Morley," Stromsvik later recalled, "besides carpentering there were lots of odds and ends to be done around the place, and I became so much of a handyman that Morley apparently got the exaggerated idea that I could do anything. One morning, as I was tinkering under the big laurel tree in front of the office, he came rushing out, tearing his hair. 'Gus, the car leaves for Dzitas in fifteen minutes and I have to get some money out of the safe. Where I have left the key I can't imagine. You'll just have to open the safe for me.' Within the allotted time I managed to fashion a makeshift key that opened the 'safe'—a steel letter-filing cabinet. Morley, wholly satisfied, carefully locked the safe and carefully put the key in his pocket. The idea that I, a complete stranger, having first made one key, could very easily make another if so inclined, apparently never entered his mind."[12]

Stromsvik had one failing. For occasional relaxation he adopted the expedient common to many sailors everywhere by resorting to semiconsciousness for days on end. Vay knew when to overlook a weakness in a valuable man, and never complained of his habit. In later years Stromsvik carried out the brilliant restoration of the ruins of Copán.

Morley had an abiding faith in men, and those working under him were given latitude to develop their ability to the fullest. Even

[10] *Morleyana*, 240.
[11] Morris, *The Temple of the Warriors*, 64.
[12] *Morleyana*, 240–41.

the youngest staff member felt that he was on his own, and consequently did his best. Paul S. Martin came to Chichén Itzá in 1928 with only his graduate study and the smallest amount of field experience as training, but he soon discovered that he was treated with professional respect. "By great good fortune, after assisting Mr. Earl Morris on the reconstruction of the Temple of the Warriors," Martin later explained, "I was assigned the task of excavating a small, late building, located near the High Priest's grave. I was given my instructions, and I went to work with a crew of ten Maya laborers. Morley paid a daily visit to the dig, but he never tried to steal the show. It was my dig. He often skillfully and tactfully ventured suggestions, and I always felt free to go to him for advice. I wanted to do a superlative job because he had trusted me and given me freedom.

"Dr. Morley was so pleased with the results that he gave me a more important job—that of excavating the Temple of the Two Lintels in 'Old Chichén.' From time to time he would visit the work and make suggestions about digging or the restoration. I shall never forget the day that we discovered a lintel bearing hieroglyphics. I sent him a frantic message, and he rushed out to the site to see the inscription. The ensuing excitement and general rejoicing were terrific. . . .

"He never once tried to take from us bits of prestige that we had rightfully earned by dint of our own efforts. Rather, he endeavored to enhance our reputations by giving us more than our due."[13]

In 1928 another man joined the staff, H. E. D. Pollock, who knew little about Morley and equally little about archaeology. By arrangement Vay interviewed him at the Harvard Club in New York City in November, 1927. "In later years," recalled Pollock, "Vay often referred to 'that delicious dinner at the Harvard Club.' I have no remembrance whatever of the dinner—other than that we ate it—which indicates how engrossed I was in this amazing little man that was assessing my qualifications for work in the tropics." Pollock was surprised at "the personality that promptly

[13] *Morleyana,* 149–50.

and without hesitation unfolded before me that evening."[14] In turn Vay wanted to look over this twenty-seven-year-old who was willing to desert Wall Street for the forests of Uaxactún as a volunteer handyman.

When Pollock arrived in Belize several months later, he was struck by the wide range of Vay's acquaintances. Everywhere he heard the questions, "How is Morley? Where is he? Will he come here this winter?" "I was later to find," added Pollock, "that wherever one traveled in Mexico and Central America . . . the name of Morley was almost legendary. Tradesman, politician, Indian, aristocrat, from country, town, and city, all spoke of *el doctor* in tones of personal affection; and their number was legion."[15]

After the season closed at Uaxactún, Pollock and Ledyard Smith came out of the Petén, met George Vaillant at El Cayo, and proceeded to Belize, where Morley joined them for the trip back to the States in the *S. S. Gansfyord*, a 700-ton fruiter. "Our passenger list was an odd assortment," Pollock remembered, "the four archaeologists, a deaf Scotsman, several other Britishers from 'the Colony,' a fellow American or two. There must have ten or twelve in all, for my memory is that there were only eight berths for passengers and several people had to sleep on deck or in the combination lounge and dining room. Vay, who enjoyed the sea as the Devil likes Holy Water, went straight to his bunk and emerged only for brief moments during the voyage.

"These were the days of prohibition and we were returning to an arid land. With the exception of Morley, who was heavily engaged in *mal de mer* and in my experience was temperate in any case, no one neglected this final opportunity. But no one seized upon it with quite such avidity as Vaillant and our Scotch friend. Hour after hour, through the day and into the night, these two would sit across the table in the lounge, bottle between them, exchanging stories that sank to lower and lower levels as the trip pro-

[14] *Morleyana*, 203.
[15] *Morleyana*, 203–204.

gressed. . . . Mind you, the entire living space, cabins and lounge, was about twenty feet square, and the Scotsman was deaf. . . .

"Out of Vay's cabin came groans interspersed with comments, mostly expletive, on the latest story, occasional bursts of laughter when the humor of some tale overcame his seasickness. Now and then he could not resist propping himself on one elbow and reciting a story or anecdote of his own, an effort that was apt to end in dead silence on his part in contrast to the laughter that came from all sides. As we came up the mouth of the Mississippi early one morning, we ran into a bank of fog that at certain times of the year enshrouds the passes into the river. There we lay athwart the ground swell, waiting for the fog to lift. Back and forth, from side to side, rocked the ship. No one liked it very much and we all fell silent. From out of Morley's cabin there came in agonized and muted tones, 'Roll, you son of a bitch, roll!' "[16]

Another young man, who joined the staff in 1932, testified to Vay's helpfulness. "When I first went to Yucatán," Robert Wauchope recalled, "still a graduate student and a very anxious one, Morley displayed the personal interest in my work that he would have lavished on that of a distinguished colleague. He shared with me all his own ideas about the topic I was working on, and gave me suggestions as to places to visit and people to look up in my field."[17] Wauchope responded to this encouragement at the very time he needed it.

From 1926, a group of specialists converged on Chichén, some to help on the Temple of the Warriors and others to pursue projects of their own. Arthur Austin experimented with finding a method of removing the pictures from the stones on which they were painted. Kenneth Conant made archaeological drawings of reconstructions of the Warriors, the Caracol, and the Thousand Columns. The American Museum of Natural History sent Clarence Hay to look into the possibility of reproducing the façade of the Warriors. And F. I. Proctor used stereoscopic photography to copy hieroglyphic texts. Joe Spinden spent some time studying hiero-

[16] *Morleyana*, 204–205.
[17] Robert Wauchope to the author.

glyphic lintels, and Walther Lehmann copied murals and sculptures in the Temple of the Jaguars.

Morley concluded by the end of the 1927 season that the Temple of the Warriors was about finished, and he dreamed of a grand celebration to mark the event. The Carnegie officials, however, were cautious, for they realized that such an official act must be followed by turning the structure over to the Mexican government. In the end, however, Morley had his way. A celebration was scheduled for March 10, 1928, even though Merriam was unable to induce President Calles to attend.

In December, 1927, the Carnegie Institution held its annual exhibition in Washington, arranged by Vay, to show archaeological progress during the year. Earl Morris was present to answer visitors' questions, and during a lull in the activity his mind wandered back to his early experiences in the Southwest. There the kivas often had dedicatory offerings of small objects. And at the Temple of the Warriors he had found evidences of disks, shells, and jade in two corners of the structure. Then the thought struck him: did the Mayas have dedicatory caches in or near altars? He determined to look into that.

Three months passed before he had the opportunity to test his hunch. Merriam arrived in Chichén a few days before the ceremony of March 10. Casually Morris told him of his idea, and when Merriam showed interest, the two men, accompanied by Danyel, a careful excavator, set out to dig into altars. They tried four without success; some had already been rifled and others contained only the bones of a bird. As the noon bell rang, Merriam went to the Casa Principal for lunch, while Morris and Danyel went to the inner structure of the Temple of the Warriors to make a try at the spot where the altar had originally been placed. Danyel's slight digging revealed nothing, and he took off. At that moment Stromsvik and Charlot came to leave their implements, and Morris told them what he was up to. Once more he took the pick and sounded the floor. Suspecting a hollow sound, he made one thrust with the implement and broke into a cavity. The three men, on hands and knees, excitedly cleared away the dirt, and Earl raised a stone lid and saw some jade in a cylinder. Realizing that he had come upon an unusual find, he resisted the temptation to examine it at once. They covered the hole with Charlot's drawing board, locked the room, and went to lunch.

At the meal the men were unusually quiet and ate with suppressed excitement. Soon Vay sensed that something was up, and asked what it was. He and Merriam were told to come to the inner chamber after lunch. Expectancy was in the air, and word of something unusual quickly got around; about eighteen people assembled at the appointed time. Morris removed the drawing board and threw a flashlight on the contents of the cylinder. Carefully he removed a jade ball and some bird bones; then he gently brushed away the dust and stared upon a splash of brilliant blue color. Morley burst out that it was a turquoise mask, and he was impatient to see its size.

The beautiful disk, a find of the first order, was in delicate condition. The wooden base, to which the three thousand tesserae had been fastened, had disintegrated. The slightest jar would jumble the pieces and destroy the design. Half a dozen coats of waterproof glue were applied to hold them in place; and the stone cylinder was carefully raised and lashed to two poles, which were carried on the shoulders of several men to the Casa Principal. At once Merriam wired to the American Museum of Natural History to send Siochi Ichikawa to Chichén immediately to preserve the disk in its original form.

While the colorless stone cylinder with its remarkable work of art rested in the Casa Principal awaiting the arrival of Ichikawa, the ceremony of March 10 took place. A special train from Mérida brought dozens of persons, including the governor of Yucatán and officials from Mexico City, who assembled in front of the Temple of the Warriors at eleven in the morning. Merriam gave the principal address, and some of the visiting dignitaries added brief remarks. Leaving the hot sun, the guests and their wives, a group of sixty in all, had luncheon in the corridor of the Casa Principal. Then two hundred Mayas from neighboring towns performed native dances, included the "O Jarana." It was a gay and gala occasion, the sort of thing Morley reveled in. Newspapers added, perhaps as a journalistic touch, that Doña Victoria sacrificed a black hog.

In response to Merriam's plea, Ichikawa arrived at the end of a week and went to work on the delicate task of saving the disk. With patience, skill, and resourcefulness, he labored over the complicated problem of preserving the design and form of the artistic treasure. In six weeks he accomplished the job of transferring the tesserae to a wooden base similar to the one it had originally been mounted on. The design showed a stylized plumed serpent constructed with brilliantly colored, perfectly shaped, minuscule pieces of turquoise. Ichikawa's restoration was a masterpiece excelled only by the artistic creation of the disk itself.

Morley gloried in this magnificent example of ancient art. He gave a lecture at the Peón Contreras Theater in Mérida and had the disk on exhibition for the event. Soon, however, he had to surrender it. The Carnegie concession was specific on that point, that all objects must be turned over to the Mexican government. And on July 7 he delivered the disk to the under secretary of public education in Mexico City. A few years later Morley could not forgive John Bolles who, as a young archaeologist feeling his oats, called Vay's attention to the fact that the "reconstruction" did not have the same number of petals as shown in the photograph of the disk taken *in situ*.

In the latter part of 1928 the International Congress of Americanists met in New York City. What could be more appropriate than to have the disk on display for the delegates and for North Americans? Thereupon opened another chapter in the history of the turquoise mosaic. It was carefully packed and taken by the Mexican delegation on board the *Monterrey*, which stopped at Progreso to pick up one or two additional delegates. Scarcely had the vessel left that port when a fire aboard forced the passengers to land again. When that danger had passed and the ship remained undamaged, the delegates set out once more and passed into the Atlantic. On September 16, the passengers celebrated the great Mexican national holiday with champagne, *vivas*, and merrymaking. Then a violent storm broke over the vessel, a hurricane that battered the *Monterrey* up and down the ocean for five days and nights. When the ship finally made port at New York, it was four days after the end of the congress. There on the pier was Morley waiting to greet his Mexican friends and the treasured disk. A special session of the congress was called to give the delayed delegates the opportunity to present their papers; and then they went to Washington for a round of dinners and receptions. The disk was placed on exhibition in the building of the Carnegie Institution on P Street.

When the delegation and the disk returned to Mexico, the turquoise object was placed in the National Museum of Anthropology. There it hangs today in one of the display cases in the Maya section with no indication of its discovery or its history.

XI

People and Places

AFTER Vay and Frances settled down to the comforts of civilized living in their $10,000 house at Chichén Itzá, Morley lost his zest for the crudities of camp life in the bush. In the years that followed he did go on several expeditions, but he carried with him all of the conveniences of modern living that he could drag along. As a result his baggage was voluminous.

He led a small expedition to Copán in April, 1926, to determine whether the ancients had constructed a giant sundial at that site. He invited Joseph Lindon Smith, the sixty-three-year-old artist who had painted archaeological subjects for many years, to accompany him. As the two men plodded through Guatemala by mule toward Copán, Smith was surprised to find that wherever they stopped natives clustered around Morley like metal files drawn to a magnet.

One overnight stay, however, left Smith dubious about the charms of native living. "I took a dim view of the situation," he remarked of Vay, "when he accepted an invitation for us to spend the night in the home of an *alcalde* who was of mixed blood. There was too much thatched roof and too many other possible lurking places for vermin, and too little floor space for the *alcalde's* large family and livestock, to make our presence seem advisable to me. But Morley was adamant.

"The wife made very superior *tortillas*. Morley was in grand form and chatted gaily in a strange jargon that apparently was understood by everyone except me. He consumed a vast number of *tortillas* before we settled ourselves to sleep on mattresses that obviously had been slept on by many others before us. I kept up a steady scratching of my legs and arms, but the torture only increased as new species of vermin joined the onslaught upon me.

"When scorpions began to drop from above, just missing us, even Morley felt that the limits of courtesy had been passed. We crawled outside into the open, where the path to a stream was outlined in the moonlight. At the water's edge we shed our inhabited pajamas and jumped in. When we had given the insects on our bodies time to sink or swim away from us, we climbed out on to the bank and enveloped ourselves from head to foot in clouds of yellow powder.

"We put on clean garments from our travel kits and, abandoning the pajamas and finding a spot at a satisfactory distance from thatched homes, we slept soundly until awakened by the morning sun shining in our faces."[1]

In the meantime Thomas Gann and his handyman Muddy landed at Puerto Barrios, secured mules with great difficulty at the height of the Easter celebrations, and managed to reach Zacapa for the appointed rendezvous with Morley and Smith. John Lindsay, of the Carnegie's department of terrestrial magnetism, made a special trip up from Guayaquil to join them, and Holy Week observances also delayed his arrival. So Gann left his photographer behind at Zacapa to join Lindsay and bring him posthaste to Copán.

The route from Zacapa to Copán, a weary trail that Vay had often traveled, was a trying experience. The path, crossing hill after hill, abounded with boulders, pebbles, and cacti; bony cattle grazed

[1] Joseph Lindon Smith, *Tombs, Temples and Ancient Art*, Corinna Lindon Smith, ed. (University of Oklahoma Press, Norman, 1956), 307–308; quotations from this book are used by permission of the publisher.

on occasional patches of dirt-laden grass; the sun poured down intense, merciless heat, and the dusty air drove the men to sip the bottled tea they carried in their saddlebags. As they passed through Indian settlements, filthy and poor, they found the natives subsisting somehow on corn and tobacco crops. At noon the party rested in a grove of mango trees, prepared hot tea, and took a siesta. At two in the afternoon, the hottest part of the day, they moved along trails over the mountainside and arrived at Jocotán and, a little farther on, Camotán; each town boasted a few hundred inhabitants and a large church.

The next day's journey provided some variety that lightened the burdensome travel through the forsaken land. At Lela Obraje the annual fish hunt was in progress. The *machaca* were moving up the Copán River for the spawning season, and had reached a lagoon near the village. Men and boys, wielding machetes, plunged through the water, happy and excited over the fun of seizing the fish with their hands or stunning them with a blow of the machete. Continuing along the trail, the Americans encountered great flocks of green parrots and small tame pigeons. When they crossed into Honduras, they found the customs station to be no more than a small bush shack; and since the lone officer did not make an appearance, they went on their way. Vay whiled away the time explaining the ruins of Copán to Smith. It was not until after dark that they arrived in the village of Copán.

This time they stayed at the house of Don Porfírio Villamil, although the owner was absent at the time. A former general in the Honduran army, Villamil had been shot in the thigh during one of the skirmishes near Copán, and he stubbornly refused to allow an operation in order to save his leg. After the wound became serious and he was reduced to helplessness, his leg was amputated, and contrary to all medical predictions he regained his health. When Morley arrived, Don Porfírio was in New Orleans being fitted with a wooden leg.

By night Copán was as noisy as ever. Dogs barked, children cried, cocks crowed, and neighbors snored. At least, that was Gann's opinion, and since the doughty Irishman could not stand the sounds, he moved his quarters to a quiet spot among the ruins and slept peacefully.

Smith listened to Vay pour out facts about the ancient inhabitants of Copán. "Morley was a stimulating companion," he recalled. "I admired him for his vast fund of scholarly knowledge about everything concerned with the Maya and their ways. Even more for his method of imparting it casually and without apparent continuity until, unexpectedly, I found that every word he uttered fitted into a whole, forming a pattern as clear-cut as a cameo and told with inimitable humor and vividness that made valuable information 'stick.' " At the site "Morley devoted the better part of a day giving me a general idea of the extent of the ruins and an explanation of them. . . . To me, Morley's interpretations, like a verbal Rosetta stone, made this city of Copán live again in its original grandeur. He summarized what it must have looked like as a flourishing cultural center, where splendid architecture and sculpture rejoiced the eye of the beholder, and ambition and glory had their moment in space."[2]

Looking for possible subjects for his canvas, Smith was amazed at what he saw. "At one charming spot, the plaza overlooked the river; at another, a gigantic wild cotton tree, known generally as the Ceiba, was growing with its wide branches stretching dramatically over the ruins of a temple and an adjacent altar. We stumbled over enveloping roots and came upon columns with complicated sculptured designs, and a colossal head, which obviously could only have been a portrait, judging from the individual characteristics of the face. For portraiture Copán was remarkable. Personalities emerged from the stone surfaces of the great stelae and from among the seated figures on friezes." After years of acquaintance with the ancient ruins of the Near East, he marveled at the carvings of Copán: "I found it hard to believe that stone chisels had accomplished such a complete mastery of the technique of stone sculpture."[3] He made drawings of some of the stelae.

Morley and Lindsay got down to the major business of the

[2] Smith, *Tombs, Temples and Ancient Art*, 308–309.
[3] Smith, *Tombs, Temples and Ancient Art*, 309.

expedition. To the west and to the east of Copán are hills four and one-half miles apart. A stela on each hill contained Maya dates that led Arthur Carpenter, Dr. Willson of Harvard, and Herbert Spinden to conclude that if a person stood at the stela on the eastern hill on April 9 he would see the sun set directly behind the western stela. Morley arranged the visit so as to test the theory on that day.

On April 9 everything went wrong. The scientists ascended the mountain, found smoke covering the valley, and then suffered from a violent thunderstorm that swept over the area. Wet and cold, they took refuge in an Indian hut, where a fire provided warmth. Vay hung up his coat to dry, and later discovered that water, coming through the roof and dropping over tobacco leaves, streaked it a bold yellow. The Indians found this very funny, but not Vay. By nightfall the party descended the steep, slippery mountainside on mules, and proceeded to get lost. Only by giving the mules the initiative did they come out on the trail.

On the following day everything worked out according to schedule, and Lindsay secured the facts to prove the theory.

The other information gathered on this visit seemed insignificant compared with the theory of the sundial. Members of the party found two heads of archaic type similar to those Gamio had found in the Valley of Mexico; natives had picked them up around the site. For Morley the crude archaic objects had no appeal, though other archaeologists began to sense the significance of these finds. And so Vay, by failing to give more attention to these little figures, lost the direction that future investigations in the Maya area would take.

One of the projects of 1926 was the investigation of Cobá in the eastern part of Yucatán. In fact four expeditions were necessary before Morley was satisfied with the reports on the multiple sites collectively known by that name. Gann and Crandall made a brief excursion there in February. Three weeks later Kidder, Eric Thompson, and two other staff members made a three-day trip to the place. When Thompson returned, he learned from Carmen

Chai, a mason at Chichén Itzá, of carved figures near Cobá. That prompted a third expedition, consisting of Thompson to decipher the glyphs and Charlot to draw the sculptures, while Carmen Chai and Eugenio Mai acted as guide and helper. With Carmen's aid, they found two new sites, Macanxoc and Kukicán.

When Thompson came back from the third expedition and showed Morley the dates he had deciphered, Vay insisted on going to Cobá at once. Thompson tells the story: "Back in Chichén again, I was unable to persuade Morley that I had read the texts correctly; only his own eyes would convince him that such early dates could exist there. Then his enthusiasm flared up, and he proposed that we set out again for Cobá that very afternoon. Another two days on muleback through that monotonous forest didn't appeal to me at that moment." But after a week he and Morley were off.

"The mule ride that time was shortened. Morley persuaded the owner of a Model-T Ford in Valladolid to drive us to Kanxoc. The nine miles along that glacier bed of a road took just on two hours; we bounced from side to side and banged our heads against the roof. The driver came out best, for, after we had mounted our mules, he did a bonanza business driving the modern-minded element around Kanxoc plaza at five to ten centavos a ride, for ours was the first car ever to reach the village.

"Next morning, on seeing Cobá, Vay turned to me and said: 'Eric, this can't be a Yucatán site. We must have traveled south for ten days and landed up in the middle of the Petén. I don't doubt your readings of those early dates any longer. They fit right in with this architecture and assemblage and even with the vegetation.'

"Two days later Vay returned to Chichén; Carmen, Eugenio, and I stayed at Cobá a few more days. In later days he used to claim that I had forced his return by the tea I served. I was cook and, as a good Englishman, served tea three times a day. The water could not be drunk untreated, so it was a choice between what I regarded as rather weak tea and chlorinated water. Vay complained that the spoon wouldn't sink in that infernal Limey brew and his stomach lining was being corroded rapidly with tannic acid. Finally, he claimed to have found a pair of my dirty, sweat-impregnated socks in the tea can, charging that I had put them there to add even more strength and flavor to the deadly poison. I never heard the end of that incident."[4]

During the field season of 1928 Morley made an excursion to Uaxactún to see what his men had been doing there in the past few years. Kidder, who accompanied him, recounted the events of the trip:

". . . Morley, Mrs. Morley, George Vaillant and I left the seaport of Belize, British Honduras, in a light-draft launch towing a dugout cargo canoe and manned by amphibious black boatmen. The water being low, we were two days and two nights getting up the Belize River to Benqué Ceiba, where mules, sent out from camp, awaited us. Then three days on the trail—my initiation to the jungle. To one brought up in the clean, open pinewoods of northern Michigan, whose field-work had all been in the semi-deserts of Arizona and New Mexico, it was strangely awesome. Hour after hour in single file on the narrow, twisting trail, the dense forest pushing in on either side with an almost physical pressure, the healthy sunlight never reaching the ground save where the fall of some giant tree had brought down others with it, opening a crack of sky and starting a new round of crowding young growth in the endless upward struggle for light. Hour after hour of moist, green gloom. Then we would break out into a *bajo*, a low area, in the rainy season a bottomless swamp, the trail now parched and cracked. The sour soil of these always dreaded stretches supports only a tangled, scrubby bush. At first it was a relief to see the sky, but travel through *bajos* is painfully slow because the hard-baked mud is deeply pitted with old mule tracks, a breath of wind is unknown, the sun beats relentlessly down, clouds of stinging flies envelop everyone. Across, it was good to be again in the cool, quiet forest. I was not prepared for its uncanny

---

[4] J. Eric S. Thompson, *Maya Archaeologist* (Norman, University of Oklahoma Press, 1963), 58–59, quoted by permission of the publisher.

silence. There would be an occasional rustle of some little animal in the thick undergrowth, but all vocal life was far above on the sunny, billowing floor of the treetops. Once night came on, however, the jungle burst into sound: shrill insects, harsh-crying nightbirds, strange unidentifiable calls; at dusk and dawn, the deep, resonant roaring of the howling monkeys.

"As we rode, I kept wondering how the ancient Maya had so thoroughly conquered this vast and hostile land; how, without benefit of metal ax or the machete, they could have made it habitable. The bush once down, the sun let in, even the Petén can be pleasant, as I learned when, tired and sweat-soaked and itching, we reached the expedition's camp.

"Knowing that the job was to be a long one, Ricketson had wisely done everything possible to make life at Uaxactún comfortable. Over several acres the trees had been felled and the clearing planted to grass. The staff quarters were in airy, screened, thatched houses on a little knoll overlooking the water-hole and the men's camp. After the long, fatiguing days on the trail and the claustrophobia of the nights in the crowding forest, it was delightful.

"Ricketson, recovering from an illness, was not there that season. Monroe Amsden, temporarily in charge, and Ledyard Smith and Harry Pollock did not say much about the work, that first evening. We thought perhaps that things had not been going well. But in the cool of the morning—one breakfasted before sunup at Uaxactún—they gave us a surprise. As we followed them through the woods they said that when we reached the diggings we were to keep our eyes on the ground until we were told to look up. Soon we came out of the gloom of the bush and sensed that we were in the open. Eyes still down, we crossed it, climbed the mound of a ruined structure on the far side. They lined us up. 'Now!' said Amsden.

"There, snowy white against the deep green wall of jungle, was a terraced pyramid, perfect in every detail, great stucco masks set on either side of the stairway that mounted to its flat summit, smaller stairways flanking the masks. Directly in front stood a weathered gray stela.

"It was one of those moments one doesn't forget.

"When we'd caught our breath and Morley, that greatest of all lovers of all things Maya, had ceased exclaiming, they told us that the structure owed its wonderful preservation to the fact that it had been entombed within a later, larger pyramid which had kept rain and prying tree-roots from harming its stuccoed surface. E–VII sub, as it is prosaically listed in the reports, is thought, as result of subsequent work on the deposits in front of, and within it, to be perhaps the oldest Maya building so far known. But its splendid proportions, the restraint and harmony of its ornamentation, and the skillful use of moldings to catch the shadows and point up the entire composition must have had behind them a long background of architectural practice.

"There were other interesting buildings in Group E. But we could not keep ourselves long away from this one. The next day, George Vaillant and I were sitting on its lowermost step and talking of the ceremonies that so many centuries ago took place on the broad platform atop the stairway. In front of us lay a section of the plaza's white plaster pavement, cleared of debris, but as yet unbroken. George stamped it with his foot. I knew what he was thinking. Our years of work together at Pecos in New Mexico had given us both a great curiosity about what might lie beneath floors.

" 'Do you think Monroe and Ledyard would let us dig a little hole?' I said.

" 'Let's ask,' said George.

"They gave us a workman. We all gathered around to watch. The first floor was pierced, a second, a third. Nothing between them but footings of marl and limestone chips. Then, from a meter down, there came out a shovelful of black dirt. As it fanned out over the growing heap there rolled to the bottom a little brown object. George leaned over and picked it up, brushed it clean— and whistled. We passed it around. There could be no doubt what it was: the hand-modeled clay head of a crude human figurine, with the double punch and poke-pupil eye that is one of the hallmarks of the Guatemala highlands and of Mexico.

"Those few minutes with pick and shovel had added centuries

to the known occupancy of Petén. Never before had evidence been found that the Petén had been inhabited by agricultural, pottery-making people during the childhood of Mesoamerican civilization. It had therefore been supposed that the developmental stages had taken place in the uplands and that only on the eve of the Classic Period, migration or the spread of cultural influences to already resident jungle hunters led to sedentary life and intensive settlement. To our little group that morning, the battered pottery head . . . had opened up deep vistas of time and a whole series of new and fascinating problems."[5]

Vay failed to respond to the figurine and what it suggested—that the elaborate structures of Uaxactún and other sites were the product of a long process of development from the simplest type of primitive life. Future research was to emphasize digging down to bedrock in order to trace the stages of development. But such an approach left Vay cold. He saw before him the flowing white beauty of E–VII sub and at his feet the three-foot hole and the figurine. If he must choose between the two, he preferred the pyramid any day to the prosaic hole and the crude, archaic pottery object. In making the choice, he let his emotional reaction win out over the weaker dictates of a scholarly mind, and in that decision he lost the opportunity for leadership in the coming generation of Maya archaeological research.

In May, 1929, Vay and Frances took a three weeks' trip up the Usumacinta River. They went by motorboat as far as Tenosique, the head of navigation, and then transferred to mules for the two-day journey to Piedras Negras. There he found six new dates and took many photographs. Unfortunately, he kept no diary, and so we lack the details of this expedition. He was so impressed, however, by Piedras Negras that he convinced the Maya archaeologists of the University of Pennsylvania to excavate that site.

He went on an elaborate three months' expedition in 1931 to

<hr />

[5] A. V. Kidder in A. Ledyard Smith, *Uaxactún, Guatemala: Excavations of 1931–1937* (C.I.W. Publication 588, 1950), 3–4, quoted by permission of the publisher.

investigate the ruins of Yaxchilán on the Usumacinta River. He took with him Ruppert and Bolles as archaeologists, Dr. Rife as physician, Frances to supervise the camp, F. K. Rhoads, her father, as assistant, and the ever useful Tarsisio Chang as general helper. Along the way they acquired a Chinese cook. Morley did not travel lightly. His baggage amounted to forty boxes, twelve kyacks, and over a dozen bundles of chairs, cots, and other luggage to make life along the trail as bearable as possible. When they took to land transportation in the bush, thirty-four mules were required, two-thirds of them for the baggage and the remainder for the eight men and women, a guide, and four muleteers. As the expedition left Chichén, an associate remarked facetiously that they lacked only an elephant, and had one got mixed up in the entourage it would never have been found.

The trip was made by boat, automobile, and mule. At Campeche they took a boat to Isla del Carmen and then to Monte Cristo at the mouth of the Usumacinta. The governor of Tabasco lent the party a truck that had a bus body perilously mounted upon it to make a side trip to Palenque. Three hours at that site exhausted everyone because of the blazing sun and dense humidity that always envelops the place.

Back in Monte Cristo, they took the *Nueva Esperanza* and ascended the Usumacinta to Tenosique. At this head of navigation they transferred to mule trains and spent two days going through the dense forest to Piedras Negras. There the University of Pennsylvania team, headed by J. Alden Mason, was carrying out its first season of exploration; and Morley thought that the team lived in luxury in a dozen bamboo houses with thatched roofs that provided for all of their needs. He took a special interest in this expedition, because he was the one who had urged it.

More plodding through the forest and then poling in a dugout canoe up the river brought them to Yaxchilán. There they camped for a month, exploring the site with intensive care, and finding many new items. At the end of their stay Morley reported their results as the discovery of twenty new sculptured stelae and lintels, a dozen new Initial Series, two dozen sculptured altars, a ball court, and two new groups of ruins to the north and south of the limits of the city.

While the party was at Yaxchilán, Mason discovered Lintel 3 at Piedras Negras, displaying a figure on a throne surrounded by twelve persons. He was so excited by its beauty that he photographed it and sent the picture up the river to Vay by the next muleteer that passed through. He included a letter in Spanish, politely inviting Morley to come up and meet "Señorita Lintel Tercera."[6]

Morley had planned, of course, to stop off at Piedras Negras on his way back, but the discovery gave his visit additional interest. Descending the river in the dugout canoe, the members of the party had to avoid the rapids of Anaïte. As they scrambled over the bare rock that hedged in the gorge beneath, they paused to watch the scene below them. The captain of their boat believed that his four crewmen could take the loaded canoe through the rapids, and he carried out the task brilliantly. On the scorching rock above, the members of the party sweltered in the heat as they took photographs of the perilous passage of the canoe with its five natives. It dived into white water and foam, while the natives fought to maintain themselves, and finally it swirled about and then moved into calm waters near the shore.

As they neared Piedras Negras, but still not within sight of it, Morley's men fired off pistols to announce their arrival. As soon as they landed at the camp, Vay, disdaining to eat, struck out for Lintel 3. He agreed with Mason about its beauty, calling it "the most superb production of ancient sculpture yet brought to light." He set to work drawing the glyphs on it and other inscriptions found during his absence. An indication of his intense concentration on the task appeared when a snake slithered peacefully across his shoe and he did not notice it.

Since he was the stepfather of the Piedras Negras project, the men in camp looked upon him and his views with respect. He inspired them to attempt to complete exploration that would confirm one of his theories. Linton Satterthwaite later wrote of Morley

[6] *Morleyana*, 152.

on that visit: "When he had got a series of *hotun* markers started, as at Piedras Negras, if there were any gaps he would search for previously undiscovered monuments to fill them. He got a great kick out of predicting to his boys the date he was going to show them on the stone they were going to find. When I arrived at Piedras Negras, under J. Alden Mason, Vay told us to get busy and find no less than eleven monuments which he still needed for the early end of his local series of *hotun* markers. Such a series, if complete, required four markers per *katun*, one for the *katun* itself, one for the half, and one each for the first and third quarters. At our site he had a sure *katun* marker for 9.5.0.0.0 and also what he considered a sure marker for the next quarter, 9.5.5.0.0. Then there was a big gap, even after throwing in plain and illegible monuments to fit the postulated pattern. Our mouths watered. We all agreed there must be an outlying ceremonial group in the bush with a dozen or so monuments for us to discover. Well, we found more groups, and by excavation we found more monuments, but none to fill the hiatus. Eight years later . . . I had decided for myself, long since, that there was no such hiatus."[7]

The only unfavorable aspect of the return trip was the boat ride from Carmen to Campeche. The *Angelita* was crowded to capacity with human beings, two automobiles, and chickens. Morley, of course, became violently seasick. The voyage required twice the twelve hours predicted by the captain, and the sea broke over the sides, giving the passengers a shower of salt water at unexpected intervals. Vay survived the trip and returned to Chichén happy and contented over the results of the expedition. As a visual report he brought back four hundred photographs and two thousand feet of movie film. Many of the photographs were of inscriptions, but the movie film, taken mainly by Frances, was intended to illustrate lectures he would give.

The Calakmul expedition resulted from the discovery of Maya sites by Cyrus L. Lundell, a twenty-four-year-old Texas botanist employed by the Mexican Exploitation Company, an American

[7] *Morleyana*, 221–22.

chicle firm. For five years Lundell had cruised through the deep interior of Campeche State in search of chicle areas. In the last days of December, 1931, led by *chicleros*, he came upon the ruins of Calakmul, with two pyramids some 150 feet high. Southeast of Campeche, it is not far from the Guatemala border. He took photographs and made a sketch map, and reported the find to James Brydon, local manager of the company in Campeche. In February, 1932, Brydon happened to return to the States on the same ship with President Merriam, and he showed him the pictures of the structures. Merriam communicated the news to Morley, who was excited over the prospect of a new harvest of glyph dates. Vay had Lundell come to Chichén Itzá, where the young man generously placed all of his information in Morley's hands. At once Vay arranged for an expedition, with Lundell as one of the party.

Although Morley made use of all modern devices to ease the hardships of such a journey, it was a wearing experience. The baggage consisted of eighteen boxes, eight bags, two kyacks, and fourteen containers, altogether weighing more than 2,400 pounds. The expedition lasted through the month of April, with two full weeks at the site. In the party were Vay and Frances, Ruppert, Bolles and Stromsvik, Tarsisio Chang, and a cook. At the last moment Lundell was prevented from accompanying the group. Vay secured the co-operation of Brydon and of Francisco Buenfil, chicle king of southern Campeche, to arrange the transportation. Using automobile, train, and sailboat, the party reached Champotón, then ascended the Champotón River by boat to the village of Kanasyab. There they transferred to mule-drawn platform cars, used to transport chicle bales. "The track is in wretched condition," Morley reported, "weaving a tortuous serpentine trail through the forest. The mules unchecked by brake or rein go like mad, the expedition's five platforms successfully maintaining an average of one derailment per car per hour." The first stop was at La Gloria, "a collection of flea-infested, thatched huts where dogs, pigs and chickens had the right-of-way and sleep was not to be had." Human beings and baggage were loaded on a five-ton truck for the seventy-mile trip over a clearing that was called a road. "Through this forest the truck fought its way over stones, and through swamps, occasionally bogging down completely and having to be pried out with logs, chains and poles, but always managing to extricate itself from seemingly impossible situations. The body plunged and jerked from side to side until it seemed as though man-made machines could no longer stand the strain but still the truck jolted onward."[8] From Central Beunfil, a chicle station, thirty mules carried the expedition the remaining seven miles to the site.

At Calakmul, camp was set up in the central plaza of the ruins, fifteen natives were employed to clear the vegetation and turn stelae, and the archaeologists were ready to go to work. The next day was one of the most thrilling in Vay's quarter-century of glyph hunting, as he took Lundell's map and moved among the stelae so clearly indicated on it. In addition to sixty-two stelae that Lundell had noted, the party discovered forty-one more. This total of 103 made Calakmul unique as the site with the most sculptured stelae. Of the date inscriptions, Morley identified fifty-one Initial Series, the largest number for any site except Copán, and four Period Ending dates. After deciphering the glyphs, he placed the city's great period at A.D. 364 to 551 by the Morley-Spinden correlation or 250 years earlier than the Goodman-Martínez-Thompson correlation. Vay also exulted over Stela 51, whose sculptured figure of a bedecked individual was in perfect condition, because, falling face down, it had been preserved from the elements. Likewise fascinating were the figures of six bound prisoners sculptured on a limestone outcrop fifteen by twenty-one feet in size.

His excitement at these finds amused and sometimes worried his assistants. "One day in Calakmul," Stromsvik recalled, "we saw a stela on the other side of a fairly wide plaza. Morley immediately started across towards it, stumbling over creepers and fallen logs and into holes, but never taking his eyes off the objective. We came after, trying to help, picking him up and cutting

8 "Calakmul—A Recently Discovered Maya City," C.I.W. *News Service Bulletin*, II, No. 34 (Aug. 19, 1932), 237, 238, quoted by permission of the publisher.

vines that entangled him. He got there, torn and bleeding, never for a moment having lost sight of the goal. We said to him, 'Why don't you look down and see where you are going?' and he answered 'I never have time to look down.' When we were turning over fallen stelae, where the inscriptions were underneath, Morley was a constant worry. He would stick his head underneath as soon as there was space enough to ram it into. Many a time I had to grab his back and drag him out lest the stelae slip and crush him."[9]

In the course of the investigation, Liborio Mar, a native worker, told Ruppert of another site some fifteen miles to the northeast near the former chicle camp of La Muñeca. At once Vay sent him and Bolles to see what they might find. Scarcely had the two men arrived at the place and began to look over the ruins when fever struck Ruppert and laid him up in his hammock. The following morning he continued to examine the place until he collapsed. The men, however, came back with a report of twenty-three stelae and four Initial Series, one of which was extremely late.

John Bolles recalls the lighter side of camp life. "Ruppert and I were accused of stealing cans of del Monte pears which had been brought along for Fanny. Karl and I were rebels; we did steal them and eat them. Henceforth this expedition was referred to as the 'Canned Peaches' (Campeche) Expedition, and Morley enjoyed the reference.

"Morley was fascinated by my survey and architectural instinct. Each night I worked up my plans under a Coleman lamp, and the others tended to their notes. One evening I bet Morley he was sitting on another stela. As I recall, I was a foot or two off!

"He was always skeptical of Karl and myself—maybe me. When I found the quarry and undercut stones at Calakmul, it was difficult to get him to accompany me. But then he was enthused like a child—again I was his dear 'Juanito.' The next day I fell from grace again. Karl and I found a small stela in the fork of a tree! Amazing! When he found out it took us and four men an hour to place it there I went back to my old status."[10]

[9] *Morleyana*, 242.
[10] John Bolles to the author.

There was a mishap on the return trip from Calakmul. Although the official report refers only to a broken steering knuckle, the delay of a full day revealed some of Vay's traits. Stromsvik recalled the incident: "Coming back from Calakmul, we were riding out on a fully-loaded, solid-wheel chicle truck, over terribly rough jungle trails. One morning the truck broke down miles from anywhere. Morley sent one of the boys ahead to try to find some mules to get us out of there. Karl Ruppert was very sick with malaria. Morley said, 'Let's play bridge while we wait.' We slung Karl in a hammock beside the road, spread a tarpaulin on the trail, ahead of the truck, and started playing, John Bolles and I against Frances and Morley. John was a fair bridge player and I was decidedly bad, and after the first six hours my interest kind of waned; still, John and I consistently won. Morley was a very keen player and so was Frances, and when they kept on losing Morley would say, 'Now Frances, you know you didn't play that hand right; you should have finessed with . . . ,' etc., and insisted that we keep on playing. Well, we kept at it for fourteen hours straight, before the first batch of mules came. Never since then have I touched cards to play bridge."[11]

As soon as Morley reached Campeche, where he had telegraphic service available, he wired news of his finds to the Mexican government and at the same time informed Kidder in the United States.

Although Lundell never became a trained archaeologist, he discovered a number of sites in the same area as Calakmul and also in the Lake Flores region. After Morley announced the results of his expedition to Calakmul, *The New York Times* ran an editorial on Lundell's intrepidity in bringing sites to light. For a brief period the young man considered the possibility of entering the field of archaeology, and Morley did what he could to encourage him, but he was also strongly pressed by professors in botany at the University of Michigan to continue graduate study in that field; when he received his doctorate in botany in 1936, Maya archaeology lost a promising scholar. Nevertheless, he made an extensive

[11] *Morleyana*, 242–43.

trip in 1932–33 to explore the unknown region between the upper Petén and the interior of Campeche State. Although he published the results in a journal, for some reason institutions with the resources to investigate the sites failed to take advantage of his information. From 1933 to 1938 he led C.I.W. expeditions in Mexico and Central America, but he concentrated increasingly on tropical botany. Occasionally Morley called on him for aid on that subject. He asked him to prepare a lengthy essay for inclusion in *The Inscriptions of the Petén*, but it did not appear because Vay's manuscript became too lengthy.

Gustav Stromsvik related several incidents of this period: "In 1934 I was working with Earl Morris at Quiriguá, straightening and repairing leaning and fallen stelae. This was done on Morley's initiative; because General Ubico, then President of Guatemala, wanted to remove the monuments from Quiriguá, and to set them up in a park in the Capital. Morley convinced Dr. Merriam, at that time President of the Carnegie Institution, that these monuments ought to remain in their original setting; he also convinced Ubico, which I believe was somewhat more difficult. During work at Quiriguá, Morley went to Honduras and got a co-operative agreement signed, whereby the Honduran Government bound itself to pay about one half of the expenditures for the study and preservation of the Copán ruins. On his way back to the States Morley came through Quiriguá. He was very enthusiastic about the work done and about the new monuments found. One evening, after dinner with Dr. McPhail, Morley took me aside and confided to me in a whisper that could be heard all over the hospital corridor, that I had been chosen to direct the work at Copán; about the contents of the agreement and what ought to be done at Copán. Then he started to explain his visions of the future; 'I am only a little over fifty and should at least have another twenty years of active life ahead of me. There are still two main Maya ruins that I should like to see being taken care of, like you are doing here at Quiriguá. They are Copán and Tikal. Now you are going to Copán and in ten years' time you should be able to finish. Then you can go to Tikal and do the same. By then I shall probably not be very active, but if nothing unforeseen happens, I shall still be very interested and will come around whenever I can.' "[12]

Ever since the days of World War I Morley had had a strong prejudice against Germans. His feeling was reinforced by his experience with Hermann Beyer in 1934. Until that time he had only nominal but friendly relations with Beyer. In August, 1923, he talked with him in Mexico City and inspected his collection of artifacts; a year later Beyer wrote a review of *The Inscriptions of Copán* that must have nettled Vay, for, after a brief commendation of the volume, Hermann spent most of the review in discussing points on which he differed from Vay's interpretation of a number of glyphs.

In 1932, Beyer, then employed by the department of Middle American research at Tulane University, was loaned to the Carnegie Institution to study glyphs at Chichén Itzá. A little later Jack Denison, Jr., also a member of the Carnegie staff at Chichén, demonstrated how rubbings could be made with Chinese paper. At once Vay had him make a full copy of the inscriptions of the Monjas by this method. On learning of this, Beyer asked Morley to lend him the rubbings in order to complete his study, and Vay, always co-operative in scholarly matters, sent them to him. Then in July, 1934, the package containing them was returned.

When Morley opened the parcel he was horrified. Beyer had cut up each inscription into the individual glyphs for convenience in studying them. Angry beyond words at what appeared to him an act of vandalism, he could hardly contain himself. It would require many days of patient work to reassemble the glyphs into the original form; moreover, Bolles had planned to use the rubbings to illustrate his report on the Monjas. After cooling off, Vay sent a protest to Frans Blom, then director of Middle American research, and without mentioning Beyer by name expressed his deep distress over the damage; it is remarkable that at only one brief point did Vay lapse into strong language.

Then followed an amazing exchange of letters. Blom replied

[12] *Morleyana*, 244–45.

with the haughty demeanor of a European-bred gentleman. "You are free to use abusive language to your mules," he began, but not to a colleague. He defended Beyer completely, accused Vay of not instructing the German how to handle the rubbings, and ended by calling for a "correction of your abusive letter."[13] Morley composed several drafts of a reply, but destroyed them. The letter he sent Blom voiced only his despair over the proceedings. It is easy to read between the lines that he could not contemplate the prospect of being on bad terms with his old-time friend Frans over this piece of vandalism committed by Hermann.

Beyer had been rude and ungenerous in the first place, when he cut up the rubbings. Now he added the crowning touch in a letter to Vay that is a masterpiece of insult. After suggesting that Morley and Bolles were unqualified to judge his work in deciphering glyphs, he admitted that he had not informed Vay of his plan to separate the rubbings, knowing that Vay would have opposed it. Also, he made light of the problem of reassembling the glyphs for photographs of the entire inscriptions. His conclusion that his actions were logical struck Vay as a case of inverse Teutonic reasoning.

The result of Beyer's research appeared in his "Studies on the Inscriptions of Chichén Itzá," published in 1937. J. Eric S. Thompson considers this his greatest contribution, not so much for the conclusions as for the meticulous manner in which he analyzed glyphs. Undoubtedly Beyer was correct in giving attention to noncalendrical glyphs, which had so far defied interpretation. But because Morley had confined himself to date glyphs, Beyer could not control his swelling egoism; in the original draft of his manuscript he made such caustic remarks about Vay's narrow approach to the subject that a professional associate toned them down considerably before the paper was published.

All things considered, Beyer was shabby and boorish in his treatment of Morley in his published study. He admitted that Vay helped him with rubbings and photographs, and that Vay had read the first draft of the manuscript and suggested many changes.

[13] Frans Blom to Morley, Aug. 21, 1934, Morley File, C.I.W.

Despite this generous aid, Hermann took every opportunity to make slighting remarks. Beyer, of course, had a right to disagree with Morley on the decipherment of certain glyphs, and he was right in moving into the study of noncalendrical glyphs, but there is more than one way to express difference with a fellow scholar. Beyer chose an approach that bristled with barbs.

Morley's expeditions gradually became tourist trips with more time in towns and cities and less time in excavation. In 1935 he and Frances took a month's jaunt through Guatemala. After a brief stopover at Quiriguá, they visited the Ricketsons, Roaches, John Armstrong, and Carlos Villacorta in Guatemala City. Then came five days through the highlands, following the usual route of today's tourist—Antigua, Tzanzuyu, Chichicastenango. At the last mecca he called on Father Rossbach, marveled at his good relations with the Indians, examined his artifact collection, and once again encountered the curious Robert Burkitt. After a visit to Utatlán and a momentary interest in Tecum Uman and the Quiché royal family, he and Frances were back in Guatemala City.

He was unusually eager to visit Copán this year, because an earthquake had shaken the region some months earlier. In January, Stromsvik wrote him a distressing report. "On arriving at Copán," Gustav reported on January 12, "a sorry sight met me. The beautiful village . . . was a bunch of cracked, buckled and cockeyed houses, the people living in tents and manaca shacks out of reach of the walls." Juan Ramón Cueva had to abandon his home and move the family into the stables. The ruins also suffered: ". . . a big chunk of the high bank fell into the river. The walls of that beautifully carved room of Mound 22" were leveled.[14] A mound beside the Hieroglyphic Stairway was shaken down; a rock struck a stela standing below but did little damage. Stromsvik wired Tegucigalpa, and a plane was sent at once to bring him to the capital, where he interviewed the president. All possible help was promised, and assistance was given to send supplies for the work of restoration.

By the time Vay and Frances arrived, much of the village had been repaired, and Cueva was able to take them into his house, as had been his custom.

After looking over the damage at the ruins, noting what had been discovered since his last visit, and complimenting Stromsvik on his work, Vay found the conversation with Gus coming around to the Hieroglyphic Stairway, that exasperating puzzle of a confused mass of carved stones. The 2,500 pieces, each with glyphs, that had composed the eighty-five steps of that stairway, had been tumbled to the ground by an earthquake in the nineteenth century. Nothing had been done, nor could anything be done, to restore them to their proper order in rows of steps on the slope of the mound. Stromsvik tells how he proposed an unorthodox solution to Vay:

"I had suggested the restoration of the Hieroglyphic Stairway at Copán, in spite of not having the complete data on the sequence of the inscriptions. Morley was against it on the ground that the inscription could not be correctly assembled, but I maintained that it was better to restore the stairway, even so. We knew its height, how many steps there had been, and we knew for certain how and where about a third of the inscription went. Morley knew the Hieroglyphic Stairway at Copán much better than any other living being, and I argued that if we didn't restore it in his lifetime, so we could utilize his profound knowledge, most likely it would never be done. At least it could never be done as well as it could be with Morley's help. Also, I said, it was better to get the stairway stones up, out of the plaza, where they were strewn about, subject to repeated grass fires and the machetes of the cleaning gangs. Morley saw my point and pledged his help as far as he could."[15]

After Copán the Morleys spent a few days in Antigua at Dr. Popenoe's house and then flew to Mérida.

On his return trip to the States, Morley stopped off at New Orleans, where he sometimes gave newspaper interviews. This

[14] Stromsvik to Morley, Jan. 12, 1935, quoted in Morley to Merriam, Jan. 19, 1935, Morley File, C.I.W.
[15] *Morleyana*, 246.

time he took the occasion to declare certain documents fakes. Theodore A. Willard, the battery manufacturer who had developed an amateur interest in Maya history, had bought a dozen manuscript sheets purporting to list the names of late Maya rulers. "You can say," Vay declared, "that in my opinion the manuscripts Mr. Willard bought are false. He honestly believes they are genuine, but the same fellow who sold them to him stung me on a document of similar nature last year."[16]

In the fall of 1935 Morley was busy with two scientific meetings in Mexico. At the American Scientific Congress in Mexico City in September, he was not an official delegate. He requested not to be named, because he believed, perhaps rightly, that he could spend the time more profitably in informal conversations with the Mexican archaeological officials than in sitting through the long sessions of papers. He did serve on a committee of resolutions and joined in the excursions that were offered to the visitors. Through some blunder the paper he had prepared for the Congress was not included on the program, and he gave it before the Alzate Society five days after the assembly of scholars had officially adjourned.

An amusing picture of Vay as he attended one of the sessions of the Congress comes from Neil Judd, who represented the United States National Museum. The "delegates and guests were seating themselves in the auditorium . . . when Morley remembered a telephone call he should have made. Hastily piling his felt hat (a hat that looked for all the world like the skin of a Maltese cat), his gloves, and Malacca cane on the seat, he scrambled over feet and knees and bolted from the hall. In a matter of minutes he was back again and forcing his way into a fully occupied row immediately in front of his own seat. He had reached the middle before he discovered the error and began retreat amidst a flurry of apologies, dislodged coats, hats, and programs. The pother followed all the way to his former place where, stooping to gather up his possessions, he caught the crook of his cane on a chair leg

16 New Orleans *Times-Picayune*, Apr. 30, 1935. In the issue of May 12 Willard insisted that he had not been duped.

and dropped gloves, hat, and papers. Watching the progressive commotion, Isabel Kelly turned to me and said, 'Morley comes into a meeting and sits down like a crate of chickens breaking open.'"[17]

The second scientific meeting, that of the Mexican Historical Congress that convened in Mérida in November, caught Morley in the middle of a political struggle. Through the proceedings he showed remarkable acumen in keeping the Carnegie project out of the conflict. He arranged two events on the program in the name of the C.I.W.—a photographic exhibit displaying the work of excavation, that filled the second floor of the museum in Mérida, and a visit of the delegates to Chichén Itza.

The exhibition that he arranged, fortunately inaugurated before politics ruined the meetings, went off well. The only hitch was that Gonzolo Vásquez Vela, minister of public education, who was scheduled to open the exhibit, was three hours late. But Morley had provided for such an eventuality and had Vela's second-in-command on hand to carry out the ceremony.

The meetings of the Congress in the Peón Contreras Theater in Mérida were soon taken over by a Communist faction. Several of the delegates from Mexico City were Marxist, and they were aided by leftist elements in Mérida, including the Communist governor of Yucatán, who did nothing to prevent the usurpation. By the third day the Communists took physical possession of the meetings and, with the conservatives absenting themselves, changed the name to the Revolutionary Congress of Mexican History.

Fortunately the visit of the delegates to Chichén Itzá on Sunday took place without political overtones. Five large buses and twenty automobiles delivered the guests at nine-thirty in the morning. Morley greeted the visitors and spent three hours guiding them over a portion of the ruins. By twelve-thirty they were tired and thirsty, and he led them to the Casa Principal for lunch. For this purpose he had on hand ten small barrels of beer, which he served cold, 600 tamales, 350 sandwiches, 300 deviled eggs, 35 tins of pineapples, and 7 pounds of crackers. He induced the

[17] *Morleyana*, 92.

brewery from which he bought the beer to donate the food as a complimentary gesture.

Vay and Frances, aided by servants in white starched clothes, catered to the needs of the hungry guests. After everyone had been served, he clapped his hands for attention and welcomed the visitors in Spanish, and in the process committed one of his usual linguistic blunders. "The Carnegie Institution of Washington," he announced, "is very happy to serve in this house today the men who are dedicating themselves to the *historios estúdicos.*" A roar of laughter informed him of his mistake, and unembarrassed he immediately corrected it. "I say, to the men who are dedicating themselves to *estúdios históricos.*"[18] Then he read in Spanish a telegram of greeting just received from Merriam and Kidder.

After showing the delegates another part of the ruins, he conducted them to the buses and said goodbye at three-thirty. He was exhausted, having climbed ten pyramids in the course of the tour. But he was gratified that no political incident marred the visit. Proudly he reported to Merriam that the only successful events of the whole Congress were the exhibit at the museum and the tour of Chichén Itzá.

The following day in Mérida, with the Congress now dominated by leftists, he had to make a delicate decision. Alfonso Toro, chief of the department of monuments of the Mexican government, was scheduled to give an address in the afternoon, to be followed by a lecture by Morley that night. But when Vay returned to Mérida, he was beset by conservatives to cancel his appearance; at the same time Vega declared that such action would affront the governor. Vay adopted a sensible solution. He reasoned that since the Carnegie project operated under the department of monuments, he would take his cue from Toro's action. On learning that Toro had canceled his address, Vay followed suit.

In a final incident he again followed Toro's example. A majority of the conservative delegates, just before leaving Mérida for Mexico City, issued an explanation of why they had withdrawn from the leftist-dominated sessions. Although Morley's sympathies were

18 *Morleyana,* 211.

with the conservatives, he refrained from signing the statement, doubtless because Toro also withheld his name.

Morley's negotiations with some chiefs from Quintana Roo, the land of the fiercely independent Mayas, originated in his desire to smooth the way for a sociological project headed by Robert Redfield, of the University of Chicago. Redfield began his studies at Chichén Itzá in 1930 and soon employed Alfonso Villa Rojas, an able young Yucatecan who had been teaching school in the village of Chan Kom twelve miles away. After Redfield and Villa made a comprehensive study of Chan Kom, the Chicago sociologist wanted Villa to penetrate the isolated area of Quintana Roo for a study of the independent Mayas who had lived there for generations. At first Villa assumed the guise of an itinerant merchant and made two visits into Xcacal country. He told the natives of the Americans at Chichén; and later when Villa was off to the University of Chicago taking graduate work, some of these Mayas made cautious overtures to the white men at Chichén.

The visits began in January, 1934, and extended to the end of the following year. The first to appear were three young men who had made the ninety-mile trip on foot from the heart of Quintana Roo. Morley welcomed them, and though he could not learn the purpose of their visit except to assume that they came out of curiosity, he sent them back with gifts and medicine, telling them he would be happy to see them again. That was in January. Ten months later one of these men, Juan Bautista Poot, showed up with a letter from a chief in the interior; he too was kindly treated and went away loaded down with gifts, medicines, and disinfectants. Then in February, 1935, José Tamay appeared at Chichén, apparently with the hope of receiving treatment for his badly infected nose. At once Morley sent him to physicians in Mérida, where he was hospitalized for several weeks until his sinus trouble subsided. While Tamay was recovering, four of his friends sought out Morley with a letter from their chief, Concepción Cituk.

At this point Morley began to learn about the background of his guests. They came from one of five groups of independent Mayas in Quintana Roo, conveniently referred to as the Xcacal group, because Xcacal was the religious capital of nine villages with a total population of 732 persons. This group maintained an army of 150 men, of which Cituk was the head with the title of captain.

Meanwhile Villa returned from the United States in the summer of 1935, went to Tusik, one of the villages in the Xcacal group, for the purpose of gaining permission to live there so as to study the natives at firsthand. In order to establish their confidence in him, he brought four of their younger men (three of them sons of chiefs) to Chichén to demonstrate his close connection with Morley. These youths bore a number of letters, setting forth the complaints of the Indians against unfair practices in the chicle trade and their fear of impending Mexican political control of their country. Vay became aware of the delicate situation that he might be in, as he read this plea in one of the letters: ". . . so the favor I ask of you . . . [is] to give me your support, to give me arms and all its implements, and all the objects to make war, so that you will take off from me all those wicked men who are at the great town of Santa Cruz, the Mexicans, because they are very bad men."[19]

Vay was confident that he could placate the natives and win their friendship at the same time. Since he considered his approach more promising if he could meet the individuals face-to-face, he invited the chiefs to visit him on December 5. He repeated the invitation in several messages to Cituk, including in one letter photographs Frances had taken of the chiefs' sons on the earlier visit.

Confident that the Indians would show up, Vay prepared for them, and in the end carried off the whole affair with great success. On Thursday morning, the fifth, three Indians prowled around the hacienda without attracting the attention of the occupants. Satisfied that there was no danger, one of their companions signaled the delegation to come forward. All told, sixteen natives, four of them chiefs, descended on Morley's quarters. He turned the guest house over to them, and calculated how much food must be provided to entertain these visitors in proper style.

Ever careful of protocol, he singled out the leaders for particular

[19] The Chiefs to Morley, Sept. 20, 1935, Morley File, C.I.W.

attention, and held the first meeting with the four chiefs. He was forthright in explaining the purpose of inviting them. He wanted them to see what the Carnegie Institution was doing at Chichén Itzá, the former holy city of the Mayas, and he explained what Villa wanted to do by living among them. Concepción Cituk, a born leader and head of their army, soon voiced their grievances. They had always feared the Mexicans and wanted to live without interference from them, but the federal soldiers at Santa Cruz de Bravo were encroaching upon the area they used for cornfields, hunting, and chicle-gathering. This statement together with the earlier written appeal for arms to repel the Mexicans put Morley on his guard; he spelled out his position very clearly. He was a stranger in Mexico, he explained, but he worked under the laws; he would be friends with these Indians, but he and the Carnegie Institution would under no circumstances become entangled in political affairs. When he was assured that his visitors understood his position, he suggested that he might be able to help them. He had a friend, James Brydon, of the American Chicle Development Company, and he would tell him that these Indians had chicle to sell. As for General Melgar, recently appointed governor of Quintana Roo, Vay explained that he would attempt to urge that official to exercise justice and right toward the Indians. When the natives requested red silk and handbells for their sanctuary, he quickly promised to secure those items as a personal gift from himself.

After this conference Morley wrote a long letter to Pedro Barreira, high priest in Xcacal, who was blind and too old to make the journey, repeating all of the points he had made to his guests orally. The letter breathed friendship, gave advice, and strongly hinted at the wisdom of keeping the peace; Morley expressed his ideas in simple language, had them translated into Maya, and sent a typed copy, noting that it had been put into a machine that printed it.

Constant entertainment was Vay's aim in pleasing his guests. He showed them his ice-making machine. Villa took them on a tour of the ruins and was amused to find them most impressed by the echoes in the Ball Court, which they believed were the voices of their ancestors. When Cituk called out in the loudest voice and received the strongest echo, he hastily assumed that it was because he was chief. The first night Morley hired an itinerant with a portable moving-picture machine to show half a dozen films, including one of the first Charlie Chaplin pictures ever made. Although the projector broke down repeatedly, the fun was not spoiled for the natives who understood the humor of the silent pictures without trouble.

The climax of the entertainment came on Saturday night with a grand fiesta. Vay secured a seven-piece orchestra from Tizimín to provide the music and invited natives from nearby villages to the festivities. Instead of the 150 guests he expected, over twice that number—men, women, children, and a host of dogs—poured into Chichén. Local custom required a master of ceremonies to conduct each girl to a young man on the dance floor; but Vay soon realized that he needed four of the social officials to accommodate the dancing throng, and he quickly pressed friends into that service. For refreshments Frances served sliced tinned fruit and cookies. Liquor was kept out of sight except for the orchestra, who needed constant reinforcement to continue playing hour after hour. Vay and Frances withdrew at midnight, but the dancing went on until two o'clock.

On Sunday morning, as a parting courtesy, Morley took photographs of the chiefs and of various groups of the visitors. Frances loaded them down with medicines, bandages, magazines, and colored advertisements; and Vay gave a half-promise that he would visit them in a few months. After formal farewells the Indians departed happy and satisfied. Villa and his wife were granted permission to live with the natives, which was the immediate object of the elaborate visit.

Vay realized that he could not rest on his oars. He must pay a return visit to those Indians if the ties of friendship were to be firmly cemented. Thus he set out in February, 1936, on an eleven-day excursion to Xcacal. In the group were Vay and Frances, his secretary Mrs. Larsen, Pedro Castillo as interpreter, and two muleteers. The party left at dawn on the twenty-sixth on a strange mission of friendship, ethnology, and adventure. Each mount had a canteen of water and saddlebags jammed with lunch foods. At the head of the group Vay jogged along on a short, unsteady horse, while Castillo acted as rear guard.

As they moved southward into unfamiliar territory, they met new sights: natives in blue aprons and henequen puttees, hunting deer, drab and pathetic hamlets, a forest where the sun had scorched all of the leaves, ghost cities with ruined churches, swarming hordes of ants, a rough band of *chicleros*, and on entering Quintana Roo forty miles of deserted rain forest.

Finally, on the fourth day, the expedition was about to reach its destination. At Tusik the natives had built a commodious new hut for the Villas. After a quick inspection of the quarters the party proceeded to Xcacal, five miles ahead. On crossing a ridge, they saw the hamlet, an assemblage of twenty thatched huts irregularly placed around a large sanctuary. Corporal Aké, the guide they acquired at Tusik, stopped the party at a rural shrine to await the arrival of the dignitaries. And shortly Captain Concepción Cituk and his brother appeared. After an exchange of greetings and double *abrazos*, the visitors were conducted into the settlement to a large thatched hut especially prepared for them. The punctilious natives—so far only men had appeared—faced their guests, and the two groups smiled self-consciously at each other. At a signal the Indians broke loose with an epidemic of handshaking.

At their quarters the guests found every thought had been given to their comfort and convenience. Hammocks, a table, and chairs were provided. When Vay hinted that food would be welcome, hot tortillas, beans, and chocolate appeared as if by magic. After the meal was over, Indian women, extremely shy and moving in single file, came in with gifts of tortillas, eggs, fruit, and flowers.

There was much curiosity on both sides. The visitors were the first Nordics in the area; and the natives, isolated from the outside world, gaped at the collapsible cots and camp tables unloaded from the cargo mules, and crowded about to watch these strange people take their meals. In turn, the visitors were equally curious about the village and its people; and Vay was on the alert to detect any vestiges of pre-Columbian practices that might have survived among these independent Mayas.

He had timed the visit so that he might see the fiesta in honor of the Virgin of the Conception. It was something like a thanksgiving celebration, held every eighteen months, though this year it had been delayed because of poor crops.

The fiesta opened with the planting of the *yaxché* tree, a fertility ritual coming down from the distant past. About sunset on the day of their arrival, the visitors saw old men and boys, laughing and shouting, bring a thirty-five-foot *yaxché*, the sacred ceiba tree, that they had cut down, through the village. Santos, a boy chosen for his ability to act and caper, impersonated a *pisote*, a badger-like animal considered a symbol of fertility, by clinging to the trunk and branches of the tree despite efforts to shake him off.

The tree was "planted" the next morning at dawn. Again shouting boys carried the *yaxché* with its *pisote* through the village and then stopped at a designated spot. There the youthful pranks and mischief ceased, and the hundreds of natives watching the proceedings became reverently silent as the tree was raised aloft and slipped into a small hole in the ground, where it stood upright. Then the *pisote*, still in the branches, scattered *calabaza* seeds in the four directions. Boys came running with clusters of fruit and gourds, which the *pisote* tied to the branches, completing the ceremony that signified fertility and fruition.

Another ceremony, that of the sacred meal, was performed every day of the fiesta at one of the four sponsors' quarters. A sponsor was a native who had the honor of providing food for the Indians who had assembled for the fiesta. At the sponsor's hut Morley and his party saw the altar loaded with stacks of tortillas wrapped in fine napkins, gourds of *atole* (a corn meal drink), and decorated with flowers, chocolate, and other esteemed foods. After religious services were performed, a procession of chiefs and natives, the sponsor, an eight-piece band, and dancing girls accompanied the food to church, where a mass was said; and then the food was distributed for the use of the people that day.

The band—perhaps it should be called an orchestra—that performed at all of the ceremonies, was a bizarre affair. Three violins with pig-gut strings and henequen fiber bows produced a strange sound, but they managed to maintain the time and tune. The cornetists, on the other hand, only added confusion; when they were not asleep, they intermittently contributed a few bars of music that had no relation to the piece the band was playing. Two drums, excellently played, provided the primitive throb for each selection.

The church, or sanctuary, was the best structure in the village and the natural focus of the religious worship. It had a fine thatched roof, walls of poles and mud, and a hard lime-plaster floor. One quarter of the interior was partitioned off to house the Santa Cruz and the Virgin of the Conception, while the remainder was open to the public for religious services.

On the second day, Cituk and Salub conducted the visitors to the church for a special mass in their honor. The inevitable band was there, rendering a polka tune that seemed incongruous for the occasion. Equally surprising was a human being sprawled on a board in a corner of the floor. It was the blind, eighty-year-old high priest. He joined the visitors before the altar and offered a long prayer that was translated for their benefit.

The visitors followed this introduction to the high priest by a formal visit to his home. Months before, Vay had promised to provide decorations for the sanctuary, and now he fulfilled the pledge. Ceremoniously, he unfolded twelve yards of bright red silk to drape the Santa Cruz. The high priest touched the material, satisfied that it was silk, and Salub assured him that it was red. Next Vay presented twelve handbells for use in religious services. And finally, he brought out a set of Christmas tree decorations, tinsel and red paper bells. The natives were delighted.

The only amusing aspect of the whole fiesta was the mock bullfight staged on two afternoons. A man inside a wooden frame, something like a hobby horse with horns and covered to represent a bull, pranced about, while half a dozen toreadors went through the motions of fighting and killing the bull. The spectators, Indian and white, found it hilarious. Although Vay enjoyed it, he found it otherwise uninteresting because it was obviously of Spanish origin.

Far more impressive and of deep ethnological interest was the ceremony of the pig's head. Resting on a large dish, the head was surrounded by honey-soaked tortillas, sweets, and other delicacies. In a room lighted by flickering candles, eleven natives went through an elaborate ritual dance, accompanied by drums. Apparently the ceremony signified fruitfulness.

A long religious service concluded the fiesta on the final day. Men carrying rifles served as a guard of the Virgin, and women appeared with square, scarlet, fringed shawls. A portable altar with the Virgin of the Conception, surrounded by candles and food, was set up in the enclosure of the *yaxché* tree. At dawn everyone knelt, facing the rising sun, heard mass, and tasted the food as a form of communion. The natives moved toward the church and celebrated mass again; eight times the rite was performed, the last time at the sanctuary. This marked the end of the fiesta.

Actually this service had been delayed for Vay's benefit. It had been originally scheduled for the late afternoon, but at that time the sun was not favorable for taking pictures; so Cituk and Salub postponed the ceremony to the following morning when the light was perfect. As an additional favor, the two chiefs stopped the proceedings at various stages so that Vay and Frances could make a full photographic record of the event.

The members of the party rose at two o'clock on Friday morning to prepare to leave. They had already made farewell rounds the preceding night. Now they packed their belongings, breakfasted, tied the packs on the cargo animals, and left just as dawn appeared. Captain Cituk, gracious host to the end, had appeared at three-thirty, when they were at breakfast, to say goodbye. He stayed on until the mule train left town, and then he stood at the edge of the village watching his guests until they were out of sight.

Morley was grateful for the days at Xcacal. The friendship of those independent Mayas impressed him deeply. He could not forget that he and his party were the first outsiders to be invited to the sacred town and that they were the first white people to be received as friends. He was impressed with the dignity and solemnity of the religious observances, and marveled that so much of the Roman Catholic services had survived since 1850. Even more significant to him were the ceremonies of the *yaxché* tree and the pig's head that appeared to be primitive Maya rites. But one thing he did not see, the Santa Cruz that was reputed to have the ability to talk; it was too sacred for the sight of outsiders.

The interchange of visits did not produce miracles, but it helped to reduce tension between the independent Mayas and the Mexican government. During his residence in Tusik, Villa used his influence for peace, and in the next year, 1937, he and Governor Melgar toured the Xcacal region. The influence of Morley's role cannot be accurately determined, but it appears that he saved the Indians from unwise warfare and aided the Mexican government in a peaceful entrance into the last stronghold of the "wild Mayas."

In 1937, Vay was off on another trip, this time for archaeological work. At Quiriguá he was happy to see that the fruit company kept the plaza well bushed, but he was worried that two altars, situated in shallow holes, were constantly washed by water and gravel with every rain; so he proposed having them tilted to correct the situation. He had to admit, too, that the temple he had helped to excavate and reconstruct two decades earlier was deteriorating, and he recommended to Merriam a season of work to put things right at Quiriguá.

Joining Kidder and a group of friends, Vay and Frances were accompanied by seven other persons on their visit to Copán. There the Kidder party stayed with Cueva, and the Morleys lived at the administration building at the airport. The flight by plane from Guatemala City to Copán gave Vay great satisfaction as he recollected the long, hot trips of the past. Stromsvik stood high in his estimation when he saw the work he was doing at the ruins, especially the way he was arranging to divert the river from the site. Gustav also had a knack for getting along well with the natives and the local and national officials. Assisting him was Aubrey Trik, who was at work reconstructing Temple 22. During his four weeks' stay, Morley spent most of his time working on replacement of the stones on the Hieroglyphic Stairway.

Back in Guatemala City he and Kidder visited the new explorations that Kidder was in charge of at nearby Kaminaljuyú, but Vay seemed more interested in the jadeite boulder of more than two hundred pounds that had recently been found. They made a courtesy call on President Ubico, who as usual promised all assistance in their work. Going on to Antigua for a meeting of the historical society, Vay read a paper in Spanish. Then he went up the Río Graciosa to try to find the place where the Leyden Plate had been found many years before.

Since Frances was not feeling well, he decided to forgo a trip to Uaxactún by mule; instead, they had the more exhilarating experience of viewing the site by air. The president of Taca airlines had ordered the pilot, Mr. Sheppard, to fly over Tikal and Uaxactún to see if landing fields might be built at each place to ship chicle out of the upper Petén. Morley and Frances were guests on the flight. Crossing the volcanic hills and then the rain forest, as they went north he recalled how he had plodded over the same terrain on muleback at the rate of two and one-half miles an hour. On reaching Uaxactún, he had the thrill of a lifetime looking down on the mounds and the headquarters of the Carnegie team there.

At Tikal the plane swooped down to 150 feet above the main plaza, zooming between the two lofty pyramids. He looked into the doorway of Temple I and saw the bats, frightened by the noise of the plane, emerge. He felt he was so close and yet so far from Tikal; overwhelmed with joyous excitement, he forgot to get airsick. Then the plane turned south to Flores and landed on the small airstrip on the south shore of the lake. Vay made a courtesy call on the governor of the Petén, and to his surprise found in his office Altar 1 from Cancuén, which Vay had discovered two decades earlier. Then he and Frances went on to Belize and back to Mérida by plane.

In the summer of 1938, Morley and his wife spent several months in Europe, mainly to attend the International Congress of Anthropological and Ethnological Sciences at Copenhagen. Vay also wanted to see the Leyden Plate again and to spend some time in a quiet spot going over proofs of the *Inscriptions of the Petén*.

The Congress apparently had little interest for him. As one of four delegates from the United States, he attended the sessions, gave two papers, and met professional friends. Only Soustelle's paper on the dwindling Lacandons appeared as an outstanding contribution. On the third day Vay gave two papers. He reviewed the quarter-century of work by the Carnegie Institution in Maya research, illustrating his remarks with motion pictures and colored slides; later in the day he read a paper on the history of the Mayas as revealed by the glyphs, also illustrated with slides of maps and monuments. Among the commentators on his paper was Hermann Beyer, who congratulated Vay on discovering that the Leyden Plate had been carved at Tikal.

Gustav Stromsvik recalled his experiences during this visit to Europe: "In the summer of 1938 I was having a vacation up in northern Norway when a telegram came from Morley, asking me to come down to Copenhagen to help him. . . . He said he wanted someone at hand who could speak the language. This I thought was a feeble excuse; Morley would always find a way to express himself, regardless of where he was. I went, mainly because I wanted to talk with Morley about the Hieroglyphic Stairway at Copán. In Copenhagen Morley was just too busy to approach with my problems, and he and Frances were leaving a Sunday morning early, taking a train across Denmark to Eidsbjerg, where they would embark for England. Deric Nusbaum and I turned up, bright and early, at their hotel, trying to help and to see them off. Besides a scare about a lost passport, which finally was found in Frances' handbag, everything went smoothly, considering their twenty-two pieces of luggage. I had to buy a ticket for halfway across Denmark to be able to have my talk with Morley."[20]

In England, Morley read proofs of the *Inscriptions of the Petén* and met friends. On the recommendation of Professor Myres, Vay and Frances settled down at Brympton Grange, ten miles from Oxford, for three weeks. There he worked in a peaceful rural setting, though it was so cold that the roses were blighted in August. Then he moved on to London for a week. The work on his book left little time for a real vacation, but he managed to meet several professional friends. He had tea with T. A. Joyce and his wife, finding Joyce in such poor health that he did not expect him to live very long. Actually, Joyce held out for three more years. Vay was also invited to the home of Lady Richmond Brown, who had accompanied Gann on the Lubaantún expedition of 1926. Gann had died some months before Vay arrived in England, and so Vay and Frances called on his widow, who was working in a bookstore to forget the loss of her husband. The British Museum also attracted Vay with its small but excellent collection of Maya material. With the co-operation of Gustav Braunholtz and Adrian Digby of the staff, Frances took color photographs of the jades the Ganns had given to that institution. Generally, Morley liked England—Westminster Abbey and the Tower struck a responsive chord in his soul—except for the cold, misty, sunless atmosphere. He claimed that Gann hated the climate and that it eventually killed him.

On the Continent the Morleys engaged in sightseeing and reviewing some famous Maya works. Frances took color photographs of the Leyden Plate in Holland, and Vay searched for the descendants of its discoverer in the tenuous hope of learning more about where it had been found. The desire to see some of Vay's distant maternal relatives took them to Brussels, where he found two third cousins, one a priest and the other a well-known brewer. He also examined two of the famous codices, the Peresianus in Paris and the one in the state library at Dresden. In Paris he and Frances stayed with André Remondet, an artist who had spent

[20] *Morleyana*, 245–46.

three months at Chichén Itzá earlier in the year. But Paris soon
lost much of its charm when the threat of war closed the museums
and art galleries. Of all places on the Continent, it was sixteenth-
century Nuremburg that gave him the most pleasure.

The international situation cut short their visit. They had
tickets to Naples and reservations on the *Rex;* but the tense atmosphere changed those plans. They canceled the Italian trip and
hastened across the Atlantic on the *Ile de France.* For Vay the
combination of seasickness and a poor cabin brought an unpleasant close to the European journey.

XII

The Middle American Project

I T is likely that Morley would have been a good money-raiser
if he had been challenged to enter the field more vigorously.
His personal charm, enthusiasm, and dedication to Maya
research attracted individuals to contribute to the cause. Not to
be forgotten were the favors he secured that were as good as
money. For example, he enjoyed passes on the United Fruit Company steamers between New Orleans and Yucatán for years; and
he induced the manager of the railroads of Yucatán to grant passes
to staff members of the Institution and to haul freight for the
Chichén project free of charge. In one year alone he thus secured
$2,000 worth of freight service. When he put on the exhibition
at the Mérida museum in 1935, a lumber company and the electric company contributed favors that reduced the expense of
the event.

How much money he procured as gifts is not known, but some
instances are on record. At least four persons gave funds to finance
special excavations at Chichén Itzá. When he heard of a new site
in southern Campeche in 1935, he received two small donations
to finance a scouting expedition to search for the ruins. In the
early 1930's, Robert Redfield discovered Alfonso Villa as a promising native, and Morley raised $600 to send the young man to the
University of Chicago for additional training. In his last years,

when Vay dreamed of a project to excavate Tikal, he felt he could raise $50,000 to $75,000 annually for that purpose; on second thought, however, he did not consider himself up to the task.

The most striking case of his money-raising ability occurred after he "discovered" Tatiana Proskouriakoff. The Russian-born draftsman, educated at the Pennsylvania State College and the University of Pennsylvania, was working at the university museum when Vay happened to visit there. Linton Satterthwaite had urged her to make perspective drawings of Piedras Negras, where the Pennsylvania team was active for several seasons. When Vay looked at her drawings, he exploded with enthusiasm, because he was always on the alert to devices that would recreate the ancient structures as they looked in their prime. Twenty-five years earlier he had found the answer in the paintings of Carlos Vierra. But now Vay saw before him a different style of pictorial restoration in the sharp, clear outlines of Maya pyramids, temples, and decorations.

At that moment he decided that he must employ her. And once he made a decision, nothing could budge him from it. Since the Carnegie budget made no provision for such a person, he buttonholed friends for money to send her to the sites for firsthand acquaintance so that her reconstructions would be absolutely accurate. He secured the funds, and as the checks came in, he sent them to Washington and had the C. I. W. set up two accounts, the Friends of Copán and the Friends of Chichén Itzá. Once he reported that of twenty-two persons he approached, twelve contributed immediately and another promised a check in the near future.

Vay had his way. Carnegie officials were considerably embarrassed by his solicitation of money in view of its great financial resources. In the meantime Vay set Miss Proskouriakoff to work, making drawings of various sites; she made her first trip to Middle America for that purpose in 1940. A few years later the C. I. W. capitulated by adding her to the staff and publishing her *Album of Maya Architecture* in 1946. It is a striking visual presentation; the panoramic view and the structures stand out in sharp, clean lines with impeccable accuracy. During the preparation of the drawings, Vay hovered over them with nervous excitement.

In the case of Miss Proskouriakoff, his intuition was better than he could have supposed. She moved on from drawing to perceptive studies of ancient Maya clothing and also suggested the possible meanings of certain hieroglyphs.

What was the purpose of all of this activity in Middle America? Morley answered the question as early as 1913, when his original plan was presented to the Carnegie Institution. Modestly, he envisioned ambitious results for the excavation of Chichén Itzá. He claimed it might solve or partially solve problems involving many facets of the prehistoric Mayas: racial origins and relationships; migration and settlement; cultural development under local environment; racial and cultural intrusion; rapid development and signs of decay; the evolution of various elements of culture, like writing, architectural style, engineering skill, social systems and governmental forms, religious systems, and esthetic taste; and, of course, the chronological record of the Mayas. In broader perspective, Maya research would contribute a chapter to the history of mankind.

After he began work at Chichén Itzá, his objectives changed little. He still aimed to utilize archaeological excavation in order to see what could be learned of the prehistoric Mayas. Five years later his purpose harked back to that of 1913. The goal was to achieve "a clearer picture of the ancient Maya contribution to the development of mankind."

Only a few years after the Chichén project began, Carnegie officials became doubtful about the effectiveness of his approach. In 1928, Ruppert was placed in charge of immediate administrative work. Vay was restricted to supervisory oversight and was told to devote his time to research, writing, and the co-ordination of fundamental problems. The following year he proposed that a committee on Maya research should be set up to grapple with a number of projects he outlined. This did not satisfy his employers, and they soon placed an officer over him. Apparently, the

Carnegie officials considered his outlook too narrow and restricted. It is likely that the newer concepts of the 1920's—the emphasis on the interaction of various disciplines and the view of culture as a complex of numerous forces—made him look a bit old-fashioned.

Regardless of the reason for the action, the C.I.W. created a new historical division, including the work in Middle American studies, and made A. V. Kidder the chairman. Kidder aimed to expand the scope and to co-ordinate the larger aims of the work in Middle America. Under the circumstances, Vay was fortunate to have Kidder as his superior; Ted liked him, and Ted also had remarkable ability as an administrator. On the other hand, Vay was surely cut to the quick by being superseded, but he never gave the least sign of it to anyone.

Kidder announced an expansion of the program which would include the study of environmental factors of Maya civilization. An array of specialists was set to work investigating the scientific aspects of Yucatán—its health and disease, biology, zoology, botany, hydrography, vegetation, fauna of caves, geology, anthropology, and folklore; and there were also detailed studies of *teosinte* and corn. At least fifty-seven scholars from various disciplines participated.

Kidder declared several years after the start of the broader program that the aim was to learn how the Mayas rose from savagery to civilization, why that civilization fell, and how the condition of the present-day Mayas came about. Although this aim was essentially the same as that put forth by Morley in 1913, Kidder added that there must be correlation of the diverse studies to produce a synthesis.

The last statement of aims that Morley made appeared in 1942. He had moved very little from his earlier views. Now he said that the study of the Mayas would throw light on the question whether the growth of human societies was governed by underlying laws or whether civilizations grew without "predictable pattern." He still maintained, as he had in 1913, that the Mayas, isolated and relatively free from outside influence, formed "an ideal laboratory for the study of human history." He gave no indication, however, that he or other scholars in the field had made progress toward fulfilling the aims. All lay in the future.

A few months before Morley died, W. W. Taylor issued a biting commentary on these aims, especially those put forth by Kidder. Taylor claimed that the important studies had been made, but nothing had been done to correlate and synthesize the results. Instead, the specialists worked more intensely in their own narrow subjects, moving farther and farther away from a central focus.

Had Morley known of this criticism, and he probably did not, it is unlikely that he would have been deeply disturbed. He always preferred the pyramids and the temples, the finely executed carvings of bedecked dignitaries, and, of course, the hieroglyphs—that is, the things that the eye could take in and the imagination could play with—over impersonal, cold abstractions like the laws of the development of civilizations.

All told, Morley and the Carnegie Institution received very little criticism of the archaeological work carried on in Mexico and Central America. In 1926 the *Revista de Mérida* carried an article commenting on criticisms made by Leopoldo Batres, which boiled down to a personal attack on Morley and Gamio made by Batres, the former disgruntled inspector of monuments of Porfírio Díaz days. But the editor of the *Revista* took the edge off the attack by defending Vay's work.

The reconstruction of ruins was one of the obligations of the Carnegie project. Assuming that excavation and reconstruction must go hand in hand, the Mexican concession required repairs and restorations. This prohibited the gutting or destruction of a structure simply for the scientific knowledge that could be gleaned from it. Reconstruction, however, provided that after excavation and examination, the building would be put in its original form and in better condition than it had been found; it would thus be available as a cultural monument for public enjoyment. The work of reconstruction vastly complicated the process of excavation and naturally increased the cost of the whole project. For example, the uncovering of the Temple of the Warriors was a simple task

The Hieroglyphic Stairway at Copán, reconstructed. Courtesy George F. Andrews.

Yaxchilán Expedition at Piedras Negras on the Usumacinta River, 1931. In the group at right are John Bolles, Karl Ruppert (rear), Mr. Rhoads (Frances Morley's father), Morley, and Dr. Dwight Rife. Courtesy John Bolles.

A presidential visit during the early 1930's. Morley is in foreground in his large sombrero, President Cárdenas of Mexico is shaking hands with R. T. Smith, and John Bolles is at far right. Courtesy John Bolles.

Calakmul Expedition, 1932. Ruppert at left, Bolles at right. Courtesy John Bolles.

The second Calakmul Expedition leaving Chichén Itzá. Karl Ruppert, Jack
Denison, and Frances Denison are at left center. According to the sign
on the back of the station wagon, this was the "17th Carnegie" expedition.
Courtesy John Bolles.

At Chichén Itzá in this 1933 photograph are R. T. Smith (second from left), Morley, Kidder, Pollack, and Stromsvik. The man at extreme left is unidentified. Courtesy John Bolles.

Morley and Dr. McPhail at Quiriguá. Dr. McPhail, physician at the United Fruit Company hospital at Quiriguá, entertained Morley on his many visits to the site. Here the two are seated in front of the doctor's quarters. In later years Morley liked to wear a stocking on his head. Courtesy Dr. Wilson Popenoe.

Morley and Juan Martínez y Hernández, well-known Yucatecan authority on Maya early colonial documents. Courtesy Giles G. Healey.

compared with the weeks of work required to assemble the wall and the panels of the front façade of the temple and to replace the carved friezes on the sides of the pyramid. Also in this case the excavation and preservation of the inner temple without endangering the outer temple required remarkable ingenuity of Morris and Stromsvik in solving perplexing engineering problems.

Reconstruction inevitably raised questions of accuracy, and there were bound to be differences of opinion in regard to details. The Carnegie officials followed a conservative policy of doing no more than replacing fallen stones in the structure. Rarely were new stones added to fill in missing pieces of a small portion of a design, and then only if the size and form of the pieces were absolutely known. The official report explained that the policy adopted in 1924 called for restoration "only within the bounds of virtual certainty."

An early criticism of reconstruction attracted the attention of the Carnegie Institution only because of the scientific repute and voluble aggressiveness of the critic. Zelia Nuttall, for a generation something of a flamboyant character in the field of Mexican archaeology, gave a lecture before the Anthropological Society of Washington, in February, 1927, in which she criticized the reconstruction of the Caracol at Chichén Itzá. Merriam conferred with Tellez, Mexican ambassador in Washington, on the subject. Merriam maintained that the Carnegie policy was one of replacement of stones rather than restoration in the usual sense of the word. It is still not clear what Mrs. Nuttall took exception to at that date, because work on the tower of the Caracol had not been started. At the moment she was addicted to her theory of the *gnomen*, and she expected to find *gnomens* everywhere. It is possible that Dr. Conant's painting of a reconstruction of the Caracol did not suit her, because it did not have a cone-shaped top, which would have made it a *gnomen* to fit her theory. At any rate, nothing more was heard of this tempest in a teapot.

The Middle American work of the C.I.W. extended over a generation, from 1914 to 1952. Within that period there were shifts in emphasis, with Chichén Itzá as the significant center of activity in the late 1920's and the 1930's. During the first eight years, 1915–23, Morley carried on annual expeditions in the search for glyphs, with excavation a secondary interest. From 1924 to 1940 he lived at Chichén Itzá and directed operations there as well as at other points in Middle America. Then after 1933 excavation was suspended at Chichén, though it remained the headquarters for all work in Yucatán until he moved to Mérida in 1940. In the meantime a Carnegie team worked at Uaxactún for twelve seasons, five annual expeditions were sent to explore the interior of Campeche State, and Stromsvik was assigned to Copán in the early 1930's and worked there before and after World War II. As early as 1931 attention was also directed to the highlands of Guatemala, and several years later excavations began at Kaminaljuyú.

Despite the investigation of various sites in the 1930's, there was the beginning of a shift away from dirt archaeology. When excavations were suspended at Chichén, Kidder attributed it to the fact that scientific facts were accumulating faster than they could be mastered. Only a few years later he announced that the major emphasis was then on the writing and publishing of reports on the work already done.

World War II crippled the Middle American program and forecast its end. The Carnegie Institution acquired a new president in 1939, whose interest was physical science, and the increasing demands of the war also put a premium on intensive scientific research. Moreover, the Institution lost a number of its best staff members in archaeology. Ricketson resigned in 1942. Others went into military service. Stromsvik enlisted in the Royal Norwegian Navy in 1943, served on Atlantic convoys, participated in the Normandy invasion, spent some time at Norwegian headquarters at Edinburgh, and returned to Institution work in 1945. H. E. D. Pollock became a major in the American Army Air Force in Italy in 1944. Karl Ruppert served in the American Field Service in Burma and Italy. And E. Wyllis Andrews was a lieutenant in the United States Navy.

The year after the war ended, the C.I.W. announced that all

projects in the Middle American area would be closed out by the end of the 1940's. When Morley and Kidder happened to meet in Guatemala City in March, 1947, they naturally discussed the future. Vay feared that the historical division, which included archaeology, would be abolished. He was not worried for himself, because he would retire within a few years, but he was concerned for the future of Maya studies. He envisioned a ten-year project to excavate Tikal at $50,000 a year and believed that he and Kidder could convince the president of the Carnegie Institution to adopt it; Vay never lost confidence in his powers of persuasion. Kidder, on the other hand, wanted to work east and south of the Maya area, hoping to find connections with the prehistoric cultures of Panama and South America.

At the time Morley was laying ambitious plans for Tikal, he did not realize that his worst fears were well founded, for the whole historical division was slated for extinction. Only by accident was it saved for a few years. When Kidder's plan was vetoed, Eric Thompson put forth the more modest proposal of excavating Mayapán. Surprisingly, this plan was adopted, because several of the Carnegie trustees resisted abandonment of archaeological work. By 1952, however, those trustees had left the board, and the historical division was quickly closed out. Fortunately, Vay did not live to see its end.

Morley had brought fame to the Carnegie Institution and distinction to himself. Over the years he received various marks of recognition from fellow scholars here and abroad. We have seen how Pennsylvania Military College, his alma mater, conferred on him an honorary doctorate in 1921 for his *Inscriptions of Copán*. The following year he was elected a member of the Société des Américanistes of Paris. But in 1923 he was passed over for the Argand Prize, which was a momentary disappointment to him.

The highest honors came in the years from 1939 to 1943. Guatemala awarded him the decoration of a Grand Officer of the Order of the Quetzal in 1939. The American Philosophical Society elected him a member the following year and two years later awarded him the Franklin Medal. In 1943 he received the Loubat

Prize of $1,000 for his *Inscriptions of the Petén*. Earlier he had received the Medal of Merit of the Geographical and Historical Society of Guatemala, and had become an honorary fellow of the Royal Anthropological Institute of Great Britain. An honor that came early in his career and appears of little moment as compared with those he received later—election as a citizen by the municipality of Copán in June, 1917—doubtless meant as much to him at that time as the more distinguished scholarly awards that came at the peak of his career.

XIII

The Later Years

AFTER Morley left Chichén Itzá in 1940 and moved to Mérida, he sensed that an important era of his career had closed. Chichén had been the center of his life. In the early years he had looked forward to the day when he would live there directing excavations, and the seventeen seasons he spent there had been so happy and satisfying that his emotions were interwoven with the place.

There is a record of only one return visit. That was in December, 1941, when he brought his brother and sister and a few other persons to Chichén for a few days. He dreaded the prospect of going back. And some sights were far from happy; the Casa Principal and his former home were down at the heel. He was pleased, however, with the neat, clean appearance of the whole area, as the vegetation had been systematically kept under control. And the ruins, seeming more beautiful than ever, gave a lift to his spirits. He even tried a phonograph concert in the Ball Court, and it too went off well. All told, the visit turned out successfully.

But he could not bring himself to return in the future. The memory of the happy days there was too poignant. When visitors came to his home in Mérida and it was imperative to show them the important ruins, he willingly guided them over Uxmal, but somehow he always found someone else to take them out to Chichén.

Chenkú suited Morley perfectly. Several miles from the center of Mérida, it was beyond the city though close to a native village. It had been the main house of a former henequen plantation. Hidden behind the usual walls, the baronial residence had a large porch and high-ceilinged rooms, and palm trees lined the walk from the entrance gate. When he acquired the place, it was in bad repair, and he enjoyed bringing it back to respectability and comfort. He made improvements wherever they were needed, built a chimney fireplace (unheard of in Yucatán), and installed a water system and an electric pump. The low rent he paid made it possible for him to afford these additions.

He found the place quiet and comfortable. "You know," he remarked to Adrián Recinos, "the tranquility of life out here in Chenkú—no telephones, a terrible road which grows worse every year, and I, surrounded by my books and photographs of my beloved Maya inscriptions."[1] There were some pets about the place. Frances had acquired two macaws on their last trip down the Usumacinta. "Their plumage is magnificent," he wrote, "barbaric in its splendor—red—yellow—orange, green, violet, blue, practically all the colors of the rainbow."[2] The macaws had the terrace as their preserve, while four ducklings possessed the lily pond. A little later the Morleys also had two police dogs, characteristically named Pop and Zip.

When Jennie Avery, Grace Bowman, and Agnes Morley Cleaveland visited Chenkú, they witnessed two incidents illustrating Vay's tender regard for the natives who worked for him.

One night the water supply, furnished by a well and an electric pump, failed completely, and Pastor, the native in charge of the apparatus, had disappeared. The next morning the story came out. Pay day was also Pastor's saint's day, and the celebration had been too much for him. The guilty delinquent sent his keys and his resignation to his employer. Morley returned the keys to their

1 *Morleyana*, 217.
2 *Morleyana*, 124.

usual place, so that Pastor would see them when he slept off his debauch and know that he still had his job.

When Vay took the three visitors to Uxmal, Jirón, another native, chauffeured the car. But Jirón was familiar with driving only on level ground, and when he tried the hill before Uxmal, the car slowed to a halt and then rolled back to the starting point. One of the women was about to volunteer to take the wheel, but Vay anticipated her by insisting that his driver could make the grade. Three times Jirón tried and failed, then he resorted to low gear and moved up the hill. At the summit Vay proudly announced that he knew that Jirón was an able driver.

The last extensive excavation in which Morley engaged was at Uxmal in 1941 and 1942, when he spent several periods of a week or two at a time at that site. The beauty and proportions of the Governor's Palace had fascinated him ever since he saw it for the first time in 1907. Now he found it more wonderful than ever and insisted that it appeared at its best in the moonlight.

The war interrupted regular fieldwork of the Middle American project, because scientists were called to military service. At the same time Vay became more immersed in writing and also more addicted to the pleasant life at Chenkú and at the new home he acquired in Santa Fe.

He and Frances set out on a two-month trip early in 1944 that was to be the last long expedition for him. Although they enjoyed days of sightseeing and pleasure, his major aim was the inevitable collecting of additional glyph dates. Now he insisted on traveling comfortably, and this aim was gratified to the hilt by his unabashed appeal to the friends he had made everywhere to secure the best modes of conveyance.

The first leg of the journey took him to his beloved Copán, and this time he went in style. Flying from Mérida to Guatemala City, he secured an automobile from the office of the Carnegie Institution located there, managed to borrow Ambassador Long's gasoline rationing coupons (Boaz Long and his wife were at the time in the United States), secured a chauffeur and a cook, and sent them on by car with his bulky luggage to Zacapa. In the meantime

Vay and Frances got John Armstrong, president of the railroad, to lend them his private coach, which was completely and luxuriously furnished with living quarters, for the trip to Zacapa. From that point the chauffeur drove them to Copán, but at the border Vay had to exert all of his persuasiveness and *simpatía* to induce the guard to let the chauffeur and cook enter Honduras without passports.

He had already wired his friend Juan Ramón Cueva of his impending arrival in Copán. At once the general prepared his best room for his old-time guest. In the afternoon Vay appeared and greeted effusively the bevy of friends awaiting him. Remembering that in earlier days Cueva maintained cocks for the favorite sport and that their crowing had disturbed his early morning sleep, Vay turned a quizzical eye on his host and inquired about the cocks. At that moment they began to crow. At once Morley left the attractive quarters and camped in a building on the airstrip near the ruins.

During his stay in Copán he noticed improvements. Now the village had a fountain and a piped supply of water, a neat building housed the museum, and the church was moving toward completion. At the ruins Stromsvik had done wonders in diverting the river away from the ancient structures; and he had rebuilt the Hieroglyphic Stairway and re-erected fallen stelae.

Returning to Guatemala City in Armstrong's private coach, Vay and Frances set out for the Chiapas region of Mexico. The institution automobile took them to the border of the country. At Tapachula they took a plane to Tuxtla Gutiérrez, where J. Eric S. Thompson and his wife joined them for the trip into the Chiapas highlands, the only part of the Maya region Vay had never visited, and then on to San Cristóbal de las Casas.

Through the grassy uplands the car took them to Chinkultic, an ancient Maya site that looks down on Lake Tepancuapán. As the two women sought a shady place for the camera, they discovered they had placed it on some leaves covering a stone with an Initial Series.

Returning to Comitán, they set out the next day for Ocosingo in a dilapidated Ford truck, with the two gringo couples seated on their baggage rolls. The trip over the long rocky road shook them up considerably. Despite Vay's extensive experience in Latin America, he still hoped that the native estimate of distance was correct, though he knew better than to be so optimistic. The trip was actually twenty-seven leagues. Thompson gives an amusing account of the distance: "At the start of the trip Vay cross-examined the driver on the distance; 23 leagues was the answer. Every forty minutes or so Vay would ask the man how far we had come and how many leagues we had yet to go. The figures never equalled the original 23 leagues or any of the previous estimates, and each time Vay would protest: 'You said, when we started, 23 leagues. Now you say we have come 6 leagues and there are 22 to go. That totals 28 leagues. *Hombre*, which is right?' '*Pues ¿quien sabe? señor,*' would reply the driver in a totally disinterested manner. An hour later the total would drop to 20 leagues, and Vay would almost forget to cross-examine in a glow of pleasure, but a little later there would be 7 leagues done with 19 to go! We would stop at one of the very rare huts along the track to check with a local inhabitant, but that was always disastrous; none of the outside guesses checked with the chauffeur.... So it went on, the chauffeur perplexed and almost angry with this gringo search for precise information; Vay still hoping for a reasonable agreement. He was always an optimist."[3]

They bogged down attempting to cross the Río Jataté. After sending for help, they walked three miles to a hacienda that swarmed with *garrapatas*, where they spent an uncomfortable night. By morning the truck had been retrieved, and they rolled into Ocosingo, accompanied by a throng of natives and barking dogs. But Ocosingo yielded nothing of archaeological interest.

Toniná, eight miles away, was a different story. The party had increased to ten, for they had acquired a cook, a policeman, and four Indians to carry the baggage. This time the transportation was by mule and the goal was Don Aureo Cruz's ranch, where they were quartered for three days. Although they were almost

[3] *Morleyana,* 255–56.

eaten up by *garrapatas*, Morley had a glyphic field day in discovering new sculptures, photographing inscriptions, and doing his best to read partly eroded carvings.

On the return from Ocosingo to San Cristóbal and Tuxtla Gutiérrez, the Morleys were out of humor with their driver. After considerable trouble, Thompson had rounded up an automobile and a chauffeur who was somewhat reluctant to make the trip. When the driver stopped along the way for a brief meal because he had not eaten before starting, Frances assumed that he was deliberately delaying their progress and Vay supported her contention. Then Vay and Frances joined in giving him a tongue-lashing. Thompson, on the other hand, tried to get along with the man in a friendly way. At the end of the trip the driver had his revenge. He refused to unload the Morleys' baggage, though he did so for the Thompsons; and he courteously said goodbye to Eric and ignored the Morleys. After he drove the car away to store it for the night, Vay discovered that his briefcase was missing—the driver had deliberately hidden it—and Vay spent two hours rounding up driver and car to recover the bag.

At Tuxtla Gutiérrez the Thompsons flew on to Mexico City, and Vay and Frances took a plane to Guatemala City. Boaz Long and his wife Eleanor gave them guest rooms in the embassy, where they enjoyed luxurious quarters for three weeks. They rose and breakfasted at their leisure, and occasionally Vay had the use of the official car to take him on errands about the city.

The stay in Guatemala City was interrupted by a three-day visit to Quiriguá, with transportation in Armstrong's private coach. Dr. McPhail housed them in rooms at the United Fruit Company hospital, and Vay and the doctor had happy conversations in an exchange of recollections over Scotch and soda on the front corridor of the physician's quarters. Changes had occurred in Quiriguá, too. The fruit company was doing everything to stem the progress of the destructive Panama disease that ruined the banana plants. But it seemed to be a losing battle, and so the company began to plant rubber as a substitute. Eventually the dread disease drove the company out of the area completely.

Vay also visited Antigua, that city of ruins that appealed so strongly to his romantic imagination. The government had just declared it a national monument, and Vay, eager to promote the cause of restoration (he had in mind more houses like the show-place of Dr. Popenoe there), wrote an article that appeared as an interview in *El Imparcial.* "Antigua is Unique and the Purest Expression of Colonial Architecture in the Whole Continent, Says Morley" was the headline of the front-page story. He praised the government for its action, called for faithful preservation, and explained how Santa Fe had recaptured its ancient indigenous style a generation earlier.

Scarcely had the Morleys returned to Guatemala City when they had to vacate their quarters at the embassy. The elaborate residence, filled with patios and halls, could easily accommodate seven hundred persons at a reception, but it had only two guest rooms. Since Mrs. Roosevelt, wife of the President, was coming, and she and her secretary would occupy the guest rooms, Vay and Frances left a day before the First Lady arrived.

The last lap of the trip was a two-week jaunt through the Petén. Again Vay called on friends so that he might enjoy the best treatment at out-of-the-way places in that area. He pulled strings to induce President Ubico to recommend him to the attention of General Mortaya, governor of the Petén, and Mortaya in turn handed the orders down to his subordinates. Vay also approached the Guatemala manager of the Chicle Development Company, who notified his field managers at settlements on the itinerary. As a result, everywhere he was received and treated as a distinguished guest, which pleased him immensely. The chicle company provided him with an outboard motorboat and orders for gasoline and oil. At one settlement the *commandante,* flanked by the whole population of the village, was on hand at the river bank to greet him. At La Libertad, his old friend Kid Tainter, now an important chicle operator, gave him the use of his Ford truck. At another place two soldiers, assigned by Governor Mortaya, accompanied the Morleys to Polol. When he reached Paso Caballos, the chicle company men had two dugout canoes and a crew of five ready to carry the travelers down the rapids of the Río San Pedro. Even at the Guatemalan-Mexican border there was no trouble; Mortaya had already sent ahead orders that the party should be allowed to pass at any hour of the day or night. Over in Mexico at El Tiradero, the chicle company representative awaited them and housed them for the night. Finally, at Tenosique they took train for Campeche and Mérida.

Despite the accommodations designed to ease their journey, the trip was wearing. They could not avoid the mosquitoes, the roaring of the howler monkeys, and the blazing sun on the Río San Pedro. Along the way Vay contracted bronchial trouble and Frances picked up an intestinal infection. One of their most trying days came at the end of the trip when they endured an uncomfortable ten-hour train ride to Campeche. At first they were put in freight cars converted for the use of passengers, crowded to suffocation with *chicleros*. Vay tipped the conductor to let them occupy the caboose, usually used by trainmen and their families. Little did that improve the situation, for two families had already taken possession of the caboose and spread filth in all directions.

In Campeche he and Frances were once more with friends and could relax from the strain of the trip. The Mexican archaeologist Alberto Ruz Lhuillier had them at his home for a meal and then invited them to dine with him again the next day before they left town. "Charmed, *hijo*, but on one condition," countered Vay, "that your wife make me *pámpanos en 'poc' chuc'* like those which we are eating now."[4]

Willingly he suffered all of the inconveniences of the trip and the loss of sixteen pounds in weight, because he returned, as in the old days, with the "archaeological bacon." All told, he had visited eleven sites, discovered six new Initial Series, five Period Ending dates, and sixteen monuments. This new information pushed the date of Altar de Sacrificios back fifty years and the date of the Maya settlements in the Usumacinta River valley by forty years. These facts, together with a new appreciation of the strategic location of Altar as a trading center for a vast area, changed his hypo-

[4] *Morleyana,* 114.

thesis of the route that Maya civilization took as it spread from Uaxactún and Tikal into the Usumacinta valley.

On his return to Chenkú, he admitted that he and Frances were exhausted by the expedition. Back home they also suffered from the Yucatecan heat and humidity. "I can't do at 60," he confessed to the Longs, "what I used to laugh at, at 30. The spirit is still willing but the good old flesh is weak."[5]

He was right. He returned to Santa Fe to spend the summer. Hardly had he recovered from attacks of malaria when he suffered a heart attack in August. Three weeks later Frances complained that she and the attending physician were unable to keep him in bed for the prescribed six weeks, because his spirits were so high. Slowly he learned to walk, but admitted that he could not restrain his excited talking. By late October he had a final physical check-up and received an encouraging report, which was what he hoped for so that he could be off on his travels again. He found an army sergeant at Los Alamos who wanted to return to his home in Louisiana and arranged to have him drive Frances and him to New Orleans. After arriving there, Vay boasted that he felt fine, and he and Frances went on to Chenkú.

In 1945 when he visited Mexico City, he made a trip north to Tula to see the remarkable ruins recently uncovered by the Mexican government. The material at Tula had a direct bearing on the Toltec occupation of Chichén Itzá.

Unfortunately, he was not a member of the expedition that set off in 1947 for the newly found ruins of Bonampak with their remarkable murals. However, he was vitally interested in the results. The C.I.W. assembled Kidder and Eric Thompson, Ruppert, Stromsvik, and Tejeda; the Mexican government sent Villagrá; and Giles Healey, discoverer of the murals, led the group.

When the party returned, Morley rushed in on them, eager to see the pictures. Copies were spread over the floor, and he plodded about enthusiastically among them on hands and knees, searching for glyphs that appeared among the figures.

He also devised the name for the ruins. Tejeda heard him ex-

[5] *Morleyana,* 125.

claim "Now we have the name" for the site—Bonampak, meaning "painted walls." Someone had suggested the name of Alfred Maudslay, but Morley confided to Tejeda that "we Mexicans" preferred a Maya name to that of the famous English explorer.[6] And so his suggestion of Bonampak was generally adopted as the designation.

Later in 1947 he took a month's trip to some of his favorite haunts. At Quiriguá he saw Dr. McPhail once more—for the last time, as it proved. Again magnetic Copán drew him to it, especially since he could cover the distance so easily by air. His spirits rose as he looked over the clean village. In the center of the plaza was the fountain designed by Tatiana Proskouriakoff, and nearby the attractive new museum building completed by Stromsvik. Gus had even carved the Honduras coat of arms that hung above the doorway of the building. The only person who was missing at Copán was Juan Ramón Cueva, who had died just short of eighty.

Back in Guatemala City, Vay visited Toxica Roach, worked with Pat McEvoy on an article designed for *Reader's Digest,* and agreed to write a fifteen-hundred-word article for *Life* magazine. Then he returned to Chenkú and Frances and his two pet dogs.

His travels were about over. In February, 1948, he took a small party to visit Uxmal, which, as far as is known, is the last time that he saw his beloved Maya ruins.

In conversation Morley did not hesitate to make known his views on politics and public affairs. In his diary, however, he was either more circumspect or perhaps less interested in discussing such subjects, for only a few of his opinions gained notice in that record. He was a staunch party man, a "dyed-in-the-wool Republican,"[7] as one of his associates described him. On learning of the death of Harding in 1923, he remarked that the President had done a good job and had a strong cabinet. But on re-reading that entry twenty-two years later, he added a pencil note that he had been sadly mistaken in his estimate. When the oil scandals of

6 *Morleyana,* 250.
7 *Morleyana,* 256.

1924 hit the headlines, he noted that fact, although he did not indicate what he thought of the exposures. His reticence may well have come from the uneasy memory that he had hoped for a diplomatic appointment through the influence of Secretary of the Interior Albert B. Fall a few years earlier.

Vay's friends had no doubt of his dislike of President Franklin Roosevelt. In this respect he was supported by the equally strong views of his wife. A friend who accompanied the Morleys on a trip through Chiapas in 1944 recalls an incident when they stopped at a hotel in one of the small cities. The Americans met the only other foreign guest in the dining-room and at the same table. But when the guest indicated great admiration for Roosevelt, Frances rose indignantly, left her place, and refused to eat at the same table in the future.

Morley sympathized from the beginning with England and France in World War II. He despised Hitler, sometimes characterizing him with unprintable words. Also, he was utterly disgusted with Lindbergh, saying that the famous aviator did not care whether the Allies won or lost the conflict. On at least one occasion Vay gave a lecture for the benefit of British war relief. He believed in United States intervention, and his enthusiasm for the cause mounted after Pearl Harbor. At Chenkú he listened to radio newscasts at five o'clock in the morning, though he had difficulty in keeping awake, and again at nine o'clock. Recalling how World War I had vastly altered his own outlook on life, he predicted in 1941 that the present conflict would bring change in the life of everyone, and he added wistfully that change is not welcomed as one advances in years.

One of his last comments on politics occurred in regard to state elections in New Mexico in 1946. He determined to stay in Santa Fe until election time so that he could vote to throw out the incumbents. He claimed that if one had little choice in voting for the man he wants, the two-party system provided the opportunity to vote against the party in power.

His views on orthodox religious belief were shattered, perhaps during the days of World War I. As early as 1917, when he was forced to listen to sermons on Hog Islands, he dismissed them as dispensing the old orthodoxies; and by the early 1920's he had lost all faith in a future life. He was fully aware of the change that had come over him when he declared that he no longer held the restricted views that had marked his early manhood. Sometimes he referred to his godlessness, noting that his Jesuit friend Father Versavel disapproved of it. On another occasion he disclaimed belief in any religious denomination. In place of a hereafter, he saw only extinction of the individual, but he solaced himself with the thought that that was not too oppressive in view of the joy and happiness one can find in the present world.

He envied those who did believe, and he wished that he too could regain some form of faith. When he and Don Rafael Regil attended church services in Mérida in March, 1923, Don Rafael went to his knees and bowed his head as the procession passed. On emerging from the church, Vay told him he would give anything to have such faith. Three days later Morley heard strains of religious music in his hotel room. Curious, he entered the church of the Tercera Orden nearby and witnessed a procession that appealed to him. Once more he wished that he might believe, but concluded that it was impossible. Then he cast up a balance sheet on what he termed his intellectual emancipation; his new attitude had compensations, but it also involved a loss of the wonder and beauty that accompanied faith.

Despite his profession of godlessness, Vay responded to the sensuous aspects of elaborate religious ceremonials like the high mass. The music, color, and drama of the spectacle stirred him, and he did not deny it. He never attacked organized religion despite his disbelief in its dogmas. Occasionally, he termed a religious practice he witnessed in Central America as superstitious, and he could not forgive the papacy for failing to come out boldly for the Allied side in World War I. But he rarely voiced these views, and they marked the ultimate bounds of his criticism of Roman Catholicism. Actually, he always harbored a yearning in his heart for Mother Church; and at the end of his life, when he asked for acceptance into that communion, friends did not realize his long, secret interest in the Roman church. It is true that he always listed himself as an Episcopalian in the accounts in *Who's Who* and other biographical dictionaries, but that was no more than a nominal statement that had lost most of its meaning .

His interest in people continued unabated through the years. A former secretary, Nina Piatt, had been in hospital service during World War II. On her return to Santa Fe on October 23, 1945, years after she had worked for him, she learned that he was lecturing one night on Maya hieroglyphics. "Naturally," she wrote, "this wasn't to be missed, and after the lecture he quickly disengaged himself from an important group when he saw me to greet me as warmly as ever."[8]

As one might expect, his record for friendship was not universal. In the 1940's, a young woman archaeologist worked in an office adjacent to his in Santa Fe. For some unexplained reason he never paid any attention to her. "We were not on chummy terms . . . ," she wrote, "about three times a week, for several months, I was addressed as 'Miss Murphy,' followed by the statement, 'I *know* that is not your name, my dear young lady, but it is something very close to Murphy.' "[9]

He loved children. He enjoyed especially the role of instructing them in simple things, particularly if he could work with the Mayas. Mrs. Nusbaum tells of his meetings with her daughter: "From the time she learned to speak, 'Uncle' Vaynus's conversations with her were little stories of the Maya and their relation to humankind. . . . On many a Sunday picnic he and Rosemary would sit in the sun or under a tree to talk 'science' until we called a halt." When the Morleys and Mrs. Nusbaum, accompanied by her two daughters, attended the state fair at Albuquerque in 1947, Rosemary and Vay sat on a bench in deep conversation while the others visited the cattle show. When they were chided for their failure to take an interest in the exhibits, Vay observed, "Well, you girls can feed the chickens and milk the cows, Rosemary and I have more important things to think about."[10]

[8] *Morleyana,* 201.
[9] Letter to the author.   [10] *Morleyana,* 175–77.

When George Brainerd visited him at Chenkú, he found Vay enjoying a boy's sport. "One morning in 1942, driving toward this village [near Chenkú] over the mud road, I saw Dr. Morley wobbling toward me on a bicycle, coat-tails waving in the breeze, horn-rim glasses on nose, a group of delighted children in the background. I pulled to one side. He rocketed past, a look of ecstasy on his face. Risking disaster, he waved a hand, shouting, 'I haven't tried one of these for thirty years.' "[11]

Although he began to show some signs of slowing his usual fast pace, he retained his enthusiasm and good spirits in his last years.

When Ben Grauer made an unannounced call at Chenkú in 1946, he was graciously received, because Vay was willing to shorten his siesta in order to accommodate the visitor. "His voice was mild," Grauer noted, "his manner friendly and informal, and he talked directly without embellishment or adornment." He was eager to hear the latest about Stirling's work on the Olmecs. But it was when Grauer mentioned Uaxactún that Vay's "energetic, slightly-squinting eyes softened and his expression grew nostalgic. It was like a man recalling a romantic experience in order to live it again." He was happy to recount the story of his discovery of that site. After Grauer said goodbye and reached the gate, he "turned and noted his short, compact body and the thatch of sandy-grey hair as he waved once, briefly, and walked inside."[12]

When H. E. D. Pollock, who had begun to work for him twenty years before, visited him at Chenkú in 1948, he noticed changes. Vay had more gray hair, and he moved more slowly and carefully. But his spirit was the same as ever. Later that season the Pollocks accompanied Morley and his brother Henry to Uxmal. "I can see the journey now—the car loaded to the ceiling, Vay sitting cross-legged like a buddha, chatting and laughing about any and every subject or incident that came to mind." After the day's work at the ruins, they would sit in the moonlight and view the ruins in the silvery bath. "As always, the conversation ran unguided and unbounded—the coming presidential election, the ancient Mayas,

[11] *Morleyana*, 13.
[12] *Morleyana*, 62, 64.

the chances of war with Russia, an incident of the day's work, an anecdote of other years."[13]

Just before Vay left for the States in May, 1948, Stromsvik called on him. He had given up plans for a grand excavation at Tikal, because his physical condition was not the best and money for the project was not forthcoming. Gustav realized that Morley was tired, and he decided to leave so as not to weary him. They parted with an *abrazo*.

In his later years he retained traits that had marked him through life. His ability to tell stories and his tendency to be extremely forgetful are illustrated by incidents during visits to his daughter, then living in Los Alamos.

Mrs. Brooks told the following classic anecdote about her father: "When Daddy returned to Santa Fe from Yucatán, in May of 1946, the Superintendent of Schools at Los Alamos asked him to deliver the Graduation Address at the Commencement Exercises. These were to be held at 8:00 P.M., and it was arranged that I would secure the visitors' passes to the project for my father and his driver. It was planned that they would arrive at Los Alamos about 5:00 P.M., which would give him (my father) time to rest and have a light supper before going to Commencement. Since this was his first visit to the project, I especially pointed out that both he and his driver would have to have some means of identification to present to the guards at the entrance to the Project.

"When no word had come from my father at 6 o'clock, I became concerned as to his whereabouts and made a telephone call to Santa Fe, from which I learned that he had left for Los Alamos about 3:30. With this information on hand, I called the Military Police Sergeant on duty at the entrance gate and asked him if Dr. Morley had called for his visitor's pass. The MP informed me that there was a man down at the gate who claimed to be my father, but he had absolutely no identification of any description with him, and besides the boy with him (his driver) couldn't speak English. The guard asked me to come down to the gate and identify this man if I thought he was my father. I assured him I would

13 *Morleyana*, 206–207.

be there at once; so, after locating my birth certificate, upon which Daddy's signature appears, I hurried to the gate. By this time it was nearly six thirty, and I could see rest and dinner being forgotten in an effort to get him in the gate and to Commencement on time.

"When I arrived at the gate, I found my father in a partial state of undress. He had shed his suit coat and vest, and was at the moment trying to find, somewhere on his trousers, with the help of the MP, some tailor's label, cleaner's mark or something which would identify him. It was all good fun and the MPs seemed to be enjoying themselves thoroughly. I quickly identified him, he as quickly dressed, and we drove home for that short rest and light supper before the Commencement Exercises."[14]

In his last years, Vay strengthened his roots in Santa Fe. He had bought a house there in the early 1940's, and for years he was given office space in the museum or the laboratory to carry out his studies in the summer and fall of each year. Also he had some connections with the School of American Archaeology by serving occasionally on one of its committees. More significant is the fact that he and Hewett were gradually healing the breach that had come between them.

The first outward sign of rapprochement appeared in the summer of 1945, when Vay gave his art collection to the museum in Santa Fe. In his official offer of the objects, he referred to Hewett with respect and affection as the first person who had employed him in archaeology. In closing the ceremony of presentation, Hewett paid fulsome tribute to Morley and announced that the museum and the school had jointly conferred on him the title of patron. Both men had accomplished what they had undoubtedly longed for over the years—the revival of friendly relations.

Morley's gift represented the choicest items of his Spanish colonial ecclesiastical art and Spanish colonial silver. His enthusiasm was evident in the description of the objects that he wrote for publication at the time of the presentation. The items on display, however, represented only half the total gift. Today the col-

[14] *Morleyana*, 15–16.

lection occupies a prominent place in the Palace of the Governors. At the same time, he arranged that his personal library of some 1,200 volumes would go to the school after his death; and his office and the books are in active use in the laboratory today.

Events moved in a direction that obviously pleased him. In the following year he was placed on the managing board of the school, and was also commissioned to act with Archbishop Byrne to seek out certain Spanish-Mexican records relating to local history. As the Carnegie Institution moved toward closing out its archaeological work and Morley was slated to retire from active service in 1949, he wisely strengthened his relations in Santa Fe.

Suddenly the school needed a new director. Hewett died on the last day of 1946, after forty years with the organization. As an individualist, he had molded the school after his own ideas, and those ideas grew less susceptible to change as he grew older. He had attempted to train a successor, but that experiment failed. Whether Hewett then recommended Morley to succeed him is not known. At any rate, some of the trustees found an ideal solution that made everyone happy. They induced the Carnegie Institution to lend Morley to the school as its director, an arrangement that gave Vay a useful post and relieved the school of the financial burden of the salary for that job. Vay, of course, was delighted with the appointment.

He was director from the middle of 1947 until his death fifteen months later. Beginning the work with enthusiasm and hope, he inaugurated a number of changes. He merged the school, the museum, and the laboratory. He established a new art program for the museum, launched an English translation of Sahagún, initiated the publication of selected illustrations called *Masterpieces of Maya Art*, and gave attention to some aspects of public relations. He listened carefully to at least one person, who suggested how to interpret scholars' research for the layman.

Much of the work he carried out at a distance, for he continued to spend considerable time in Mexico. After assuming the post, he remained in Santa Fe for about five months. But in November he made his annual trip southward and lived at Chenkú until the following May. During his absence Albert Ely, executive secretary, carried on routine matters for him, and made several plane trips to Yucatán to confer with him.

Morley had a third heart attack in August, 1948, and was sent to the hospital in Santa Fe on the thirteenth. He held on for three weeks. Fortunately for him, Kidder was a daily visitor, for Ted happened to be recuperating in a room next to Vay's. Sensing that the end was near, Vay called for Archbishop Byrne, who was happy to admit him to membership in the Roman Catholic church. If this action did not please some of Morley's friends, one can assume that it gave him strong spiritual comfort in those last days. On Wednesday, September 1, the board met, heard Morley's annual report as delivered by Albert Ely, and voiced concern over the director's illness. The next morning, at 7:20, he died. On the following Monday, the sixth, funeral services were held in the cathedral; Archbishop Byrne celebrated the Requiem Mass and delivered the eulogy.

One of the projects that Vay had failed to carry out was a large-scale examination of Tikal. He could not have dreamed that by the mid-1950's the University of Pennsylvania expedition would begin a vast excavation of the site that extended beyond the decade originally contemplated, and that the plans called for restoration so that the public could view the ancient stelae and temples in prime condition.

February 18, 1964, was a big day at Tikal. Outsiders swarmed into the place by plane from Guatemala City and even by truck from Flores. Among the visitors were Vay's daughter and his granddaughter, state officials, and archaeologists. They gathered at the museum, a new, modest, modern structure that was to be dedicated to the memory of Sylvanus G. Morley. Appropriately enough, J. Eric S. Thompson, dean of Maya epigraphers, gave the major address, first in Spanish and then in English. Perhaps it was coincidence that the dedication occurred fifty years after Vay's first visit to Tikal. With the conclusion of the formal ceremonies, everyone indulged in refreshments, and a marimba band, composed of native workers on the project, furnished the music. The guests began to dance, and soon they were tripping the Yucatán *jarana*. Good spirits and happiness filled the air, another tribute to the spirit of Vay Morley, who relished the sheer joy of living.

XIV

Writings and Lectures—2

THE pattern of Morley's publications after 1923 continued to include scholarly productions and popular works. His serious contributions appeared in the annual reports of the Carnegie Institution, in monographs, and in articles in scholarly journals and books. After his monumental *Inscriptions of the Petén* appeared, he encountered trouble over the publication of his researches. His employer began to doubt the wisdom of the subjects he selected and the significance of the results that he achieved. He reached the height of his fame with professional associates in his great contribution to Maya epigraphy that appeared at the end of the 1930's.

His second great work on hieroglyphic dates, *Inscriptions of the Petén*, appeared in five volumes in 1937–39. It presented the results of three decades of travel and collecting, of study and restudy of the extant inscriptions. The project was a partial fulfillment of the plan he had outlined to Merriam in July, 1914, when he was employed by the Carnegie Institution.

He spent five to six years of intensive work in completing the project in the 1930's. As early as 1932 he said that he had finished four-fifths of the manuscript, which amounted to 2,400 typed pages, legal size, triple spaced; and by the next year he had selected the photographs. It seemed, however, that this was only the beginning rather than the end of his labors, for by 1935 and 1936 he was devoting almost full time to the manuscript during the regular season in Chichén Itzá and in the summer and fall at Santa Fe.

When he and Frances returned from Yucatán to the States in June, 1936, he made elaborate provision to bring the bulky manuscript with him. It was priceless to him, because there was only one copy. As he boarded the ship, he duly wrapped the valuable package in a life preserver to insure its survival, even if the Morleys were not that fortunate. Some friends who tell the story insist that the bundle bore an American flag in which each star represented a Maya city. All went well, however, and the Morleys and the bundle landed at New Orleans. Then they took a Pullman for Washington, and Vay reserved an upper berth for the sole occupancy of the package. Just before the train pulled out, he discovered that the manuscript was not in its place. With a shriek of despair, he wailed over the loss, racing hither and yon, losing his glasses, and stumbling over luggage. At the next stop the Pullman porter had located the precious bundle, which had only been misplaced, and once more the manuscript was stowed away in the upper berth and rode safely to Washington.

The work was assuming mountainous proportions, and Carnegie officials, alarmed at the prospect of its costly publication, attempted to keep it from becoming a monster. When Vay decided to add appendices, as he had done in the *Inscription of Copán,* he appealed to various scholars for essays on collateral aspects of the subject. But the editorial committee put its foot down on three of these addenda—Lundell's account of flora, Van Tyne on fauna, and E. Wyllis Andrews on the Supplementary Series—explaining that these topics had already been treated in other publications of the Institution.

Reading proof and checking all of the references was a tremendous task. When Morley approached the job in Santa Fe in the summer of 1937, he made arrangements to have the Peabody *Memoirs* and Maudslay's great work available for reference. Actually Frances did most of the dreary work of confirming the citations to these standard works. The following year he was still at the task of reading proof, this time working in Washington where he had the aid of Alexander Pogo and Linton Satterthwaite. The tedious work of reviewing the mathematical calculations was entrusted to Pogo, while Satterthwaite carried on other functions.

Since a sizable portion of the manuscript dealt with the dates at Piedras Negras, where Satterthwaite had worked with the University of Pennsylvania team for a number of years, Vay asked him to read that part of the proof. "We spent two or three days at it," Linton later recalled. "He would 'rest' on the bed in his room at the Cosmos Club while I waded through a thick pile of proof sheets on a table." Vay had always insisted that a series of eleven katún markers should have been found at Piedras Negras to complete a given sequence; but those stones never turned up. Satterthwaite had become suspicious of this theoretical hiatus, and had then carefully examined Stela 29 on which Vay had based his assumption. Since the lower half of the inscription was missing, Satterthwaite found it possible to assume another date than the one Vay had adopted, and thus he could dispense with the eleven undiscovered markers which he did not believe existed. Vay, however, could not give up a long-cherished theory at once. "But crossing the street later on, as we dodged a taxi and with complete change in the subject of conversation he said, 'Lint, you're right. I'll re-write Stela 29.' "[1]

Satterthwaite had also become annoyed with Morley's ingrained habit of repetitious writing. Prolixity of this kind was perhaps necessary in works for the general public in order to clarify technical information, but Satterthwaite could not approve of it in a scholarly work that would be read by specialists familiar with the subject. So he did what he could to induce Vay to trim out excess verbiage. "As I read, periodically I would object to what I described as 'window dressing.' We would argue about it for a while, then I would read the whole passage through continuously, sometimes I am afraid with sarcastic overtones. Generally at this stage Vay would concede that it *was* window dressing and render

[1] *Morleyana*, 220, 223.

the verdict—'All right, cut it out.' I, not he, would wield the pencil, sometimes eliminating a foot or more of text."[2] He marveled at the way Vay agreed to this "wholesale murder" of his brainchild with no ill-feeling.

Friends apparently never knew that Vay paid a stiff price for all of these changes made in the proof. The Carnegie Institution had unusually generous rules governing authors' alterations. They allowed such changes up to 20 per cent of the printing costs, and they were willing to consider additional changes in the event that new discoveries occurred after the manuscript had been submitted. Apparently Vay never thought of these regulations as he went ahead making wholesale alterations in the proof. Nor did his first action augur well for what was to come. After the Institution had secured an estimate on the manuscript he turned in and had set up its budget accordingly, he submitted 126 additional pages. Then when he returned the proof sheets, they bristled with changes, deletions, and additions. Since the Institution had a sacred regard for a scholar's manuscript, it did not wish to quibble with what he said; but it also had to use its funds judiciously. Vay's proof-sheet corrections cost $7,176 or about 60 per cent of the total cost of printing the several volumes of the text.

The Institution had to take action in self-defense. Vay attributed the numerous changes to new material that had come to light while he was writing. This explanation was difficult to accept since he had collected the data over a period of a quarter of a century and had been writing the manuscript for five years. The Carnegie officials gave him considerable benefit of the doubt on this point and credited half of the cost of changes under that head; then they allowed him the maximum of 20 per cent of the total printing charges for author's alterations. By these calculations Vay owed the Institution $1,240, which was deducted from his salary over a period of three years. The officials were reluctant to do this and were almost apologetic when they broke the news to him, but he uttered no complaint.

[2] *Morleyana*, 220.

The *Inscriptions of the Petén* was an expensive work to produce. The two volumes of photographs and oversize maps cost twice as much as the three volumes of text. The Institution spent $33,940 to print eight hundred copies of the set of five volumes. If Vay's annual salary and the expense of the numerous expeditions he took in search of the glyphs were added to the cost of printing, the total investment in this production is staggering.

By sheer bulk alone this was his great contribution to Maya epigraphy. It was a masterly compilation, bringing together all of the known date glyphs of the Petén area. This was a necessary service, for in the early stage of any science the factual data must be collected and made available for study; in this respect he carried out a noteworthy project.

One of his protégés later remarked that he was no theoretician, that is, he failed to work out interpretations of the material he had collected. From one point of view the charge is true, because his major purpose was accurate compilation rather than theoretical interpretation. From another point of view the statement is open to question or is even unfair. His original aim, which he achieved, was to construct a chronology of Maya civilization. He entertained a few theories, like the conception of the Old and the New Maya Empire and the Spinden correlation of the calendar. Unfortunately, he adopted both of these ideas at the outset of his career as working hypotheses and gradually looked upon them as facts. He never surrendered the idea of the Old and the New Maya Empire, but the Spinden correlation he scrapped in favor of the Thompson-Martínez system by the time he wrote the *Inscriptions of the Petén.*

His failure to theorize more about Maya chronology must also be viewed against the age in which he lived and the kind of mind he possessed. He began Maya studies at the opening of the twentieth century, when a handful of serious students like Goodman, Seler, Bowditch, and Tozzer attempted to provide a solid, scholarly basis of factual information on the subject. They were reacting against the trends of the preceding generation, when fantastic theories, emanating from men like Brasseur de Bourbourg and Le Plongeon, clouded the whole field of Maya studies with useless argument and unsupportable claims. Morley entered the profession at the time when a new movement called for incontrovertible fact, and he carried out that aim in the area of epigraphy. Moreover, he found this task congenial and absorbing, while his general professional attitude shunned theorizing. This was perhaps a happy circumstance, because too much speculation could have endangered the objectivity he sought to bring to his work. If others were later to use his materials to achieve interesting and fruitful hypotheses, that was precisely what Morley had hoped would be the result of his arduous labors.

In addition to the bulky work on the *Inscriptions of the Petén*, he produced three monographs, in each case in collaboration with another person. Far more investigation went into *Age and Provenance of the Leyden Plate*, written with his wife, than is suggested by the brief eighteen pages of text. With the history of the Xiu family and the account of five Books of Chilam Balam, he ran into trouble over publication.

For years Vay had been fascinated by the genealogy of the Xiu family in Yucatán, dating from the time of the Xiu rulers of Uxmal about A.D. 1000 to the descendants he found scattered in the different parts of the country in his own day. As early as 1918, when he visited Oxkutzcab, major center of the modern Xius, he did his first work on the family tree by questioning descendants. By the 1930's he resumed the quest in earnest with the aid of Ralph Roys and Ignacio Rubio Mañé. They ransacked local archives, talked with every Xiu they could track down, and used the Xiu documents in the Peabody Museum library. Often they ran into blind alleys. Once Vay excavated a mound near Oxkutzcab to prove that it was the site of the colonial church where Xius worshiped; he found no traces of a church. Then on his trip to Xcacal in Quintana Roo he encountered an Antonio Xiu, but Antonio could not recollect the name of his paternal great-grandfather who came from Oxkutzcab, and so Vay could not place him on the family tree. The extensive exhibition that Morley prepared for the Mérida museum in honor of the meeting of the

Mexican Historical Congress had a whole section devoted to Xiu lineage and photographs of Xiu homes.

Because Vay considered Nemesio Xiu and his son Dionisio direct descendants of the rulers of Uxmal, he took great interest in them. He was on friendly terms with members of the family and helped them in minor ways. He advised Dionisio on finding a bride, and Vay and Frances became godparents of several of the children. But he could never bring himself to acknowledge that Dionisio's marriage failed. When he wrote *The Ancient Maya,* he included the story of the Xius with pictures of their homes over the centuries to illustrate their decline from rulers to ordinary citizens. Also he saw to it that Dionisio was taken to Uxmal to pose against the ruins of his ancestors' palaces when Kessel took photographs to illustrate the article on the Mayas in *Life* magazine.

Morley's research on the Xius was one of the most ill-advised tasks he ever undertook. The manuscript, completed in 1941, amounts to four volumes, including a volume of plates. He wrote the section on the family history and Ralph Roys the second part on the Xiu Chronicle. The text runs to 813 pages and is fattened by the inclusion of 145 documents. Two copies of the manuscript, an original and a carbon, are on deposit in the Peabody Museum library, because Kidder refused to sanction the expense of printing such an elaborate work that produced so little useful results. Not only is it dreary reading, but unfortunately Vay could not fill the gap of four hundred years in the genealogical framework. In this project his enthusiasm overcame his good sense, and his zeal to exhaust the subject distorted his scholarly judgment. Perhaps someone some time might find the elaborate manuscript useful.

Morley's study of five of the Books of Chilam Balam, written with Alfredo Barrera Vásquez and published as *The Maya Chronicles* after his death, presented problems. He spent considerable time and money running down and photographing the most reliable copies of some of the documents. When he submitted the completed manuscript to the Carnegie Institution for publication, the editorial office raised several questions. Was there justification for the expense of producing fourteen pages of photographs show-ing sheets from the documents? Kidder agreed that the costly luxury could be dispensed with. Next came the question of Mor-ley's interpretation of the results of his study, because other scholars did not agree with his views. On this point Kidder, it must be recorded to his credit, staunchly defended the author's right to publish his views regardless of what other specialists thought of those interpretations.

As in the earlier period, Morley reviewed books sparingly. He gave a favorable account of Tozzer's *Landa*, and a somewhat less enthusiastic review of Gruyter's volume on Maya hieroglyphics and Satterthwaite's on the Maya calendar.

In his last years he also worked on a compilation of all known hieroglyphs. He employed a draughtsman to make an exact copy of the figures on cards, on which Vay supplied the pertinent in-formation. On completing the Initial Series and the Supplemen-tary Series, he submitted that part of the project to his superiors; the Carnegie Institution mimeographed, although it did not for-mally publish, it for the use of scholars.

He also put his hand to the production of guidebooks for the use of visitors to Quiriguá, Chichén Itzá, Copán, and Uxmal. At his best, he had a gift for this type of writing, which sprang essen-tially from his desire to explain and teach.

Guide Book to the Ruins of Quiriguá was the only publication of that genre actually completed by Morley. Written in the early 1930's, when he was still in top form, it was an excellent book that happily combined information with personal experiences. A compact work of two hundred pages, it carried splendid photo-graphs made by Jesse Nusbaum on early expeditions and con-tained a simple explanation of Maya history and the Maya calen-dar. He dedicated the volume to the people of Guatemala and to the Geographical and Historical Society of that country.

Although this was not the kind of book the Carnegie Institution normally issued, officials considered its general educational value so significant that they departed from their rules to publish it. Moreover, President Merriam induced Adrián Recinos to translate it into Spanish, and that version was also published by the Institution. Twelve years later, when the English edition was about exhausted, it went through a second printing.

Morley's plans to write similar handbooks for other sites were less fortunate. In the 1940's, Kidder pressed upon him the idea of guides for Chichén Itzá and Uxmal, partly to distract him from completing the remaining work on date inscriptions not covered in the publications on Copán and the Petén. Finally, in February, 1948, Vay abandoned the project on hieroglyphs, only because he realized that the Institution was unwilling to publish it. In the meantime he made headway on one of the guides.

He submitted the manuscript of the guide to Chichén Itzá three months before his death, and was probably spared the knowledge of its fate. Kidder and officials of the C.I.W. could not bring themselves to print it because the weaknesses were too obvious. The text was repetitious; it was filled with unnecessary descriptions of objects the visitor could see for himself; and the author injected opinions that other scholars did not accept, a practice not consistent with a guidebook.

He never wrote the guidebook on Copán. As early as 1937 he had told Merriam offhandedly that some time he wanted to produce such a work. But he did not get around to it, and so Stromsvik, who had spent years at the site, prepared a guide that the Carnegie Institution published in 1947. But Morley still nursed his ambition; he considered Gustav's book unsatisfactory and made it clear that he would write his own regardless of who published it. When Kidder explained that the Stromsvik book would take care of the need for some time to come, Vay did not budge. However, when an official at the Institution asked Morley to consider how Stromsvik would feel if Vay carried out his plan, the point went home. So at the first opportunity, when Gustav visited Chenkú in May, 1948, Vay asked if he had objections to his writing a new guide, and the bighearted Norwegian assured him of his approval and referred to his own book as "merely a stop-gap." Vay made no headway on the plan before his death a few months later.

One of the last short items to come from his pen was an introduction to a shortened version of Prescott's *Conquest of Mexico* that appeared in 1948. In these few pages, Vay, again in the role of the teacher and instructor of the lay public, justified the elimination of the uninteresting passages of this classic work and concluded with reasons to account for Cortés' success.

His desire to see important sources available in English showed up in two projects in his last years. One was the inauguration of an English translation of Sahagún, a work that continued in progress for years after his death. The other was his appeal to the Rockefeller Foundation for funds for an English rendering of Adrián Recinos' Spanish version of the *Popul Vuh*, which was published in 1950. Recinos made his own English translation from the original Quiché-Maya, with the assistance of Delia Goetz and advice from Morley, who wrote an introduction for the volume.

To appeal to the general public, Vay used any avenue that was open to him. He utilized daily newspapers, popular magazines, motion pictures, and illustrated lectures.

When the purpose suited him, he resorted to the newspapers to create a favorable atmosphere for some project at hand. As he maneuvered for the important concession in Mexico in 1923, he used this approach on several occasions, once to gain popular support for the Mexican officials with whom he was dealing. Occasionally when he landed at New Orleans on his return from Yucatán, he announced discoveries of the past season in newspaper interviews in that city. There was an understanding between him and the C.I.W. that he could speak to the press on such things, but that more detailed accounts of archaeological finds would emanate from the Institution in Washington.

His articles of a general nature appeared in a variety of magazines. He seemed, however, to be at his best with the text-and-picture format of the *National Geographic Magazine*, which carried three of his articles between 1925 and 1936. The *Illustrated London News* in 1923 had a similar article though briefer in extent. *Mentor, Forum,* and the *Bulletin of the Pan American Union* also printed his material. Perhaps his best account of the work of the Carnegie Institution in Mexico and Central America appeared in the Franklin Medal lecture he delivered to the American Philosophical Society in 1942. He told the story with broad strokes, informative detail, and well-chosen illustrations. His most widely read account, however, was the article that accompanied Kessel's photographs in *Life* in 1947. He was careful to submit this article to the Carnegie Institution before it appeared.

He participated in at least one Fox Movietone documentary of Chichén Itzá. The twenty-minute film included air views of the site and featured Morley before important structures giving a commentary on their significance.

His most extensive work for the general public was a book that provided a vast panorama of the Mayas. The writing and publication of *The Ancient Maya* demonstrated Vay's judgment, perseverance, and good luck. He was inspired to begin the project by a casual conversation. When the manuscript was completed, his closest friend could not give him encouragement for its publication and several New York publishing houses rejected it; and when it did appear and gained great applause, his employer was perturbed by the thought that Morley might receive royalties from the work.

Its inception was in March, 1939, when Barklie Henry visited Chichén Itzá for several days as Vay's house guest. There was nothing remarkable about this, because he had entertained hundreds of guests over the years. Sometimes, however, Carnegie officials in Washington wrote ahead, asking him to pay particular attention to certain visitors. Mr. Henry was one of those recommended for kid-glove treatment, although the reason for making his visit especially pleasant was not disclosed.

In an after-supper conversation on the porch of the Casa Principal, Mr. Henry inquired about Vay's plans for future writing. Had he considered a general book about the Mayas? Yes, as a matter of fact, he had; and he explained his plans for an autobiography that would feature his experience in exploring the bush and forest of Central America. At that his guest asked him to give the firm of Reynal and Hitchcock first consideration of the manuscript.

Henry planted the seed in 1939; it did not sprout until 1942. In the meantime Morley was clearing up unfinished business. He was completing the *Inscriptions of the Petén* in 1939, and he concluded the history of the Xiu family in 1941. After the working season in Yucatán was over in 1942, he tackled the new book. When he actually got down to writing, he soon changed his aim from an autobiography to a broad account of the Mayas past and present because he believed that such a work would be more useful. Here the teacher and instructor triumphed over the yarn spinner of tropical adventures. In this change of plan he judged correctly that a comprehensive volume would have great educational value for the general public.

He wrote the manuscript, including a complete revision, and collected the illustrations in the year ending in June, 1943. At first he expected to complete the text in a short time, but it actually took him seven months. In January, 1943, he informed his chief at the Carnegie Institution that he was about to cut the text from 140,000 words to 125,000. That task he completed in three months, and by June he had finished the arduous job of assembling the photographs. During this last stage of the work he informed Mr. Henry of the book he had written, and Henry asked him to send in the manuscript.

Before submitting the work, Vay asked his friend Kidder to read it and make comments. Ted gave a critical report that must have disheartened the author. Although he found the text readable, he considered it too detailed for the general public; on the other hand, it would not fulfill the purpose of a textbook, because it lacked scholarly annotations. Also, the text was marred by two grave defects: Vay's addiction to superlatives overdid the case for the Mayas, and his failure to place that group in the broader framework of other prehistoric peoples of America displayed a lack of perspective. He advised Morley to put the manuscript aside for the time being; actually Kidder never expected to see it in print.

Vay did not put the manuscript on the shelf. He sent it off to Reynal and Hitchcock, where it was carefully considered and then rejected. Its length, the large number of illustrations, and the current wartime shortage of paper were given as reasons for not accepting the work. About a year later he tried Scribner's, and John Hall Wheelock replied in October, 1944, that the major drawback was the cost of the pictures; Scribner's would consider the book if it had a subsidy of $10,000, and he suggested that perhaps the C.I.W. might be interested in advancing that amount.

Morley never questioned the wisdom of his attempt to have the book commercially published. He had informed his superior at the Carnegie Institution of the progress of his writing; Kidder had always assumed that the real test of the manuscript was whether a commercial firm would accept it, and he also believed that it was not an appropriate work for the Carnegie Institution to issue. Then when the Institution declined to grant a subvention of $10,000, Vay assumed that his employer had no interest in the matter and that he was free to offer the manuscript anywhere. So, late in the summer of 1945, he sent it to Stanford University Press, and it was accepted. Vay resolved the problem of the costly illustrations by arranging with the Fondo de Cultura Económica in Mexico City to bring out a Spanish edition in Mexico, the two publishing houses dividing the cost of the pictures and using the same plates.

Another happy accident occurred when he enlisted Adrián Recinos to make the translation into Spanish. To pay Recinos, who was out of political favor in Guatemala and willing to undertake the task, Vay planned to use the money received from royalties on the American edition. A decade earlier President Merriam had asked Recinos to make a Spanish translation of the guide to the ruins of Quiriguá. Morley was so impressed with the favorable reception of the Spanish edition that he invited Recinos to come to Chenkú to perform the same miracle of translation on *The Ancient Maya*. Recinos described his experiences:

"The work was very interesting and the company of my old friend exceedingly pleasant. Besides, I was away from home, as a result of political developments in Guatemala, which were highly unpleasant to me, so that I accepted Sylvanus' invitation with pleasure. For three months we worked without respite, until we finished the Spanish translation. . . . Whenever possible I would make a literal version of the English text, so that Morley, who carefully read each page as it came from the typewriter, used to say that in my Spanish translation he could read his English original. Nevertheless, sometimes he came across some uncommon word, or one unknown to him in the rich Spanish vocabulary, and, interrupting his reading, he would come running to me to ask where I had found that word. Fortunately, my authority was always upon my desk, and the *Diccionario de la Real Academia Española* would show him that I was inventing no unusual terminology. 'This certainly is a sixty-four dollar word,' was his remark on such occasions."[3] Recinos worked at Chenkú during the winter of 1945–46.

Again, Recinos' rendition, published under the title of *La civilización maya,* met a favorable reception. And Morley was so pleased that he generously declared that the entire presentation in Spanish was superior to his own English version.

By early 1946, J. P. McEvoy, a roving editor of *Reader's Digest,* prepared an article about Morley for that periodical. At once Vay sensed that the timing of the article might have some bearing on the forthcoming book. On writing to the editor of Stanford University Press, he was told that the article would provide excellent advance publicity for *The Ancient Maya,* but that it must appear between August and October since the book was scheduled for publication on November 1. For some reason, the article never appeared.

Within a few weeks after the book was published, the president of the Carnegie Institution told Kidder that he considered it improper for Morley to draw royalties from a work based so largely upon his years of research financed by the Institution and written on Institution time. Kidder was worried by this turn of events, because he, as Vay's immediate superior, had approved plans for the book. He informed Vay of this new development, and at the same time wrote a long letter to the C.I.W. assuming entire

[3] *Morleyana,* 214.

responsibility for what had happened. Morley wrote a full explanation of how the book came to be written and published, how he had kept Kidder informed of every stage of the work, and how the refusal of the Institution to grant a subvention indicated to him that he was free to offer the manuscript elsewhere. The president, still not completely reconciled, replied that Morley's action set an unfortunate precedent for other scientists employed by the Institution.

The success of *The Ancient Maya* pleased Morley and surprised his colleagues, most of all Kidder, who was certain it did not have general trade possibilities. The sale of the book, though not phenomenal, was encouraging for an informative nonfiction volume selling at ten dollars. By 1947 a second edition appeared that differed from the first only in the improved reproduction of the pictures. In Mexico City, the Fondo de Cultura Económica issued the Spanish translation in an edition of three thousand copies, half of which were sold by the end of 1947.

The Ancient Maya is comprehensive in scope, compact in treatment, and attractively presented. In seventeen chapters Morley dealt with the ancient people and their civilization and also introduced results of other scholars' research on the contemporary natives. The text culminates with an appraisal of the Mayas, in which Vay put his finger on maize as the keystone of their culture; he also afforded an appreciation of their civilization by emphasizing their achievements. The text ends with a typical flourish: ". . . in the light of the *known cultural limitations* . . . we may safely acclaim the ancient Maya . . . as the most brilliant aboriginal people on this planet."[4] The text can be understood by the general reader, and Morley was careful to explain all unusual terms; he also used the technique of moving from the known to the unknown and from the simple to the more complex.

Illustrations, tables, and a bibliography enhance the volume. Ninety-six photographic plates and fifty-seven line drawings, carefully integrated with the text, provide an extra dimension to the presentation. The pictures came from various sources, and one

[4] *The Ancient Maya* (Stanford University Press, 1947), 455.

can well believe Morley's claim that assembling and arranging them required almost as much work as the writing. Thirteen tables give an encyclopedic touch to the book. There are tables of linguistic stocks, physical characteristics, history, monuments, ceremonies, ceramic periods, and other information that lends itself to tabular presentation. Fellow archaeologists were amused or exasperated by Table XI listing fifty superlatives about Mayas, a compilation that illustrates Vay's penchant for numbers and his zeal for popular presentation. The bibliography, covering thirty-six pages, has books for general reading specifically indicated.

Reviewers agreed on the attractive aspects of the volume. Its scope and style were praised. Conceded to be the best volume on the subject, it was ranked with Breasted's *History of Egypt*, Means's *Ancient Civilizations of the Andes*, and Vaillant's *Aztecs of Mexico*. It was characterized variously as warm and intimate, artistic, fascinating, and impressive.

Fellow scholars were quick to point out the flaws about which Kidder had warned Vay. The lack of scholarly apparatus, the failure to place the Mayas in the context of all prehistoric Americans, and the refusal to deal with debatable interpretations were the major charges entered against the book. Speaking the specialists' language, George Brainerd and William D. Strong gave penetrating critiques.

From one point of view the scholarly reviewers were barking up the wrong tree. Many of them did not realize that they were criticizing Morley for violating the rules of a game he was not playing. They refused to accept the book for what it purported to be. It was the presentation of a vast panorama of the Mayas as Vay saw them, and felt them, and, one might add, as he loved them. He could communicate his enthusiasm and dedication in a way that appeals to the nonspecialist. Intuitively, he realized that in such a work you cannot have your cake and eat it, too; that it is impossible to present divergent interpretations, to magnify fine points so as to satisfy all of the scholars and still retain the reader's interest. Considered in one way, *The Ancient Maya* is a work of art, and one reviewer was right in considering the scholarly defects "the vices of great virtues."[5] Fellow archaeologists continued to carp at the volume, because they refused to consider it as intended for the general reader. Rightly or wrongly, the volume is still more widely used in public libraries than the scholarly but less colorful writings by his critics.

Morley was pleased to find his book rated along with those by Breasted, Vaillant, and Means. But apparently he had never read the volume by Means, and so he went through it while visiting Popenoe in Antigua in March, 1947. The more he read the more impressed he was with the style. Likewise, he considered Means a scholar in weighing the evidence and arriving at valid conclusions. When a younger archaeologist told Vay that the factual information in Means's book was outdated, that made no difference to Morley.

By the 1920's Morley had already launched his career as a public speaker on the Mayas. The extent of his lecturing is not known, but every fall he had many engagements. On one occasion he referred to his one-night stands. In August, 1931, he already had sixteen appearances on his calendar for the coming months, and other dates were pending. The audiences varied from university groups to women's clubs. In 1928 he gave three lectures in Spanish at the summer school of the University of Mexico, and two years earlier several of his addresses were broadcast on the radio from Mexico City.

No transcriptions of his lectures, as he actually delivered them, have been found. *The Story of the Maya, "The Greeks of the New World,"* which he prepared as a souvenir for guests at the opening of the Fisher Theater in Detroit in 1929, probably summarizes the historical facts that he presented. In the construction of that edifice he helped the builder to achieve authentic Maya detail in the decoration of the lobby and the auditorium. At the gala opening, Vay was one of the principal speakers, but it is unlikely that he delivered the contents of the brochure in his presentation. The

[5] Robert Redfield, *Journal of American Folklore*, Vol. 61 (1948), 400.

cold print of those four pages gives no hint of the secret of his appeal as a speaker.

Nor do the lengthy descriptions of two appearances in Latin America, recorded in his diary, suggest the charm of his delivery. Those accounts show that he knew exactly what effect he wanted to create and that he devoted much preparation to every detail of the performance.

He appealed to the eye as well as to the ear. He used photography, at first black-and-white slides, then colored slides, and finally motion pictures. He always had a camera with him on expeditions, taking pictures for his lectures as well as for scientific purposes. After a voyage on the Usumacinta in 1931, he proudly remarked that he had taken over four hundred pictures as well as two thousand feet of movie film. He also utilized his ability to draw, sketching with ease and precision the individual glyphs of numbers, always with a running commentary.

In addition to visual devices, he used humor in his lectures. This was spontaneous and unexpected. His humor was kindly, rarely at the expense of others, and often directed at himself. One time, when showing movies of an expedition, he added without change of tone, "And here I come carrying of all things—a pillow."[6] In the midst of an account of hieroglyphs, he might suddenly tell how a can of beans exploded in camp. With Latin-American audiences he exploited his extremely faulty Spanish, not so much as an astute device to make his audience feel superior but for the amusing atmosphere it created. On one occasion he spoke of a leader commanding his *tripas* (insides) when he intended to say his *tribas* (tribes).

In the last analysis his intense enthusiasm for the Mayas was the major factor in his appeal to hearers. His interest in "my Mayas" gushed forth with tremendous enthusiasm; it dripped from every word; and it spread his own intense conviction to those who heard him. This evangelical faith in the significance of the Mayas was not simulated or "put on" for the lectures; it was gen-

[6] *Morleyana*, 57.

uine. In his daily work and in conversation with friends he displayed the same zealous interest. On the lecture platform he was completely natural, stimulated of course by the prospect of relaying his message to a large number of people. His careful preparation of every detail, the use of pictures and drawings, and the infectious humor were fused into a unified effect by his dynamic enthusiasm.

After devising a successful pattern for his public appearances, he rarely changed the format except as special occasions might demand. Each year he added an account of recently made discoveries, the only new feature he introduced.

Sometimes he admitted to a close friend that the public craved entertainment and not instruction. It was not a cynical comment on human nature; it was to him no more than the observation of a truth. In view of the highly specialized subject he treated, he was undoubtedly right. As a professional scientist, he not only realized this fact but was able to fulfill the want to perfection. In so doing, he was not deceiving the public or himself; he was utilizing a legitimate device to carry out his ultimate purpose of "selling" other people his own intense zeal in the Mayas.

Epilogue

ESSENTIALLY, Morley's great gift was his personality. The interaction of his personality with persons and places created the expansive world in which he lived. Each individual he met was one part of that great humanity he loved to observe, and each place he visited left strong associations in his soul.

He was endowed with a greater power of personality than most persons. He communicated his sincerity and friendship instantly, he felt with deep intensity, he reined in egoistic impulses with a taut bridle, and the unending flow of his enthusiasm propelled him and his associates forward to the goals that had been set.

With him, personality and character were one. He put on no calculated pose, no fake front. He was sincere throughout his being. He had faith in the goodness of people and he expected the same in return. He used friendship for worthy ends, always choosing immediate aims that would eventuate in goodwill in the future.

Rafael Heliodoro Valle, Honduran ambassador to the United States, spoke this tribute after Vay's death: "He did not notice that he was giving me a lesson in beauty when he showed me proofs of the last pages of his book on Copán, the second time that I visited him in his apartment in Washington.

"I always saw him that way, with his laugh as of a gentle river coloring the beauty of a landscape; with his optimism as of a bird out early only to drink in the first stir of air and the dawn; with that simplicity which won him so many friends, and which made it easy for him to come and go without hindrance as a citizen of America, who had succeeded—this eager, generous archaeologist —in doing much for the friendship and acquaintance of the United States with Mexico, Guatemala, and Honduras.

"This only was his reward—to have used the ties which the constructing geniuses of the Maya world created in order that the four nations might take advantage of the ways of life of the past as foundation for a future which might create humanistic forms. For this we, in Honduras, have owed him homage; and for that reason we are here, like catacumens arriving from the four cardinal points, bringing white maize, yellow, brown, and blue, with the same noble austerity with which he scattered the dynamic seeds of his wisdom.

"We could offer him turquoises, like those which he discovered in the Temple of the Warriors, at Chichen, which we would conserve in the mosaic of enlightened tenderness; but we prefer to give him the humble testimony of the maize, one of the symbols of wisdom in this land, and one of the stimuli which in Copán, the Wind-god receives whenever day breaks and it is calm all about. The conception of the sage whom we do not mourn dissipates the sorrow and gloom in order to display the light with which he passed through life, charged with carrying the seeds that sing."[1]

[1] *Morleyana,* 264–65.

Writings of Sylvanus G. Morley

Manuscript Materials

Diary, 1905–1908, 1912, 1914–25, 1931, 1932, 1935, 1937, 1939, 1941–42, 1944, 1946, 1947. The manuscript notebooks, except for 1925, are in the C.I.W. Collection, Peabody Museum; typescript volumes for all of the years except 1935, 1939, and 1946 are in the library of the American Philosophical Society.

Notebooks and papers in the library of the Peabody Museum: notebooks of lectures in Anthropology 1, 4, 7, 9; "Deluge Myths of Central America and Mexico," December, 1904; "Pigmentation as an Index of Vital Superiority," December, 1904; "A Comparison between the Material Culture of the Alaskan Eskimo and the Chukakee," May, 1905; "The Basques," January, 1907; "The Occurrence and Representation of the Death Deity in Maya Codices," 1908; "The Four Principal Gods of the Maya Codices and their Name Glyphs," M.A. thesis, 1908.

"Dr. Morley's Notes on Tulane Expedition—1925 Monuments," typescript, Tulane University Library. Technical data on stelae and glyphs.

"Preliminary Report on The Ruins of La Honradez, Petén, Guatemala" [1915], Morley Files, C.I.W.

"The Xiu Chronicle. Part I: The History of the Xiu Family," typescript, 1941. Copy in Peabody Museum library. Part II is by R. L. Roys.

Letters to and from Morley are in the Morley File, C.I.W., Washington; in Hodge Papers, Southwest Museum, Los Angeles; in the Archives of the Bureau of American Ethnology, Smithsonian Institution, Washington; in the School of American Research, Santa Fe; and in the American Museum of Natural History, New York; a few items are in the National Collection of Fine Arts, Washington, and at Tulane University. The following collections in private hands were made available to the author: J. Eric S. Thompson, Ashdon, Saffron Waldron, Essex, England; C. L. Lundell, Renner, Texas; and Mrs. Frans Blom, San Cristóbal de las Casas, Chiapas, Mexico. George Stuart examined Morley correspondence in the National Geographic Society for me.

Articles

"An Ancient Maya City in Yucatan," *Science*, July 4, 1924, Supplement #1540, p. x.

"Ancient Temples and Cities of the New World: Chichen Itza," *Bulletin of the Pan American Union*, Vol. XXXII (1911), 453–68; "Uxmal, the City of the Xius," *ibid.*, 627–42; "Copan, the Mother City of the Mayas," *ibid.*, 863–79.

Annual Reports in *Carnegie Institution of Washington, Year Books*, Nos. 13–46, 1914–47.

"Antigua es Única y la Expresión mas pura de la Arquitectura Colonial en Todo el Continente, dice Morley . . . ," Guatemala *El Imparcial Diario Independente*, March 25, 1944, p. 1.

"Archaeological Investigations of the Carnegie Institution of Washington in the Maya Area of Middle America, during the Past Twenty-Eight Years," *Proceedings of the American Philosophical Society*, Vol. LXXXVI (1943), 208–19. Franklin Medal lecture, delivered April 23, 1942.

"An Archaeological Research . . . ," *Science*, Vol. LXXI (1930), 546. Co-author A. V. Kidder. An abstract.

"Archaeological Research at the Ruins of Chichen Itza, Yucatan," *Reports upon the Present Condition and Future Needs of the Science of Anthropology Presented by W. H. R. Rivers, A. E. Jenks, and S. G. Morley at the Request of the Carnegie Institution of Washington*, 61–91, Washington, 1913. C.I.W. *Publication* 200.

"The Archaeology of the McElmo Canyon, Colorado, Part I," *El Palacio*, Vol. IV (1917), 41–70. Co-author A. V. Kidder. Part II did not appear.

"Basketball Bets Were Mayan Mania," *The New York Times*, August 3, 1924, II, 1:2. Quotes from Morley's report.

"Bringing Forth Glories of Ancient Mayas," by Nell Ray Clarke, Syracuse *Post Standard*, May 23, 1926. Quotes from Morley's reports.

"The Calakmul Expedition," *The Culture of the Maya*, C.I.W. *Supplementary Publication* 6 (1933), 30–43. Also in *Scientific Monthly*, Vol. XXXVII (1933), 193–206.

"Chichen Itza, an Ancient American Mecca," *National Geographic Magazine*, Vol. XLVII (1925), 63–95.

"Combination of Glyphs G and F in the Supplementary Series," C.I.W. Division of Historical Research, *Notes on Middle American Archaeology and Ethnology*, No. 49 (1945).

"The Correlation of Maya and Christian Chronology," *American Journal of Archaeology*, 2d ser., Vol. XIV (1910), 193–204. Also in *Papers of the School of American Archaeology*, No. 11.

"El dintel 42 de Yachilan," *Yan*, Vol. II (1953), 135–39. Accounts by Morley and by Maler.

"The Earliest Mayan Dates," *Congrès International des Américanistes*, XXI Session (1924), pt. 2 (Göteborg, 1925), 655–67.

"The 'Egypt' of American Antiquities. The Great Maya Ruins Buried in Tropical Forests," *Illustrated London News*, March 24, 1923, pp. 468–71.

"La escritura jeroglífica maya," in R. Pavón Abreau, *Cronología maya*, xv–xlv. Campeche, 1943.

"The Excavation of Cannonball Ruins in Southwest Colorado," *American Anthropologist*, new ser., Vol. X (1908), 598–610. Also in *Papers of the School of American Archaeology*, No. 2.

"Excavations at Quiriguá, Guatemala," *National Geographic Magazine*, Vol. XXXIV (1913), 339–61.

Extracts from Morley's diary on the discovery of Uaxactún, 1916, in Leo Deuel, *Conquistadores Without Swords: Archaeologists in the Americas*, 287–95. N.Y., St. Martin's Press, 1967.

"The Foremost Intellectual Achievement of Ancient America," *National Geographic Magazine*, Vol. XLI (1922), 109–31.

"From the Archives," in Edgar L. Hewett, *Pajarito Plateau and Its*

Ancient People, 149–54. Albuquerque, University of New Mexico and School of American Research, 1938.

"El grabado en madero en la civilización Maya," *La Justicia* (México), March, 1958, p. 205.

"Great Mayan City Overrun by Forest," *The New York Times*, June 9, 1932, 44:6. Contains quotations by Morley.

"The Greatest Murals of Ancient America at Bonampak, Chiapas, Mexico," *El Palacio*, Vol. LV (1948), 99–102.

"A Group of Related Structures at Uxmal, Mexico," *American Journal of Archaeology*, 2d ser., Vol. XIV (1910), 1–18. Also in *Papers of the School of American Archaeology*, No. 6.

"The Guatemala Earthquake," *American Museum Journal*, Vol. XVIII (1918), 200–10.

"Historia general de los antiguos mayas," *Enciclopedia Yucatenense*, II, 5–52, Mérida, 1945.

"The Historical Value of the Books of Chilam Balam," *American Journal of Archaeology*, 2d ser., Vol. XV (1911), 195–214. Also in *Papers of the School of American Archaeology*, No. 19.

"History and Chronology in Ancient Middle America," *American Historical Association Annual Report for 1922*, I (1926), 281–82. An abstract.

"Honduras, La Tierra Prometida," Tegucigalpa *El Nuevo Tiempo*, August 15, 1917.

"The Hotun as the Principal Chronological Unit of the Old Maya Empire," *Proceedings of the 19th International Congress of Americanists* (1915), 195–201. Washington, 1917.

"How Holon Chan Became the True Man of His People," in E. C. Parsons, ed., *American Indian Life*, 251–64, 403–406. New York, Heubsch, 1922.

"The Initial and Supplementary Series of Stela 5 at Altar de Sacrificos, Guatemala," C.I.W. Division of Historical Research, *Notes on Middle American Archaeology and Ethnology*, No. 58 (1945).

"Inscriptions at the Caracol," in Karl Ruppert, *The Caracol at Chichén Itzá, Yucatán, Mexico*, 276–93. C.I.W. *Publication* 454 (1935).

"The Inscriptions of Naranjo, Northern Guatemala," *American Anthropologist*, new ser., Vol. XI (1909), 532–62. Also in *Papers of the School of American Archaeology*, No. 9.

"Introduction," in *Prescott: The Conquest of Mexico. Designed for Modern Reading by Marshall McClintock*, v–viii. New York, Messner, 1948.

"Un jarro maya pintado," *Forma* (México), Vol. I, pt. 5 (1927), 22–24.

"Joseph Thompson Goodman," *American Anthropologist*, new ser., Vol. XXI (1919), 209–13.

Letter to W. H. Holmes, Sayaxché, May 3, 1914, in J. E. S. Thompson, "1914: La Carnegie Institution of Washington ingresa al campo Maya," *Estudios de Cultura Maya*, Vol. IV (México, 1964), 170–72.

Letter from Morley, November 24, 1917 (extract), in "New Light on the Mayas," *El Palacio*, Vol. IV (1917), 98.

Letter to Marjorie Tichy in "The Bonampak Expedition," *El Palacio*, Vol. LIV (1947), 98–99.

Masterpieces of Maya Art. The Corn God. N.p., n.d. [1947 or 1948]. Hand printed from silk screen by Louis Ewing, and described by S. G. Morley.

Masterpieces of Maya Art. Piedras Negras, by Tatiana Proskouriakoff, and described by S. G. Morley. N.p., n.d. [1947 or 1948].

"The Maya: The Greeks of the New World," *Mentor*, pt. 1. Vol. XIII (1925), 51–54.

"The Maya Civilization," in Watson Davis, ed., *Science Today*, 228–34. New York, Harcourt, Brace & Co., 1931.

"Maya Civilization, 100% American," *Forum*, Vol. LXXII (1927), 226–36.

"Maya Epigraphy," in *The Maya and Their Neighbors*, 139–49. New York, Appleton-Century, 1940; limited ed., 1962.

"The Maya New Empire," *Co-operation in Research*, 533–65. C.I.W. Publication 501 (1938). In Spanish translation, *Historia antigua de Yucatán: el nuevo imperio maya*. Mérida, 1942.

"Maya Origins," *Masterkey*, Vol. XXII (1948), 1–18.

"Maya Ruins Reveal New Treasures," *New Orleans Item*, July 24, 1927. If not written by Morley, this article is based on information supplied by him. Another article in the same paper, July 3, 1927, quotes Morley in praise of Blom and Spinden.

"Maya Society," *Life*, Vol. XXII (June 30, 1947), 51–76.

"Mayan Records False Declares Research Leader," New Orleans *Times-Picayune*, April 30, 1935, 3:4. Quotes Morley.

"Mexico Es El Egipto del Nuevo Mundo," México *Excelsior*, April 15, 1923, 2d section, p. 1.

"The Morley Collection of Spanish Colonial Ecclesiastical Art," *El Palacio*, Vol. LII (1945), 175–90. Also in *Archaeological Institute of America, Papers of the School of American Research*.

"Museum-Laboratory Merger," *El Palacio*, Vol. LIV (1947), 207–208.

"New Art Program for the Museum of New Mexico," *El Palacio*, Vol. LIV (1947), 190–91.

"New Light on the Discovery of Yucatán, and the Foundation of the New Maya Empire," *American Journal of Archaeology*, 2d ser., Vol. XXXI (1927), 51–69.

"Notes on the Hieroglyphic Inscription of the Polychrome Cylindrical Vase Shown in Plates 4 and 5," in A. L. Smith, "Two Recent Ceramic Finds at Uaxactún," *Contributions to American Archaeology*, No. 5 (1932), 21–25. C.I.W. *Publication* 436.

"El nuevo imperio Maya," *Yikal Maya Than* (Mérida, México), año 4, No. 41, Vol. IV (1943), 9–10, and No. 43, 62–65.

"Prehistoric Quiriguá, the Unfinished City," *El Palacio*, Vol. I (1914), 1–3.

"Quiriguá—An American Town 1,400 Years Old," *Scientific American*, Vol. CVII (1912), 96–97, 105.

"Recent Epigraphic Discoveries at the Ruins of Copán, Honduras," *So Live the Works of Men, Seventieth Anniversary Volume Honoring Edgar Lee Hewett*, 277–93. Albuquerque, University of New Mexico Press, 1939.

"The Rise and Fall of Maya Civilization in the Light of the Monuments and the Native Chronicles," *Proceedings of the 19th International Congress of Americanists* (1915), 140–49. Also in *Proceedings of the Second Pan American Scientific Congress* (1915–16), Vol. I, 192–208. Washington, 1917.

"The Ruins of Tuloom, Yucatan: The Record of a Visit of the Carnegie Institution Central American Expedition, 1916, to an Important but Little Known Ancient Maya City," *American Museum Journal*, Vol. XVII (1917), 190–204.

"Santa Fe Architecture," *Old Santa Fe Magazine*, Vol. II (1915), 278–301.

"The South House, Puyé," *Out West*, Vol. XXXII (1910), 121–33. Also in *Papers of the School of American Archaeology*, No. 7, and in *Bulletin of the Southwest Society of the Archaeological Institute of America*, No. 6.

Statement on Tuxtla figure in William H. Holmes, "On a Nephrite Statuette from San Andrés Tuxtla, Vera Cruz, Mexico," *American Anthropologist*, Vol. IX (1907), 696–700.

The Story of the Maya, "The Greeks of the New World." [Detroit, Fisher Theater]. 4 pp. Issued in connection with the opening of the theater on November 16, 1929.

"Study of Maya City Fills Historic Gap," *The New York Times*, August 14, 1932, 17:1. A report on Calakmul, with quotations by Morley.

"Summary of Archaeological Investigation in Middle America, 1925," Pan American Union, *American Archaeology*, No. 1 (1927), 10–15.

"Summary of Archaeological Work in the Americas in 1926: III—In Mexico and Central America," *Bulletin of the Pan American Union*, Vol. LXI (1927), 108–21.

"Summary of Archaeological Work in Middle America in 1927," *Bulletin of the Pan American Union*, Vol. LXII (1928), 228–41. Also in a Spanish translation.

"Summary of Archaeological Work in the Americas in 1928: III—Research in Middle American Archaeology in 1928," *Bulletin of the Pan American Union*, Vol. LXIII (1929), 230–35. Also in a Spanish translation.

"The Supplementary Series in the Maya Inscriptions," *Holmes Anniversary Volume, Anthropological Essays Presented to William Henry Holmes in Honor of his Seventieth Birthday*, 366–96, Washington, priv. print., 1916

"Unearth Proofs of Maya Civilization. Northern Yucatan Ruins Show Evidence of Culture of Fifth Century," *New York Herald*, April 3, 1923, p. 9.

"Unearthing America's Ancient History," *National Geographic Magazine*, Vol. LX (1931), 99–126.

"Yucatan, Home of the Gifted Maya . . . ," *National Geographic Magazine*, Vol. LXX (1936), 591–644.

"Yucatán Fué la Cuna del Arte Maya. Dice el Doctor Morley," México *El Universal*, April 4, 1923, p. 1.

Books and Pamphlets

The Age and Provenance of the Leyden Plate. Contributions to American Anthropology and History, No. 24. C.I.W. *Publication* 509 (1938). Co-author Frances R. Morley.

The Ancient Maya. Stanford, Calif., Stanford University Press, 1946; London, Oxford University Press, 1946. Second edition, 1947. Third edition, revised by George W. Brainerd, Stanford, Calif., Stanford University Press, 1956. Spanish translation by Adrián Recinos, *La civilización maya.* Mexico City, El Fondo de Cultura Económica, 1947, 1950, 1953, 1955.

Annual Report of the School of American Research, 1947. Report of Morley as Director.

Bibliography of the Maya Area. Washington, C.I.W., 1929. 4 pp.

Check List of the Corpus Inscriptionum Mayarum, and Check List of All Known Initial and Supplementary Series. Mimeographed. Washington, C.I.W., 1948.

Guide Book to the Ruins of Quiriguá. C.I.W. Supplementary Publication 16 (1935). Spanish translation by Adrián Recinos, *Guía de las ruinas de Quiriguá,* C.I.W., 1936, 1952.

An Introduction to the Study of the Maya Hieroglyphs. Smithsonian Institution, Bureau of American Ethnology Bulletin 57, Washington, 1915.

The Inscriptions of Copán. Washington, 1920. C.I.W. *Publication* 219.

The Inscriptions of Petén. 5 vols. C.I.W. *Publication* 437 (1937–38). Several excerpts were later published in Guatemala.

The Maya Chronicles. Contributions to American Anthropology and History, No. 48. C.I.W. *Publication* 585 (1949). Co-author A. Barrera Vásquez.

Popul Vuh: The Sacred Book of the Ancient Quiché Maya. English version by Delia Goetz and Sylvanus G. Morley from the translation of Adrián Recinos. Norman, University of Oklahoma Press, 1950. Half-title: *The Civilization of the American Indians.*

Book Reviews

G. B. Gordon, *The Book of Chilam Balam of Chumayel, Current Anthropological Literature,* Vol. II (1913), 157–59.

W. J. de Gruyter, *New Approach to Maya Hieroglyphics*, American *Journal of Archaeology*, ns., Vol. L (1946), 444–45.

L. Satterthwaite, *Concepts and Structures of Maya Calendrical Arithmetic*, *Journal of American Folklore*, Vol. LXI, (1948), 321–22.

H. J. Spinden, *A Study of Maya Art, Its Subject Matter and Historical Development*, *Current Anthropological Literature*, Vol. II (1913), 154–57.

H. J. Spinden, *Ancient Civilizations of Mexico and Central America*, *American Anthropologist*, ns., Vol. XX (1918), 209–13.

A. M. Tozzer, *Landa's Relación de las Cosas de Yucatán*, *Hispanic American Historical Review*, Vol. XXII (1942), 138–40.

Notes on Sources

General

The most useful sources of information, Morley's diary and his correspondence, remain unpublished. Although a number of years are missing from the diary, the extant volumes provide scientific field notes and data on his personal activity. It should be noted, however, that the entries often cover only a part, sometimes a very small part, of the year.

Friends who remember Vay's outbursts of anger and strong language will be surprised to learn that the text of the diary is calm and matter-of-fact. It appears that he wrote the record so that anyone might read it; it is free of profanity, malicious gossip, or statements that might reflect unfavorably on persons about whom he wrote. But it does reveal his sense of humor and flair for the dramatic.

A claim that the diary was censored is open to question. An examination of the original notebooks in the Peabody Museum and of the typescript volumes in the American Philosophical Society failed to reveal marked changes between the two versions. The absence of certain years of the diary has also been attributed to suppression, but internal evidence shows that no diary was kept during some of those years.

The correspondence made available to the author varies from routine matters to informative, interesting description. Of the several collections examined, the Morley File in the C.I.W. is the largest and also the most helpful.

Recollections of Vay's friends describe the man as others saw him and also provide amusing anecdotal material. Individuals who shared their reminiscences with the author in interviews or by correspondence are listed under "Acknowledgments." *Morleyana* (Santa Fe, 1950) provides the best collection of reminiscences in print, and I have made liberal use of it. A few anecdotes appear in G. Edward Pendray, "Men Who Dig," *New Outlook*, Vol. 165 (March, 1935), 41–47.

Public notice about Morley and the Middle American Project can be traced through the Index and files of *The New York Times*. For a more limited period, the Scrap Books, "Archaeology," in the C.I.W. contain clippings from numerous newspapers.

Biographical accounts, varying in length, appear in *Who's Who in America*, from 1918; *Who's Who in New Mexico*, I (1937); *National Cyclopedia of American Biography*, Vol. 38, p. 19. More informative are the obituary notices of J. Eric S. Thompson in *American Anthropologist*, Vol. 41 (1949), 293–97; A. V. Kidder in *El Palacio*, Vol. 55, No. 9 (1948), 267–74, reprinted in *Morleyana*, 93–102; R. L. Roys and M. W. Harrison in *American Antiquity*, Vol. 14 (1949), 215–21; and the *Santa Fe New Mexican*, September 2, 1948, p. 1. For other notices, see Ignacio Bernal, comp., *Bibliografía de arquelogía y ethnología: Mesoamerica de México* (México, Instituto Nacional de Antropología e Historia, 1962), items 12682–12698.

I. Introduction

This material has been drawn from a comprehensive view of the man.

II. The Early Years

Childhood. *Morleyana* contains a few items. Mrs. Elinor M. Vail (Morley's sister) and Mrs. Charles R. Macaulay (his niece) provided helpful information. Mrs. Constance Fussell (Morley's sister) also supplied data about the family. Some reminiscences of this period occur in later years of Vay's diary. The story that he attended Harvard to take courses under George A. Reisner, Egyptologist, is in error, because Reisner did not join the faculty until a year after Vay arrived on campus. The Putnam Papers, Harvard University Archives, might contain Morley's youthful letters, but when the author made inquiries the collection was not arranged so as to disclose them.

College Years. The diary is the major source. His notebooks for four anthropology courses are in the library of the Peabody Museum. Tozzer offers a few lines in *Morleyana*. The courses and the grades come from the diary and from a loose sheet of paper on which Vay tabulated his grades for the first year. Morley to J. Eric S. Thompson, Nov. 26, 1946, contains reminiscences; where they conflict with the diary, I have relied on the latter account.

III. Apprenticeship

First Mexican Trip. The diary gives a full record, but Vay's letters to his Aunt Virginia, appended to the diary as a separate part of 231 typed pages, add much interesting detail.

Out West. The diary must be supplemented by the reminiscences of Hewett and Kidder, cited in the footnotes, and by John Gould Fletcher, *Life Is My Song* (New York, Farrar and Rinehart; Toronto, Oxford, 1937), 26–32.

Working with Hewett. The diary is available for several years of this period. A formal summary appears in *Official Records of the School of American Archaeology*, 1908–13, and in a historical sketch in the school's *Annual Report* for 1946; official reports of some of the expeditions are in *Archaeological Institute of America Bulletin*, I–III (1909–12). Tozzer, Buckley, Hodge, and Laughlin offer recollections on the summer expeditions in *Morleyana*. Morley to J. Eric S. Thompson, Nov. 26, 1946, recalled the illness at Kabah. For the 1910 expedition, see Morley, *Guide to Quiriguá* (1935), 103, 105–106, and an article in *Santa Fe New Mexican*, May 3, 1910. Several letters in the Hodge Papers, Southwest Museum, give data on Quiriguá in 1912. For the expedition of 1913, see *Santa Fe New Mexican*, April 15, 17, 25, May 2, July 23–25, 1913, and a few letters in the Hodge Papers, Southwest Museum. The campaign to restore the old architecture in Santa Fe receives excellent treatment by Jesse Nusbaum in *Morleyana*; Morley, "Santa Fe Architecture" (1915), gives his ideas on restoration.

IV. The Carnegie Institution of Washington

Appointment. The Morley File and the manuscript Minutes of the Executive Committee, C.I.W., give the significant facts. Letters in the Hodge Papers, Southwest Museum, and the diary reflect Vay's worries. *Reports upon the Present Condition . . .* by Rivers, Jenks, and Morley

(C.I.W., 1913) present the three proposals. Bowditch's resentment is explained by J. Eric S. Thompson, "1914. The Carnegie Institution of Washington Enters the Maya Field," manuscript supplied by Thompson to the author; the paper appeared in Spanish translation in *Estudios de Cultura Maya,* IV (Mexico, 1964), 167–75. The C.I.W. employed Vay at $200 a month, a marked increase over the $125 a month he earned with the school.

First Trip to the Petén. The diary for 1914 gives the fullest account. Some of Vay's letters to Holmes are in the Morley File; one of them is in the article by Thompson, cited above. Some letters in the Hodge Papers, Southwest Museum, supplement the diary. An article on the early stage of the expedition appears in *Santa Fe New Mexican,* Apr. 11, 1914. Morley to Spinden, Sept. 20, 1914 (American Museum of Natural History), explains how he financed most of the trip himself.

La Honradez and Copán. The diary and the Morley File provide the major facts. There is an informative letter by Vay in the Hodge Papers, Southwest Museum. The *C.I.W. Year Book* for 1915 indicates that he visited nine other sites in addition to those mentioned in the text.

Domestic Problems. The diary for 1912 and 1914 and recollections in later years of the diary contribute some information. Several letters in the Hodge Papers, Southwest Museum, add interesting details. El Nido was the name Vay gave to his home in Santa Fe.

V. Death in the Bush

Again, the diary and the Morley File are the major sources. S. K. Lothrop, "Archaeology Then and Now," Lothrop, ed., *Essays in Pre-Columbian Art and Archaeology* (Harvard University Press, 1961), 1–2, offers material on the trips to and from Copán. An envelope with various documents on Lafleur's death is in the Morley File. Thompson's article, cited above, reports Vay's nightmares.

VI. Secret Agent

World War I. Boas' article in the *Nation,* Vol. 109 (Dec. 20, 1919), was brought to my attention by Ross Parmenter, who also supplied information about the men in the Secret Service. One of the former ensigns refused to discuss the subject. Mrs. John Held, Jr., provided extracts of letters from H. J. Spinden and Boaz Long about the Intelligence work. The *United States Navy Register*, 1918, indicates Morley's official status.

For other adventures, most of the information comes from the diary and the Morley File. Mrs. John Held, Jr., provided data about her husband. While waiting for the boat in New Orleans, Held attracted the attention of a journalist, Flo Field, who wrote an article about him in the *Times-Picayune*, May 6, 1917. The account of the first meeting of Morley and Held is assumed from circumstantial evidence. The watercolors made on the expedition are in the possession of Mrs. Held, but John's archaeological drawings have not been found. Hebard's brief recollections appear in *El Palacio*, Vol. 62 (Apr., 1955), 122, and in a letter from Hebard to Mrs. Held. An extract of a letter from Vay to Hewett, written on Hog Islands, is in *El Palacio* (1917). A copy of Vay's article in *El Nuevo Tiempo*, Tegucigalpa, Aug. 15, 1917, is in the Morley File. The Bluefields newspaper, to which he contributed an article, has not been located; and a search under the direction of Alfredo Martínez Moreno, of San Salvador, failed to find the article by Morley and Spinden that caused the trouble described by Long.

Yucatán. Thomas Gann, *In an Unknown Land* (London, Duckworth & Co., 1924), gives the most detailed account. The Morley File provides some information, and the diary covers only three weeks of the expedition. Alfredo Barrera Vásquez recalls the lecture in Mérida in *Morleyana*.

VII. *In the Petén*

The major source is the diary. Material on Gates comes from J. Eric S. Thompson to the author. For the founding of the Maya Society, see *The New York Times*, May 2, 1920, II, 6:2. By 1922, Vay was its secretary and treasurer. About a decade later Morley wanted to reconstitute the organization, but he was unsuccessful; Gates had incorporated the name, and he revived it largely as a one-man affair.

VIII. *Writings and Lectures—1*

Details on the writing and printing of the *Introduction* appear in the diary and in the Hodge Papers, Southwest Museum. For the *Inscriptions of Copán*, the diary and the Morley File contribute most of the facts. *Morleyana* contains references to each work. P. A. Means reviewed the Copán volume in *Hispanic American Historical Review*, Vol. 3 (1920), 388–92; T. A. Joyce in *Nature*, Vol. 106 (1921), 656–58; and H. Beyer in *El México Antiguo*, Vol. 2 (1927), 313–18.

IX. The Great Year—1923

Mexico and Guatemala. The diary for 1923, amounting to seven volumes, provides elaborate detail. The Morley File adds a few sidelights. Newspaper articles are helpful. *The New York Times*, Mar. 2, 1923, 3:1, gives E. H. Thompson's revelations of his past activities; and an article in Feb. 4, 1923, IV, 3:1, forecasts the visit of Merriam, Parsons, and Morley. The visitors' excursions to Uxmal and Chichén are reported in the issue of March 25, IV, 7:1, by Alma Reed, and in April 1, IV, 14:1. Morley's interview with the Associated Press appears in the *New York Herald*, April 3, p. 9. For his interviews for *La Universal* and *Excelsior*, see his writings, 1923. The author's interview with Mrs. Elinor M. Vail, Morley's sister who was in Yucatán during the dignitaries' visit, provided vivid recollections, especially of the trip to the Cave of Loltún.

The diary for 1924 covers Feb. 22–July 7. The Morley-Blom correspondence indicates the close friendship of the two men. *International Congress of Americanists*, XXI Session, 2d part (Göteburg Museum, 1925), gives the official record. Three letters in the Morley File tell the story of Vay's European experience. Blom's work at Uaxactun appears in the *C.I.W. Year Book* for 1924.

X. At Chichén Itzá

Much information about life at Chichén comes from the diary and the Morley File. Ann Axtel Morris, *Digging in Yucatan*, and Earl Morris, *The Temple of the Warriors*, explain the use of native laborers. Dr. J. O. Kilmartin to the author, Feb. 28, 1968, provides details of the early work at Chichén. Some scattered items are in *Morleyana*. The engagement and wedding receive notice in the same volume, 257–59; a biographical account of Frances is in *El Palacio*, Vol. 62 (April, 1955), 120–22. The Hodge Papers, Southwest Museum, contain a printed invitation to the wedding. J. Eric S. Thompson to the author supplied the story of the imitation Maya lintel. *The New York Times*,

Feb. 6, 1929, 32:6, carries the article about visitors to Chichén. One account of a Ball Court concert is in Lawrence Dame, *Yucatan* (New York, Random House, 1941), 111. Josephus Daniels, *Shirt-Sleeve Diplomat* (Chapel Hill, 1947), 488, prints an extract from his diary about his visit.

Morley's Assistants. The diary and the Morley File are the major sources. For the technical story of the Temple of the Warriors, see Earl H. Morris, Jean Charlot, Ann Axtel Morris, *The Temple of the Warriors at Chichén Itzá* (C.I.W. Publication 466, 1921, 2 vols.); for a popular account, Earl Morris, *The Temple of the Warriors.* J. Eric S. Thompson, *Maya Archaeologist,* is readable and informative. For dedication of the Temple of the Warriors, see *Diario de Yucatán,* Mar. 11, 1928, p. 1, and *New York Hotel Pennsylvania Daily,* Apr. 21, 1928. The story of the mosaic disc and its journey to the United States is in *The New York Times,* Mar. 8, 1928, 41:3, and May 13, 1928, X, 2:4, and in the *Washington Star,* Sept. 28, 1928. Illustrations of the Temple of the Warriors, with accompanying articles, are in *Art and Archaeology,* Vol. 30 (1931), 291–322. John Bolles to the author, July 3, 1967, supplied interesting details.

XI. *People and Places*

For the trip to Copán, see Thomas Gann, *Ancient Cities and Modern Tribes* (N.Y., Scribner's Sons, 1926), 191–95. J. Eric S. Thompson, *Maya Archaeologist,* 52–59, describes the several expeditions to Cobá; C.I.W. Scrap Books contain newspaper notices of the discovery of Macanox in the Cobá complex. The *Baltimore Sun,* July 5, 1926, with dateline El Paso, Texas, gives Morley's account of discoveries of the season. The official report on Uaxactún is in the *C.I.W. Year Book* #27 (1928), 307–17. For the expedition to Yaxchilán, see full account in the diary for 1931, two volumes, and a long letter in the Morley File. There is considerable material on Calakmul. C. L. Lundell, "Archaeological Discoveries in the Maya Area," *American Philosophical Society Proceedings,* Vol. 72, No. 3 (1933), 147–79, describes the sites he found. The Lundell-Morley correspondence shows how Vay tried to encourage a promising man to enter the field of archaeology. Morley, "The Calakmul Expedition" (1932) and the diary for 1932, two volumes, provide the full story. Notices of the new site appeared in *The New York Times,* May 1, 1932, 3:2; June 9, 44:9; Aug. 14, 17:1; and Aug. 16, 12:1.

A lengthy letter in the Morley File describes the Historical Congress in Mérida in 1935. For the visit of the chiefs of Quintana Roo and for Morley's expedition to that region, see the diary for 1936, the Morley File, and Helga Larsen, "Trip from Chichen Itza to Xcacal, Q.R., Mexico," *Ethnos,* 1964, 5–41. Alfonso Rojas Villa, *The Maya of East Central Quintana Roo* (C.I.W. Publication 559, 1945), Introduction, gives Villa's story. The diary for 1937 provides the facts for that year. Vay's trip to Europe in 1938 is treated in letters in the Morley File, and in Morley to J. Eric S. Thompson, Oct. 16, 1938. The official report is in *Congrès international des Sciences anthropologiques et ethnologiques . . . ,* 2d Session (Copenhagen, 1938).

XII. The Middle American Project

Raising Money. Scattered references in the Morley File and in the diary provide the information for this topic. Miss Proskouriakoff told the author the story of how Vay found her and added her to the staff.

Middle American Project. See reports of the *C.I.W. Year Books* for the increasing scope of the project. Walter W. Taylor, *Study of Archaeology* (American Anthropological Association Memoir Series, Vol. 50, No. 3, pt. 2, July, 1940), 45–94, gives criticisms of the project. Concern over Zelia Nuttall's strictures appears in the Morley File. J. Eric S. Thompson to the author explained how the work was continued for a few more years. For Morley's honors, see *The New York Times,* July 6, 1939, 7:1, for the Order of the Quetzal; Apr. 24, 1942, 19:8, for the Franklin Medal; and Apr. 20, 1943, 21:4, for the Loubet Prize.

XIII. The Later Years

Chenkú: Letters in the Morley File describe the move to Mérida and his last visit to Chichén. *Morleyana* gives the recollections of Adrián Recinos and Jeannie Avery.

Last Expedition: The diary for 1941–42 covers the visits to Uxmal, but field notes fill most of the entries. For the trip of 1944, the two-volume diary for that year and a long letter in the Morley File provide the details. Vay to Long in *Morleyana*, 122–24, treats the last lap of the journey. J. Eric S. Thompson to the author added significant data on another part of the expedition. Morley's newspaper article, calling for a committee of experts to supervise the restoration of Antigua, is in *El Imparcial*, 1944. Antonio Tejeda in *Morleyana* explains why Vay left Cueva's quarters; Morley confided to his diary that barking dogs also prompted his departure.

In August, 1944, Vay had his first heart attack in Santa Fe, and Frances and his physician had a hard time keeping him in bed.

The trip of 1947 is detailed in the diary for that year.

Politics and Religion: The story of the Morleys' anti-Roosevelt feeling comes from J. Eric S. Thompson. Vay's interest in current events appears in the Morley File, and his views on religion are scattered through many years of the diary.

Slowing Down: Stromsvik tells of his last visit in *Morleyana*. For Vay as a raconteur, see the same volume, 2–3. Morley described his antiques in "The Morley Collection," (1945); the diary for 1922 and letters in the Hodge Papers, 1922–23, Southwest Museum, show how his collecting began in the early 1920's. For his new job in Santa Fe, see *Santa Fe New Mexican*, May 31, 1947; *Annual Report of the School of American Research* for 1946–48; Morley, "New Art Program for the Museum" (1947) and "Museum-Laboratory Merger" (1947), and other notices scattered through *El Palacio* for that year. The author's interview with Albert Ely, assistant to Morley as director, yielded interesting information.

His death prompted a long notice in the *Santa Fe New Mexican*, Sept. 2, 1948, p. 1; his funeral received a sparse note, Sept. 7. The account of the dedication of the museum at Tikal is based on the diary of J. Eric S. Thompson.

XIV. Writings and Lectures—2

The Morley File contains much data on his publications of this period, and the diary occasionally notes his work in preparing the volumes. The story of the failure of Dionisio Xiu's marriage comes from J. Eric S. Thompson. The Petén volume was reviewed by J. A. Villacorta C. in *Sociedad de geografía e historia de Guatemala Anales*, Vol. 16 (1939), 8–21, and M. Mariscal in *Boletín Bibliográfico de antropología*

Americana, Vol. 3 (1939), 237–47. For reviews of *The Ancient Maya,* see Mrs. Harrison's bibliography in *Morleyana,* 82.

At the annual meeting of the Association for the Advancement of Science, held in Nashville in December, 1927, Liberty Hyde Bailey, the president, was ill, and Vay was called upon to give the major address. The lecture received notice in a number of newspapers, e.g., *The New York Times,* Dec. 27, 1927, 18:8. "Fisher Nears Its Opening," *Detroit Free Press,* Nov. 4, 1929, indicates that Morley provided the Maya detail. A. S. Graven's article in *Exhibitors Herald-World,* Jan. 19, 1930, describes the theater, with a photograph of the interior. Vay's opinion that the public craves entertainment occurs in his diary and was also reported to the author by a close associate of Morley in his last years.

Index